HEALTHY **DEVELOPMENT**

THE WORLD BANK STRATEGY FOR
**HEALTH, NUTRITION, &
POPULATION RESULTS**

HEALTHY **DEVELOPMENT**

THE WORLD BANK STRATEGY FOR
HEALTH, NUTRITION, & POPULATION RESULTS

THE WORLD BANK
Washington, DC

The findings, interpretations, and conclusions expressed herein are those of the author(s) and do not necessarily reflect the views of the Executive Directors of the International Bank for Reconstruction and Development/The World Bank or the governments they represent.

The World Bank does not guarantee the accuracy of the data included in this work. The boundaries, colors, denominations, and other information shown on any map in this work do not imply any judgement on the part of The World Bank concerning the legal status of any territory or the endorsement or acceptance of such boundaries.

Rights and Permissions
The material in this publication is copyrighted. Copying and/or transmitting portions or all of this work without permission may be a violation of applicable law. The International Bank for Reconstruction and Development/The World Bank encourages dissemination of its work and will normally grant permission to reproduce portions of the work promptly.

For permission to photocopy or reprint any part of this work, please send a request with complete information to the Copyright Clearance Center Inc., 222 Rosewood Drive, Danvers, MA 01923, USA; telephone: 978-750-8400; fax: 978-750-4470; Internet: www.copyright.com.

All other queries on rights and licenses, including subsidiary rights, should be addressed to the Office of the Publisher, The World Bank, 1818 H Street NW, Washington, DC 20433, USA; fax: 202-522-2422; e-mail: pubrights@worldbank.org.

ISBN-13: 978-0-8213-7193-0
e-ISBN-13: 978-0-8213-7194-7
DOI: 10.1596/978-0-8213-7193-0

Cover design: Naylor Design, Inc.
Cover photo: C. Carnemark/World Bank.

Library of Congress Cataloging-in-Publication Data

Healthy development : the World Bank strategy for health, nutrition, and population results.
    p. ; cm.
 ISBN 978-0-8213-7193-0 (alk. paper)
1. Public health--Developing countries—Finance. 2. Public health—Developing countries—International cooperation. 3. Nutrition policy—Developing countries—Finance. 4. Population assistance—Developing countries—Finance. 5. World Bank. I. World Bank.
 [DNLM: 1. World Bank. 2. Developing Countries. 3. Public Health. 4. Financial Support. 5. International Agencies. 6. Public Policy. WA 395 H4347 2007]
 RA410.55.D48H45 2007
 362.109172'4—dc22

                                                                         2007022159

Contents

Tables

Foreword

Reducing poverty and improving the quality of people's human and economic welfare constitute vital steps for developing countries as they strive to achieve sustainable economic growth and create lasting national development. With ill health both a major contributor to, and a result of poverty, the state of people's health is therefore highly relevant to governments and communities as they work to improve the education and skills of their citizens, raise national incomes, and chart more promising directions for their countries.

The challenges to achieving better health and human capital, however, are profound. One noteworthy analysis of 30 countries shows that poor people living on less than $1 a day use health care services at a consistently lower rate than richer groups. Low-income countries also have difficulty ensuring physical access to clinical services for large numbers of their people.

Almost 11 million children die every year, mainly from preventable causes such as diarrhea and malaria. More than 500,000 women die during pregnancy and childbirth every year. In 2006, almost 3 million people died from HIV/AIDS. About 380,000 of these deaths occurred among children younger than 15 years of age. Tuberculosis is curable, yet 1.7 million people die from it every year. Malaria kills a child every 30 seconds somewhere in the world, infects millions of people with its debilitating illness, and undermines national economies as adults become too sick to work and lose income.

Studies have found that almost one-third of all households in a given group of low-income countries have had to sell assets or borrow to pay for medical expenses to treat a sick family member over the course of the previous year. Other reports have found that a country's economic growth rate is significantly influenced by the health of its general population.

It is little wonder, therefore, that illness is often a cause of poverty as well as a catalyst for sudden impoverishment, as families tap into savings or sell what they own to cover the costs of medical care. As a result, all too often people end up falling below the poverty line. Improving the perilous health of millions of the world's poorest people is rightly one of the essential priorities of the global development community in this new century.

In another worrying trend, poor countries are catching up with their wealthier counterparts in the North in the growing numbers of premature deaths caused by chronic diseases—cancer, diabetes, hypertension, pulmonary diseases—linked to tobacco-addiction and obesity pandemics. Malnutrition is problematic, not only in poor countries (with both under-nutrition and obesity), but also in rich countries that are confronted with a rapidly growing prevalence of obesity.

Furthermore, strong commitment is required to address the lack of progress in improving sexual and reproductive health, which is not only a key development priority, but is also central to successfully achieving the 2015 Millennium Development Goals for maternal and child mortality, as well as to addressing HIV/AIDS.

Given its mission to reduce poverty and inequity in low- and middle-income countries worldwide, the World Bank has updated its health, nutrition, and population (HNP) strategy to help developing countries strengthen their health systems to improve the health and well-being of millions of the world's poorest people, boost economic growth, reduce poverty caused by catastrophic illness, and provide the structural "glue" that combines multiple health-related programs within partner countries.

On the ground, it means putting together the right chain of events to ensure that poor people get sustained access to the good quality health services needed to save and improve their lives.

In its new HNP Strategy, the Bank envisions that its support and advice will help countries achieve better health results in a way that also boosts their economic growth, global competitiveness, and good governance. Good health has proven to be not just an outcome of economic growth. At the same time, good health and sound health system policy have also been recognized as major, inseparable contributors to economic growth.

The international community's expanded commitment to better health has opened an unprecedented window of opportunity for the Bank to further contribute to HNP results both at the country and global levels. Consultations in partner countries and with many global and country leaders in health, executive directors of the World Bank, and Bank management and staff have confirmed their expectations that we rise to the new challenges—and expeditiously. This Strategy presents the Bank's global short- and medium-term response to meet these new challenges.

Joy Phumaphi
Vice President for Human Development
The World Bank Group
Washington, DC

Preface

This new Health, Nutrition, and Population (HNP) Strategy was prepared in two phases. The first phase of preparation was completed at a briefing to the Committee on Development Effectiveness (CODE) in June 2006, as presented in the Background Note on the New HNP Strategy, dated May 30, 2006. That briefing culminated in a process of extensive consultations with global partners, Bank staff, and management and confirmed the proposed Strategic Directions. The second phase finalized necessary technical work to address the main comments from the CODE discussion and comments received from global partners before the CODE briefing and began consultations with client countries from all Bank Regions. More than 9 client countries in the field, 65 global partners—including civil society organizations, bilateral and multilateral organizations—and 160 Bank managers and staff from HNP and other sectors were consulted.[1] The new Strategy benefits from the comments and suggestions given to the team during these enriching consultations. The Strategy is intended to inform the decisions of client–country policy makers, Bank country teams and Bank management, and global partners on country- and Region-specific strategies and action plans for achieving HNP results on the ground. This final strategy also benefits from comments and suggestions made during the CODE discussion held on March 14, 2007.

This Strategy does not attempt to make in-depth, specific technical recommendations on the diverse and complex range of issues involved in HNP policy today. In-depth technical recommendations must be country-context specific. Therefore, this Strategy does not, for example, list specific health system reforms to improve performance in specific country contexts, nor does it recommend the best approach to support much-needed improvements in HNP in post-conflict and fragile states or propose international arrangements necessary for sustainable donor HNP financing in low-income countries. Instead, this Strategy outlines a new strategic vision for the World Bank in improving its own capacity to respond to these urgent questions globally and with a country focus, ensuring that this capacity will be mainstreamed in Bank lending and nonlending country support and support to global partners in areas of Bank comparative advantages.

Although this HNP Strategy does not include country-specific technical recommendations, its preparation has been informed by abundant in-depth policy work, conducted by the Bank, setting forth analyses on health financing,[2] on nutrition policy,[3] a Bank Global Program Action Plan for HIV/AIDS[4] (World Bank 2006h), and a renewed commitment to sexual and reproductive health (World Bank 2006j).[5] It provides the vision of the Bank on the need to strengthen health systems and refers to key challenges for the HNP sector in contributing to combating the HIV/AIDS pandemic, in repositioning nutrition on the development agenda, and in renewing its commitment to population policy in line with, inter alia, the Programme of Action of the International Conference on Population and Development (UNFPA 2004). Readers are referred to this specific technical work for further in-depth technical analysis. Through the implementation of this new HNP Strategy, the Bank plans to strengthen further its analytical and operational work in these important areas.

The new Strategy identifies a plan of action and internal functional adjustments for its implementation to bring about essential improvements in Bank work on HNP. It identifies necessary changes that would allow better support for government leadership and programs as well as global partners' efforts to achieve results. Country-driven and country-owned programs are key to good HNP results on the ground.

Acknowledgments

This World Bank Health, Nutrition, and Population (HNP) Strategy was prepared by a team led by Cristian C. Baeza (Lead Health Policy Specialist, LCSHH /Acting Director, HDNHE) and composed of Nicole Klingen (Senior Health Specialist, HDNHE), Enis Baris (Senior Public Health Specialist, ECSHD), Abdo S. Yazbeck (Lead Economist, Health, WBIHD), David Peters (Senior Public Health Specialist, HDNHE), Eduard Bos (Lead Population Specialist, HDNHE), Sadia Chowdhury (Senior Health Specialist (HDNHE), Pablo Gottret (Lead Economist, HDNHE), Phillip Jeremy Hay (Communications Adviser, HDNOP), Eni Bakallbashi (Junior Professional Associate, HDNHE), Lisa Fleisher (Junior Professional Associate, HDNHE), Jessica St. John (Junior Professional Associate, HDNHE), Elisabeth Sandor (Health Specialist, HDNHE), Andrianina Rafamatanantsoa (Program Assistant, HDNHE), and Victoriano Arias (Program Assistant, HDNHE).

Special gratitude is due to the government officials of client countries, global partners, and Bank management and staff who generously provided the team with valuable recommendations and guidance on how the Bank can better support client country efforts to improve the lives of those who are most vulnerable. A comprehensive list of acknowledgments is presented in annex B.

Overall guidance to the team was provided by Jacques Baudouy (former Director, HDNHE), Nick Krafft (Director Network Operations, HDNVP), Joy Phumaphi (Vice President, Head of Network, HDNVP), Jean-Louis Sarbib (former Senior Vice President, HDNVP), James Adams (Vice President & Head of Network, OPCVP and Regional Vice President, EAPVP), Danny Leipziger (Vice President & Head of Network, PRMVP), Xavier Coll (Vice President, HRSVP), Shanta Devarajan (Chief Economist, SARVP), Steen Jorgensen (Sector Director, ESDVP), Jamal Saghir (Director, EWDDR), James Warren Evans (Sector Director, ENV), Evangeline Javier (Sector Director, LCSHD), Julian Schweitzer (Sector Director, SASHD), Michal Rutkowski (Sector Director, MNSHD), Guy Ellena (Director, IFC), Debrework Zewdie (Director, HDNGA), Kei Kawabata (Sector Manager, HDNHE), Akiko Maeda (Sector Manager, MNSHD), Anabela Abreu (Sector Manager, SASHD), Armin Fidler (Sector Manager,

ECSHD), Eva Jarawan (Sector Manager, AFTH2), Fadia Saadah (Sector Manager, EASHD), Keith Hansen (Sector Manager, LCSHH), Ok Pannenborg (Senior Adviser, AFTHD), Bruno Andre Laporte (Manager, WBIHD), Elizabeth King (Research Manager, DECRG), and Susan Blakley (Senior Human Resources Officer, HRSNW). We also acknowledge the assistance of the Office of the Publisher—Paola Scalabrin, Dina Towbin, and Stuart Tucker—in preparing the manuscript for publication.

Abbreviations

AAA	Analytic and advisory activities
AAP	Africa Action Plan
ACT	Artemisinin-based combination therapy
ADB	Asian Development Bank
AFD	French Agency for Development
AfDB	African Development Bank
AFR	Africa Region, World Bank
AHI	Avian and human influenza
AMC	Advance Market Commitment
APL	Adaptable Program Loan/Credit
ARPP	Annual Review of Portfolio Performance, World Bank
ART	Antiretroviral therapy
ARV	Antiretroviral drug
AusAID	Australian Agency for International Development
BAPPENAS	National Development Planning Agency, Republic of Indonesia
CAS	Country Assistance Strategy
CCT	Conditional cash transfer
CDC	Centers for Disease Control and Prevention, United States
CDP	Comprehensive Development Partnership
CEM	Country Economic Memorandum
CMU	Country Management Unit, World Bank
CODE	Committee on Development Effectiveness, World Bank
CPIA	Country Performance Institutional Assessment
DAH	Development assistance for health
DANIDA	Danish International Development Agency
DEC	Development Economics, World Bank
DFID	Department for International Development, United Kingdom
DGF	Development Grant Facility, World Bank
DP	Development Partner
DPL	Development Policy Lending
EAP	East Asia and Pacific Region, World Bank
ECA	Europe and Central Asia Region, World Bank
ESW	Economic sector work, World Bank
EU	European Union
FAO	Food and Agriculture Organization
GAIN	Global Alliance for Improved Nutrition
GAVI	Global Alliance for Vaccines and Immunisation

GDP	Gross domestic product
GFATM	Global Fund to Fight AIDS, Tuberculosis and Malaria
GMR	*Global Monitoring Report*
GNI	Gross national income
GTZ	German Agency for Technical Cooperation
HA-LIC	High-aid low-income countries, for which DAH is a large proportion of government or total expenditures in health
HD	Human Development Network, World Bank
HNP	Health, nutrition, and population
HNPFAM	Health, Nutrition, and Population Network of the World Bank
HPAI	Highly pathogenic avian influenza
HR	Human resources
HSPT	Health System Policy Team, World Bank
IADB	Inter-American Development Bank
IBRD	International Bank for Reconstruction and Development, World Bank Group
ICPD	International Conference on Population and Development
ICR	Implementation Completion Report, World Bank
IDA	International Development Association, World Bank Group
IEG	Independent Evaluation Group, World Bank Group
IFC	International Finance Corporation, World Bank Group
IFFIm	International Finance Facility for Immunisation
IFPMA	International Federation of Pharmaceutical Manufacturers and Associations
IFPRI	International Food Policy Research Institute
ILO	International Labour Organisation
ISR	Implementation Status Report, World Bank
LA-LIC	Low-aid low-income countries, for which DAH is a small proportion of government or total expenditures in health
LCR	Latin America and the Caribbean Region, World Bank
LIC	Low-income country
M&E	Monitoring and evaluation
MCA	Multisectoral Constraints Assessment for Health Outcomes
MDG	Millennium Development Goal
MENA	Middle East and North Africa, World Bank
MIC	Middle-income country
MMB	Marginal budgeting for bottlenecks
MMR	Maternal mortality rate
MOF	Ministry of Finance
MOH	Ministry of Health
MTEF	Medium-term expenditure framework
NCD	Noncommunicable disease

NGO	Nongovernmental organization
NHA	National health accounts
Norad	Norwegian Agency for Development Cooperation
ODA	Official development assistance
OECD	Organisation for Economic Co-operation and Development
OECF	Japanese Overseas Economic Cooperation Fund
OOP	Out-of-pocket spending
OPCS	Operations, Policy, and Country Services, World Bank
PDO	Project development objective
PEPFAR	United States President's Emergency Plan for AIDS Relief
PER	Public expenditure review
PREM	Poverty Reduction and Economic Management Network, World Bank
PRH	Population and reproductive health
PRSC	Poverty Reduction Strategy Credit
PRSP	Poverty Reduction Strategy Paper
PSD	Private Sector Development, World Bank
QAG	Quality Assurance Group, World Bank
R&D	Research and development
RTA	Reimbursable technical assistance
SAL	Sector Adjustment Loan/Credit
SAR	South Asia Region, World Bank
SARS	Severe Acute Respiratory Syndrome
SIDA	Swedish International Development Cooperation Agency
SMU	Sector Management Unit, World Bank
SSA	Sub-Saharan Africa
SWAp	Sectorwide approach
TA	Technical assistance
TB	Tuberculosis
TF	Trust fund
TFR	Total fertility rate
TGHE	Total government health expenditure
U-5	Children under five years of age
UNAIDS	Joint United Nations Programme on HIV/AIDS
UNFPA	United Nations Population Fund
UNICEF	United Nations Children's Fund
USAID	United States Agency for International Development
WBI	World Bank Institute
WDR	*World Development Report*
WFP	World Food Program, United Nations
WHO	World Health Organization

Executive Summary

Healthy Development: The World Bank Strategy for Health, Nutrition, & Population Results updates the 1997 World Bank Health, Nutrition, and Population (HNP) Strategy in light of the momentous changes of the past decade in the international architecture of development assistance for health (DAH)[6] and of persisting and new HNP challenges worldwide. Ten years ago, the Bank was the main financier of HNP. Today, in addition to the Bank, new multilateral organizations, initiatives, and foundations have assumed a prominent role in financing HNP, among them the Global Fund,[7] the Global Alliance for Vaccines and Immunisation (GAVI), the Global Alliance for Improved Nutrition (GAIN), and the Bill and Melinda Gates Foundation. Bilateral aid has also increased substantially. Much of this new funding is earmarked for combating priority diseases such as HIV/AIDS, malaria, tuberculosis, and some vaccine-preventable diseases; less for health system strengthening at country level, for maternal and child health, for nutrition, and for population priorities.

The ultimate objective of World Bank work in HNP, reinforced by this new Strategy, is to improve the health conditions of the people in client countries, particularly the poor and the vulnerable, in the context of its overall strategy for poverty alleviation. To achieve this objective, this new Strategy states the vision and the action plan necessary to strengthen Bank capacity to better serve client countries by excelling in areas of Bank comparative advantages and by improving its collaboration with global partners.

The increased awareness and expanded international financing for HNP constitute a great opportunity for the Bank to help client countries and global partners improve HNP results on the ground, particularly for the poor and the vulnerable. However, the new environment also poses significant challenges for the Bank, requiring important changes in the way the Bank operates in HNP to be able to rise to these challenges. This 2007 HNP Strategy outlines the Bank vision for improving its own capacity to respond globally and with a country focus to the urgent issues posed by these challenges.

Throughout this Strategy, the case is made for sharpening Bank focus on results on the ground; for concentrating Bank contributions on its comparative advantages, particularly in health system strengthening, health financing, and economics; for supporting government leadership and international community programs to achieve these results; and for exercising selectivity in engagement with global partners. This focus is not intended to constrain what the Bank does—country circumstances must drive Bank programs. However, a selective and disciplined framework is advocated, particularly for policy advice and knowledge generation, to ensure that the Bank is appropriately staffed and ready to support country efforts and requests for assistance in a core set of key areas where the Bank can play a major role. This framework is also essential for the Bank to collaborate with global partner efforts to ensure aid effectiveness.

Background

Health, nutrition, and population policies play a pivotal role in economic and human development and in poverty alleviation. For a century and a half, HNP improvements, achieved through the contributions of multiple sectors of the economy, have contributed to economic growth everywhere.

At the same time, improved economic growth has enabled improvements in health outcomes, creating a virtuous cycle—good health boosts economic growth, and economic growth enables further gains in health.[8] The dramatic increases in development assistance for health and shifts in the major players involved in the global health architecture show the widespread recognition of the tight link between investments in health and economic development.

A multisectoral approach is essential for achieving HNP results. Many advances in health status achieved during the 20th century were the result of close synergy among HNP and multiple sectors of the economy such as water and sanitation, environment, transport, employment, education, agriculture, energy, infrastructure, and public administration. For example, investments in girls' education improve household decisions on nutrition and demand for basic health care. At the same time, investing in basic nutrition during pregnancy and infancy has a substantial positive effect on early childhood development, which, in turn, significantly contributes to educational attainment, employability, and future income (Bloom, Canning, and Jamison 2004; Jamison 2006; World Bank 2003b, 2004, and 2006j).

The Bank Contribution to HNP in the Last Decade: The 1997 HNP Strategy

The Bank has contributed substantially to HNP in client countries in the last decade. Since the 1997 HNP Strategy, the Bank has decisively committed to focusing its work on health gains for the poor. The Bank has also played a crucial role in advocacy, awareness, and development of new international initiatives and organizations such as the Global Fund and GAVI.

As one of the world's largest single international financing organization of HNP activities in the last decade, the Bank has been a significant source of funding and has made substantial contributions in policy advice for priority–disease and HNP interventions. The Bank assisted more than 100 countries with more than 500 projects and programs, with cumulative disbursements of US$12 billion and cumulative new lending of US$15 billion from 1997 through 2006.[9] Through more than 250 Analytical Sector Work reports and advisories, the Bank also provided substantial policy and technical advice.

Despite the many excellent projects and programs in various Regions, the implementation impact of the 1997 Strategy on HNP results on the ground cannot be systematically evaluated. Focus on monitoring and evaluation (M&E) was weak during the last decade, and impact data are scarcely available.

During the last decade, the Bank has also faced significant challenges. Its total active portfolio (active commitments) in HNP decreased[10] by 30 percent from FY01 to FY06, and the implementation quality of the HNP lending portfolio had the lowest performance among all sectors in the Bank since 2001. Although the HNP sector operations are inherently complex and high risk as compared with many other sectors, much improvement is needed in the quality at entry and strategic focus of operations to improve HNP portfolio performance. In addition, the focus of Analytical and Advisory Activities (AAA) has been insufficient, with less than 35 percent of all AAA during the decade focused on areas of Bank comparative advantages.[11]

New and Persisting HNP Challenges in the New International Environment

The last three decades have brought important achievements in HNP in the developing world, *but formidable challenges persist*. Actual and potential pandemics and regional epidemics have continued to emerge, and some have expanded (e.g., HIV/AIDS, malaria, drug- and multidrug-resistant TB, SARS, avian flu). A significant increase has occurred in premature deaths related to chronic diseases (diabetes, pulmonary diseases, hypertension, cancer) linked to the tobacco-addiction and obesity pandemics. The world population more than doubled in the second half of the 20th century, mostly from population growth in developing countries. High population growth poses significant challenges to country efforts to alleviate poverty and to facilitate access to basic services. Malnutrition is problematic not only in poor countries (with both undernutrition and obesity), but also in rich countries confronted with a rapidly growing prevalence of obesity.

The new opportunities brought about by the changes in DAH also present three special challenges: the need to focus beyond increasing available financing for HNP, ensuring that additional funds produce tangible results on the ground to improve the living conditions of the people, especially the poor and the vulnerable; the need to align and harmonize global partners' activities with country needs to prevent duplication, economic distortions—and excessive administrative costs—ensuring country-owned and country-led DAH; and the need to ensure synergy between enhanced priority–disease financing and strengthening of health systems, essential for achieving results and improving DAH effectiveness on the ground.

Results on the Ground

In this Strategy, *HNP results* encompass not only HNP outcome indicators, such as the United Nations Millennium Development Goals (MDGs), stunting, or fertility rates but also health system performance, as reflected, for example, in financial protection[12] and utilization of essential health services by the poor. Other results targeted are: empowerment of the poor (as outlined in *World Development Report—2004* [World Bank 2003]), good sector governance, sector financial sustainability and its contribution to sound fiscal policy and country competitiveness; key outputs such as the proportion of children immunized, proportion of children born under safe delivery conditions, and other outputs closely linked to achieving the HNP-related MDGs; and availability of essential drugs and personnel in rural clinics. All these results are examples of Bank HNP objectives in client–country work. For these results to be achieved, a multisectoral approach is essential. Annex D presents the World Bank Results Framework for HNP, which summarizes the main outcomes and outputs for the Bank in HNP. The Framework is intended as the guidance for country teams for developing country-specific and detailed results frameworks for Bank operations and programs.

Strengthening Health Systems

"Strengthening health systems" may sound abstract and less important than specific-disease control technology or increased international financing to many people concerned about achieving HNP results. But, well-organized and sustainable health systems are necessary to achieve results. On the ground, in practical terms, it means putting together the right chain of events (financing, regulatory framework for private-public collaboration, governance, insurance, logistics, provider payment and incentive mechanisms, information, well-trained personnel, basic infrastructure, and supplies) to ensure equitable access to effective HNP interventions and a continuum of care to save and improve people's lives (see box 1.1 in "Introduction and Overview"). Strengthening health systems is not a result in itself. Success cannot be claimed until the right chain of events on the ground prevents avoidable deaths and extreme financial hardship due to illness because, without results, health system strengthening has no meaning. However, without health system strengthening, there will be no results.

Achieving HNP results requires a well-organized and sustainable country health system, capable of responding to the HNP needs of the community. Strengthening health systems to achieve HNP results requires a multisectoral effort at the country level. There is consensus that a major, urgent effort must be made to strengthen health systems if financial commitments enabled by the new DAH architecture are to succeed in improving the health conditions of the poor and achieve the HNP-related MDGs. The international community agrees on this principle after much debate in the early 2000s, centered on the false dichotomy between focus on priority diseases and focus on system strengthening.

To make sure people's health and daily lives are really being improved with the money invested, actual results on the ground have to be evaluated. Measuring results requires systems for close and effective monitoring and evaluation, which are effectively linked to policy design and management.

New Opportunities, Challenges, and the Bank Role in the New DAH Scenario

The new aid architecture, persisting HNP challenges, and the urgency for strengthening health systems to achieve results represent major challenges, particularly to low-income countries and fragile states. The quality of Bank policy and technical advice will be critical for client–country response to these challenges. While still strategically very important, Bank financing, at roughly US$1.5 billion a year, is relatively small, compared with the overall large and increasing funding for the control of specific diseases. Financing no longer drives relationships with client countries. For example, as measured by new annual financial commitments for HIV/AIDS, for malaria, and for tuberculosis, Bank financing in FY2005 represented about 5 percent,[13] 3 percent,[14] and 7 percent,[15] respectively, of total annual international commitments for each of these diseases.[16] In this scenario, it is the quality of the policy and technical dialog and the strategic focus of Bank lending that will define the true magnitude of the Bank contribution to country efforts in HNP in the next decade.

It is important to highlight that, although the share of Bank financing in total DAH has decreased, Bank lending, particularly through the *International Development Association (IDA), is strategically crucial to ensure much-needed health system strengthening (for which dedicated international financing is scarce), and it is essential to set the enabling environment for effective disease-specific financing to achieve results.* This was stated again and again by client countries during preparation of this new Strategy.

This new Strategy for HNP Results asserts the global vision of the Bank role in the new global architecture in HNP (box ES.1). It also attempts to give Bank regional and country teams guidance for addressing these questions with a sharp focus on HNP results, working closely with global partners. For that purpose, it defines the strategic and operational changes necessary to assist these teams more effectively and suggests opportunities for collaborative division of labor among global partners.

Box ES.1: Healthy Development—The World Bank Strategy for Health, Nutrition, & Population Results

---

Strategic Vision

With the implementation of this new HNP Strategy, the Bank aims to bolster client–country efforts to improve health conditions for the poor and the vulnerable and to prevent them from becoming impoverished or made destitute as a result of illness. The Bank envisions that its support and advice will help client countries achieve these HNP results in a way that also contributes to their overall fiscal sustainability, economic growth, global competitiveness, and good governance. This new Strategy is embedded in the core mission of the Bank to alleviate poverty worldwide. To achieve these objectives, countries need to articulate a response from multiple sectors that influence HNP results. The Bank, with its 19 sectors working globally in 139 countries, is uniquely positioned to support client–country efforts.

Strategic Objectives: What HNP Results?
- Improve the level and distribution of key HNP outcomes (e.g., MDGs), outputs, and system performance at country and global levels in order to improve living conditions, particularly for the poor and the vulnerable.
- Prevent poverty due to illness (by improving financial protection).
- Improve financial sustainability in the HNP sector and its contribution to sound macroeconomic and fiscal policy and to country competitiveness.
- Improve governance, accountability, and transparency in the health sector.

Strategic Directions: How should the Bank support country efforts to achieve results?
- Renew Bank focus on HNP results.
- Increase the Bank contribution to client–country efforts to strengthen and realize well-organized and sustainable health systems for HNP results.
- Ensure synergy between health system strengthening and priority–disease interventions, particularly in LICs.
- Strengthen Bank capacity to advise client countries on an intersectoral approach to HNP results.
- Increase selectivity, improve strategic engagement, and reach agreement with global partners on collaborative division of labor for the benefit of client countries.

Long-Term Country-Driven and Country-Led Support

Country-driven and country-owned programs are the key to good HNP results on the ground. A strong country presence, country focus, and country-driven support are at the core of the Bank business model and are some of the most important comparative advantages of the Bank. Country teams working with Country Management Units (CMUs) embody the Bank country focus and its intersectoral approach to development. Strengthening and empowering CMUs to better serve client countries in collaboration with global partners working at the country level is therefore essential to ensure country-driven implementation of the HNP Strategy and, ultimately, sound HNP results.

Results on the ground, especially outcome improvements, rarely occur in the lifetime of a single project nor are they achieved by any single sector. It is long-term Bank policy advice, technical assistance, and its strategically focused lending program as a whole that can influence client–country HNP policy actions, inputs, and structural changes in the health system and influence HNP-relevant policies from other sectors. Therefore, proposed objectives and directions in this new HNP Strategy are geared to support the central role of CMUs in leading the Bank country support and in further improving the effectiveness of the Bank country focus in HNP.

Upon country demand, the Bank will continue to lend in all areas deemed necessary to improve health status and financial protection for people, especially the poor and the vulnerable. This includes support for controlling priority diseases in countries where they constitute a large part of the burden of disease. However, the Bank will increasingly endeavor to ensure that Bank operational and policy advice support for priority diseases will strengthen the health system to solve systemic constraints that impair the effectiveness of country, Bank, and international community financing in achieving HNP results.

Bank Comparative Advantages

The Bank has special strengths *(comparative advantages)* for providing policy and technical advice to client countries and global partners in their efforts to achieve HNP results. The Bank will focus and enhance its capacity to generate knowledge and provide policy and technical advice in these areas. They include: its health system strengthening capacity; its intersectoral approach to country assistance; its advice to governments on regulatory framework for private-public collaboration in the health sector; its capacity for large-scale implementation of projects and programs; its convening capacity and global nature; and its pervasive country focus and presence.

Some of these strengths are fully developed in the Bank. Others, such as policy and technical advice on regulating the private sector and improving public-private collaboration for HNP results, health system strengthening capacity, and intersectoral work for HNP results, need significant strengthening if the Bank is to scale up its efforts in this area and realize its full potential for supporting client countries and the international community effectively.

Analytical capacity in economics and evaluation is also a Bank comparative advantage. The Bank will substantially increase both its analytical work on health systems and its monitoring and evaluation capacity to ensure that the renewed commitment to HNP is actually rendering results on the ground. It is also essential that this increased capacity and commitment to M&E be effectively linked to and inform policy design and policy management in the health sector.

The Bank has comparative advantages for health system strengthening mainly in the areas of health financing, insurance, demand-side interventions, regulation, and systemic arrangements for fiduciary and financial management. The Bank will actively seek collaborative division of labor with global partners, based on respective comparative advantages. For example, leading agencies such as WHO, UNICEF, and UNFPA have clear comparative advantages in areas such as the technical aspects of disease control (e.g., determine what is the best drug to treat malaria or how to overcome micronutrient deficiencies), human resource training in health, and internal organization of service providers (e.g., how to run medical services in clinics or hospitals).

The Challenge of Implementation

The resource requirements for implementing the HNP strategy will be a function of the pace of implementation of the Strategy (pace of change), the demand from countries, and the availability of resources in an environment of zero growth in the overall Bank budget. It is expected that the cost of implementing the new HNP strategy will involve a modest increase in the base budget for the Human Development (HD) Network over the FY2007 base budget, after taking into account one-off transitional adjustments. An extraordinary allocation to the HD Network above the regular base budget will be utilized to finance these transition expenses, as justified.

A Window of Opportunity for Scaling Up Support to Country HNP Results

The expanded commitment of the international community in health has opened an unprecedented window of opportunity for the Bank to further contribute to HNP results at country level and globally. Consultations in client countries and with many global and country leaders in health, including leaders of donor agencies, foundations, Ministries of Health and Finance of client countries, leaders of civil society organizations, Executive Directors of the World Bank, and management and staff from HNP and other sectors in the Bank have confirmed their expectations that the Bank needs to rise to the new challenges—and expeditiously. This Strategy presents the global short- and medium-term response of the World Bank to meet the new challenges.

Box ES.2: Key Next Steps for Implementation

The following are the key initial steps at country level to implement the Strategic Directions and Objectives defined in the Strategy. This box outlines key country-level actions to be taken in the next 18 to 24 months.

- *Launch health system strengthening assessment.* Estimate the investment and policy reform gaps.
- *Assess fiscal space.* Estimate the space for closing the financing gap at country level.
- *Rapidly mainstream system strengthening into priority–disease operations.*
- *Multisectoral assessment of constraints to achieving HNP results (e.g. MDGs).*
- *Offer policy advice on health system integration.* Address the challenge of country systems fragmentation and, in close collaboration with IFC, improve policy environment for public-private collaboration.
- *Scale up output- and/or performance-based financing.*
- *Strengthen client–country capacity in monitoring and evaluation (country-based) to measure results.*
- *Enter into specific agreements with the WHO and the Global Fund on collaborative division of labor at country level (next 12 months).*
- *Implement the harmonization and alignment agenda at the country level.*
- *Improve the quality of the Bank HNP portfolio.*

CHAPTER 1

Introduction and Overview

Health, nutrition, and population (HNP) policies play a fundamental role in economic and human development and poverty alleviation. For more than a century and a half, health, nutrition, and population contributions to the improved health status of individuals and populations have also contributed to economic growth. In turn, improved economic growth has led to better health outcomes, creating a virtuous cycle: good health boosts economic growth, and economic growth enables further gains in health.

Healthy Development: The World Bank Strategy for Health, Nutrition, & Population Results for the next decade updates the 1997 World Bank Health, Nutrition, and Population Strategy to enhance Bank capacity so that it continues to contribute to this virtuous circle in light of the momentous changes of the past decade in the architecture of development assistance for health (DAH) and of persisting HNP challenges worldwide. This 2007 HNP Strategy outlines the Bank vision for improving its own capacity to respond globally and with a country focus to the urgent issues posed by these changes and challenges. It seeks to ensure that this capacity will be mainstreamed in Bank lending and nonlending country support and support to global partners in areas of Bank comparative advantages.

The Importance of HNP in Socioeconomic Development

Health is often thought to be an outcome of economic growth. Increasingly, however, good health and sound health system policy have also been recognized as a major, inseparable contributor to economic growth.[17] Advances in public health and medical technology, knowledge of nutrition, population policies, disease control, and the discovery of antibiotics and vaccines are widely viewed as catalysts to major strides in economic development, from the Industrial Revolution in 19th-century Britain to the economic miracles of Japan and East Asia in the 20th century. Sound health policy, one that sets the correct incentive framework for financing and delivering services, also has important implications for overall country fiscal policy and competitiveness (Schieber, Fleisher, and Gottret 2006).

Many advances in health status during the 20th century are the result of close synergy among multiple sectors of the economy. For example, investing in basic nutrition during pregnancy and infancy has a substantial positive effect on early childhood development, which, in turn, significantly contributes to educational attainment (Bloom, Canning, Jamison 2004; Jamison 2006).

The complex HNP-development dynamic operates in both directions. Higher incomes allow capacity expansion, which, in turn, may inspire investment in better access to safe water, sanitation, cleaner indoor environments, education, housing, diet, and health care. It also changes household decisions on fertility, usually increasing birth space—all greatly improving health outcomes. This virtuous circle means that, particularly in low-income countries (LICs), ensuring economic growth is also crucial to achieve HNP results. How equitable improvements in health outcomes will be in a growing economy will depend on an effective pro-poor public policy in the health and other sectors (World Bank 2003b, 2004).

Longer-lasting achievements in HNP can improve the investment climate and attract foreign direct investment, once labor forces no longer bear a heavy disease burden. Foreign companies are often deterred from investing in countries with high burden of disease because of concerns about their own workers' health, the possibility of high turnover and absenteeism, and the potential loss of workers with "institutional knowledge" of the firm (Haacker 2004).

In addition to the effect of returns from improving health to improve learning, countries in demographic transition witness a "baby boom" cohort that participates in the education, labor market, and pension systems. Because cohorts before and after the baby boomers are generally much smaller during the transition, the labor force is large relative to overall population size. This means less dependency and greater potential for economic growth, which enables governments to raise investments in health and education and also to increase their economic investments (Jamison 2006; World Bank 2006j).

Significant HNP Gains but Large, Persisting Challenges

The last three decades have brought impressive achievements in HNP: steep reductions in infant mortality and malnutrition in almost every country, unprecedented innovation in health technology and discoveries in medicine, and a steady decline in mortality. An aware international community has become a vocal and active financier of progress in HNP, dedicating massive financial resources to bring it about.

However, almost 11 million children die every year, mainly from preventable causes such as diarrhea and malaria.[18] Malaria kills a child somewhere in the world every 30 seconds.[19] More than 500,000 women die during pregnancy and childbirth every year.[20] In 2006, almost 3 million people died from HIV/AIDS.[21] About 380,000 of these deaths occurred among children younger than 15.[22] Tuberculosis is curable, and yet 1.7 million people die from it every year.[23]

Infant and maternal mortality have marginally improved, if not worsened, in many African countries. Millions more face premature death due to both undernutrition and chronic diseases related to the obesity pandemic. The HIV/AIDS and malaria epidemics are still uncontrolled in most LICs. Illness throws millions into poverty and destitution every year (Baeza and Packard 2006). Well-organized and sustainable health systems and sound health financing policies (national and international) have proven essential to meet these challenges and achieve HNP results on the ground. Both are also vital for sound fiscal policy and country competitiveness, crucial to eradicating poverty in a global economy.

By 2015, noncommunicable diseases (NCDs) will be the leading cause of death in low-income countries (Lopez, Mathers, Ezzati et al. 2006). Many of these deaths will occur prematurely, at an early middle age of adulthood. NCDs impose a significant economic burden, not just on patients, but also on their households, communities, employers, health care systems, and government budgets. An increasing burden of NCDs in developing countries will put an enormous strain on their weak health systems. Sound health policies are essential, for example, to protect households from the impoverishing effects of catastrophic costs associated with NCD-related medical care. Furthermore, health system strengthening is vital to address the growing burden of NCDs because their management and prevention requires long-term, sustained interaction with multiple levels of the health system (World Bank 2007).

Effective interventions and increased financing exist for many of the health problems afflicting the world's poor and vulnerable (Wagstaff and

Claeson 2004). However, in countries with weak health systems, reaching the people needing these interventions through health service delivery mechanisms and improved basic nutrition is challenging. Strengthening health systems—so that these services can be delivered effectively, sustainably, and when needed—is critical to ensure that investments in health continue to foster economic growth to overcome poverty in generations to come.

The Bank Role in HNP Improvements in the Past Decade

As one of the pillars for eradicating poverty, the World Bank has supported countries' efforts to improve health, nutrition, and population policies and results for more than three decades. However, much has changed since the last Bank HNP Strategy was approved by the Board in 1997—and for the better. In the international community, awareness of the pivotal role of HNP policy in poverty eradication, and in economic development itself, has heightened. The central importance of HNP policy to development is reflected, for example, in the emphasis given to HNP in the United Nations Millennium Development Goals (MDGs). Three of the eight MDGs target HNP outcomes, and HNP policy greatly influences results for other MDGs such as poverty, environment, education, and partnerships.

The Bank has substantially contributed to this increased awareness of the international community. Since the 1997 HNP Strategy, it has decisively committed to focusing its work on winning health gains for the poor. The Bank has also played a crucial role in advocacy, awareness, development of new initiatives, and financing of priority diseases and HNP interventions. From 1997 through 2006, the Bank lent US$15 billion and disbursed US$12 billion in HNP for more than 500 projects and programs in more than 100 client countries, making the Bank one of the world's largest international financing organizations of HNP activities in the last decade.

In this new Strategy for the coming decade, the Bank envisions that it will bolster client–country efforts to improve health conditions for the poor and to prevent households from becoming impoverished or made destitute as a result of illness. The Bank envisions that its support and advice will help client countries achieve HNP results in a way that also furthers good governance and their overall fiscal sustainability, economic growth, and global competitiveness. To achieve these four objectives, client countries need to articulate responses from multiple sectors that influence HNP results. The Bank, with its 19 sectors working globally in 139[24] countries, is uniquely positioned to support client–country efforts. This Strategy provides guidance to country teams on steps forward to ensure effective intersectoral work for HNP results.

Opportunities and Challenges: The New International Environment and DAH

The heightened awareness of HNP globally has dramatically changed the international architecture for development assistance in health.[25] In addition to the Bank, new multilateral organizations, initiatives, and foundations have assumed a prominent role in financing HNP, among them are the Global Fund, GAVI, GAIN, and the Bill and Melinda Gates Foundation. Innovative financing mechanisms such as UNITAID,[26] IFFIm,[27] and Advance Market Commitments (AMCs) have also been developed to help to improve the predictability of donor funds. Much of this new funding is earmarked for combating priority diseases such as HIV/AIDS, malaria, tuberculosis, and some vaccine-preventable diseases; less for health system strengthening. Bilateral aid, such as the United States President's Emergency Plan for AIDS Relief (PEPFAR), has also increased substantially. Thus, financial commitments from all sources have doubled in five years, from US$6 billion in 2000 to almost US$14 billion in 2005 (Michaud 2007) (figure 1.1). Annex C presents an overview of trends in DAH in the last decade.

The new opportunities created by the changes in DAH also present three special challenges to: ensure tangible results on the ground for the money invested; align and harmonize global partners' activities with country needs to prevent duplication, economic distortions—and excessive administrative costs—ensuring country-owned and country-led DAH; and ensure synergy between enhanced priority–disease financing and interventions to strengthen health systems.

Ensuring Tangible HNP Results

HNP results in this Strategy encompass not only HNP outcome indicators such as MDGs, stunting, or fertility rates, but also prevention of poverty due to illness *(financial protection)* and health system performance indicators such as equity in utilization of health services and in health insurance[28] coverage. Other results included are: empowerment of the poor, good sector

Figure 1.1: Development Assistance for Health by Source, 2000 and 2005

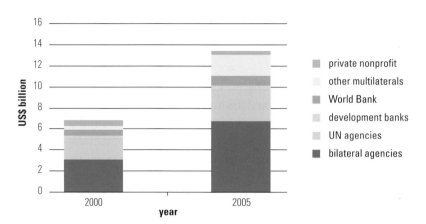

Source: C. M. Michaud 2007.

Note: "Other multilateral" includes the European Union, Global Alliance for Vaccines and Immunisation (GAVI), and Global Fund to Fight AIDS, Tuberculosis and Malaria (GFATM).
"World Bank" total includes only IDA lending.

governance, sector financial sustainability and its contribution to sound fiscal policy and country competitiveness; key outputs such as the proportion of children immunized, proportion of children born under safe delivery conditions, and other outputs closely linked to achieving the HNP-related MDGs; and availability of essential drugs and personnel in rural clinics. All these results are examples of Bank HNP objectives in client–country work. They are determined not only by the inputs of the HNP sector but also by the effects of many other sectors and their interactions.

To make sure people's health and daily lives are actually being improved with the money invested, results on the ground have to be closely monitored and evaluated. However, both client countries and the international community have lacked effective M&E systems for gauging the impact of increased financing on people, particularly the poor in low-income countries. This lack deprives development policy makers of basic knowledge about what works and what does not, essential knowledge for effective use of resources now and for any future scaling up.

The Bank has not escaped this knowledge-gap dilemma. Although there are good examples of individual projects, programs, and policy advice to client countries, and research, the impact of its 1997 HNP Strategy is hard to measure. The impact on the ground of the 1997 HNP Strategy has not been systematically monitored or assessed, nor are there sufficient monitoring data to do it today. Assessment difficulties have been problematic not only for the Bank but also for most of the international community. In the past two years, the Bank has multiplied its HNP evaluation efforts, but the benefits of this effort will be useful only for assessing the impact of the new Strategy. A thorough assessment is not available at this time. However, the Independent Evaluation Group will conduct in 2008 an evaluation of the Bank's client–country assistance in HNP since 1997. This evaluation will inform the implementation of this new Strategy and adjustments will be made as appropriate.

The Bank also faces important challenges in the implementation of its current lending and nonlending portfolio. The active HNP portfolio (active commitments) has declined since 2001 and the quality performance of the portfolio has been the lowest among all Bank sectors. In addition, AAA is not focused enough on Bank comparative advantages.

The Bank, as a public international organization, is accountable for its expected contributions to country HNP results, especially for results of concessional lending under the International Development Association (IDA). The focus on increasing the link of Bank financing to results as well as on effective measurement and impact assessment is therefore essential.

Harmonization and Alignment

The multiplicity of actors offering generous financing has put an additional management and administrative burden on recipient countries. Essential to overcoming this burden are the use of effective country fiduciary systems *(alignment)*—financial management, procurement, logistics (which the Bank can help strengthen)—and the implementation of the Paris Declaration (OECD/DAC 2005) on harmonization of procedures, policy advice, strategies, and program implementation at country level among Bank and other global partners. The Bank is committed to contributing to alignment and harmonization efforts in the HNP sector at country level and will selectively strengthen its engagement with global partners.

Synergy between Single-Disease Priority Programs and Health System Strengthening in LICs

For most of the last decade, the changes in DAH have gone hand-in-hand with a focus on single-priority–disease programs (e.g., HIV/AIDS, malaria) or single interventions (e.g., vaccines), often in the form of vertical pro-grams.[29] However, the new focus of DAH on priority diseases has encoun-tered tight bottlenecks in LIC health systems at country and subnational levels. There is now consensus that, for the renewed commitments of client countries and the international community to realize their full potential, synergy must be ensured between efforts to strengthen the health system and a focus on priority–disease results in LICs. Focus on key priority dis-eases is essential in LICs, given the importance of a few priority diseases in the overall disease burden (e.g., HIV/AIDS, malaria, tuberculosis, vaccine-preventable diseases, micronutrient deficiencies, and perinatal diseases), their limited financial and fiscal space, and health system constraints. For this focus to be successful, a well-functioning health system is fundamental.

In principle, there is no contradiction between a focus on a single priority disease and a system strengthening approach. When well implemented, they are complementary and synergistic, and the only practical way of addressing the multiple causes of morbidity and mortality that might at first appear to be caused only by a single disease. Increased awareness and financing offer client countries and the international community excellent opportunities to improve overall health system performance at marginal cost while concentrating the new resources on controlling priority diseases. Expanded financing has allowed considerable scaling up of HIV/AIDS treatment and is facilitating the scale up of malaria and tuberculosis treatments. If well-directed, scaling up holds great potential for improving access to priority services for the poor well beyond these three diseases in LICs. Countries and the international community have yet to take full advantage of this potential. Ensuring synergy between priority diseases and system strengthening will require a significant effort and discipline from client countries and all development partners, including the World Bank. This will be particularly challenging in Africa, the focus of most priority–dis-ease programs, global initiatives, and funds. The role of IDA financing in health system strengthening, with its capacity to flexibly address system con-straints, will be crucial to ensure this synergy and integration.

A Well-Organized and Sustainable Health System: Essential to Achieve HNP Results on the Ground

"Strengthening health systems" may sound abstract and less important than specific-disease control technology or increased international financing to many people concerned about achieving HNP results, but it is not. On the ground, in practical terms, it means putting together the right chain of events (financing, governance, insurance, logistics, provider payment and incentive mechanisms, information, well-trained personnel, basic infrastructure, and supplies) to ensure equitable access to effective HNP interventions and a continuum of care to save children like Elizabeth (box 1.1). Success in strengthening health systems cannot be claimed until the right chain of events on the ground prevents avoidable deaths and impoverishment due to illness. Without results, health system strengthening has no meaning; yet, there will be no results without health system strengthening.

Box 1.1: Could Elizabeth Have Been Saved? Why Health Systems Matter

Elizabeth was Mary's seventh child. She died at the age of three due to complications of *malaria* on February 17, 2003, at a clinic in San Pedro (a pseudonym), one of the poorest municipalities, in an all-too representative country. Why did Elizabeth die? What does health system strengthening have to do with saving her life? Elizabeth's death had everything to do with a broken health system in desperate need of repair.

The Single Disease
Why Elizabeth died perhaps seems obvious. She caught malaria, developed a cerebral form of the disease, and a common, treatable infection killed her. But why Elizabeth? Had her family not received free bednets to prevent the infection? Was she not diagnosed and treated in time? What happened?

The Broken System
Finding out why Elizabeth died took so much time that Dr. Joy Macumbo, the local public health authority, almost gave up trying. So many children die every day in her district, how could she spare time to investigate just one? Finding out anything was so hard. There were *almost no records* of Elizabeth's last few hours in the hospital or of her previous health history in the clinic. Dr. Macumbo was puzzled. According to her *district data,* for three years San Pedro, Elizabeth's town, had been receiving *free bednets and antimalarial drugs* from the Ministry of Health (MOH). However, the district hospital was still reporting many cases of complications from malaria from the San Pedro area. Dr. Macumbo went to San Pedro to investigate.

   Dr. Macumbo discovered that the health center where Elizabeth should have received the bednets and been diagnosed and treated early on, had had *no health worker for at least 18 months*. Bednets and drugs arrived from the MOH program, but often there was nobody to distribute the nets, or nobody trained to early-diagnose and treat the children. Some community volunteers helped *visiting health workers* catch up with distribution and treat-

(continues on the following page)

Box 1.1: *(continued)*

ment, but there were *no guarantees (or records)* of whether drugs had been *stored properly* (so they stay active) or *administered correctly* to San Pedro's children. In some cases there were no records of what happened to the free bednets. Elizabeth had either not received (or used) a bednet, had not been diagnosed and treated in time, and/or had not received treatment at all.

Why had the health center gone so long without trained workers? Dr. Macumbo asked San Pedro's mayor—*management of health centers had been decentralized from district to municipalities* five years earlier. Any *trained health workers* San Pedro managed to hire *did not stay long in the poor town.* The mayor said the job had been advertised for months, but the few qualified applicants did not want it. Working conditions in San Pedro were much harder than in South Port, the district capital, but the *pay was the same under civil service regulations.*

To make matters worse, health workers on the center's payroll often showed up late— because, the mayor discovered, they were *moonlighting during center working hours.* Some small, private providers paid them case by case, a *supplement to their monthly salary.*

The scant records from Elizabeth's stay at the district hospital and interviews with her mother, Mary, and hospital staff showed that Elizabeth, with very advanced malaria complications, *had arrived at the hospital on a weekend, long after the onset of the symptoms.* Why did she arrive so late?

Elizabeth's mother said *she could not afford* to take her children to the hospital on a weekday. Dr. Macumbo was surprised—public hospital services are free in San Pedro. However, Mary said she had to sell one of her two cows, spend all her savings, and borrow money to cover expenses related to Elizabeth's sickness. A trip to the hospital takes a full day because doctors show up late, so Mary would *lose a day of work. She had to pay for transportation, under-the-table fees for treatment, as well as additional supplies* (antimalarial drugs are free but the supplies are not). Years ago when her first child died, Mary endured a similar financial catastrophe. The *community mutual aid scheme* she joined after the death of her second child *had gone broke* after only three years.

Around the world every day, there are thousands of cases like Elizabeth's. Strengthening health systems is vital to prevent other deaths like Elizabeth's. It is about ensuring that the international community's commitment to supply an area like San Pedro with bednets and drugs will not be wasted by the *wrong chain of events. Strengthening health systems is about setting up the right sequence of events so that others survive.*

The Right Chain of Events

The right sequence of events might have saved Elizabeth. Strengthening a health system means:

- Ensuring the *right logistics* so that bednets (and other drugs and supplies) will reach poor families at risk and that antimalarial drugs will not lose potency through poor storage.
- Helping the government change *salary incentives* so that workers show up for work at health centers to diagnose and treat children, and, at a marginal cost, do well-child consultations at the same time, educate parents, and distribute micronutrient supplements to

Box 1.1: *(continued)*

expectant mothers (to help prevent low birth weights and malnutrition, which compound the effects of malaria), and deliver other services.

- Enhancing *public-private partnerships* (e.g., with community and/or faith-based organizations) in the delivery of services to complement each other and reduce supply gaps.
- Setting the right *payment mechanisms* for providers and linking workers' salaries to both attendance and performance and reducing incentives to spend health center and hospital time on income-generating activities outside their workplace.
- Instituting *governance arrangements* that empower patients and the community to address issues such as informal payments and provider responsiveness.
- Setting the *right insurance and/or public financing mechanisms* (including donor financing) so that the cost of illness will not prevent a mother from taking a sick child for treatment and will not throw her and her family into destitution, forced to sell the few assets they possess.
- Taking advantage of *decentralized decision making and management* while, simultaneously, putting in place *compensatory mechanisms for capacity and equity issues*.
- Having many *more doctors and dedicated health professionals* like Dr. Macumbo, so that countries and districts can *identify and follow systemic problems* without needing external assistance.
- Having *information systems* that address all the key diseases so that doctors and health personnel can treat patients instead of filling out multiple, duplicative reports for each disease to each donor and/or government agency.

Achieving HNP results requires a well-organized and sustainable country health system. A major, urgent effort must be made to strengthen health systems, if financial commitments enabled by the new DAH architecture are to succeed in improving health conditions of the poor and achieve the HNP-related MDGs in middle- and low-income countries. Improving HNP sector governance is also essential. On this, the international community agrees after much debate in the early 2000s, centered on the false dichotomy between priority–disease and system strengthening focus. Policy makers in LICs and MICs face difficult challenges to make their health systems work and to protect people from poverty caused or deepened by illness. Middle-income client–country demand for policy and technical advice also makes it clear that health system strengthening is essential to ensure and sustain more comprehensive approaches to HNP results.

A Shift in the Driver of the Bank-Country Relationship toward High-Quality Policy Advice and Strategic Focus of Bank Lending on Structural HNP Issues

The new DAH architecture, the persisting challenges, and the increasing importance of health systems in addressing them create a scenario in which Bank financing, though still very important, is increasingly small compared with the growing volume of disease-specific financing and no longer is the sole driver of relationships with client countries. In this scenario, it is the quality of policy and technical dialog and the strategic focus of Bank lending (particularly IDA lending) that will define the true magnitude of the Bank contribution to country efforts in HNP.

Strategic focus of Bank advice and lending is essential. Bank financing is strategically crucial to ensure much-needed health system strengthening (for which financing is scarce in the new DAH architecture) and to set the enabling environment for increased disease-specific financing to be effective. This was stated again and again by client countries during preparation of this new Strategy. For example, Bank financing, as measured by new annual financial commitments for HIV/AIDS (figure 1.2), for malaria, and for tuberculosis represented in FY2005, respectively, about 5 percent,[30] 3 percent,[31] and 7 percent[32] of total annual international commitments.[33] That the role of Bank financing is increasingly small, compared to overall international financing for health, is true mainly for middle-income and low-income countries for which DAH is a minor proportion of government or total health expenditures (low-assistance LICs, LA-LICs). Bank financing is still an important source of financing for LICs that count on DAH to cover a large part of government expenditures on health (high-assistance LICs, HA-LICs).

How to Best Serve Client Countries in This New Scenario?

Within this new development assistance scenario, how can the Bank best serve client countries in their efforts to achieve their priority HNP results? How can the Bank contribute to the effectiveness on the ground of global partners' increased financial commitments? What is the role of Bank financing in the context of globally expanded financing for HNP? This new Strategy for HNP Results states the vision of the Bank role in the new global

Figure 1.2: Total Global and World Bank Commitments for HIV/AIDS, 2000, 2002, and 2004

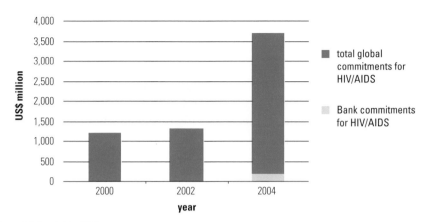

Source: J. A. Izazola-Licea 2006.
Note: World Bank commitments reflect projects identified as having HIV/AIDS as a theme. World Bank commitments for HIV/AIDS in 2002 were approximately US$9 million.

architecture in HNP. It also attempts to give Bank regional and country teams guidance for addressing these questions with a sharp focus on country-led and country-owned Bank assistance for HNP results, working closely with global partners.

Results on the ground, especially outcome improvements for the poor and the vulnerable, rarely occur in the lifetime of a single project, nor are they achieved by focusing on any single sector. It is long-term Bank policy advice, technical assistance, and its lending program as a whole that can influence client–country policy actions, inputs, and structural changes in the health system; HNP policy; and relevant policies from other sectors (e.g., environment, water, transport, social protection, education, agriculture). Therefore, the effectiveness of the Bank country focus in HNP is determined by the quality of policy advice and the strategic focus of Bank lending, as developed in the overall Country Assistance Strategy (CAS), to identify long-term constraints to improving outcomes and country system performance and to define a set of multiple-sector lending and nonlending interventions to support countries' efforts. Under "New Bank Strategic Directions," a strategy is outlined for ensuring that this assessment becomes standard practice in the preparation of the CAS.

The Bank has special strengths *(comparative advantages)* for providing policy and technical advice to client countries in their efforts to achieve

HNP results. The Bank will focus and enhance its capacity to generate knowledge and provide policy and technical advice in these areas.

Bank Comparative Advantages in Helping Client Countries Achieve HNP Results

The Bank has significant comparative advantages to help client countries improve HNP results in this new environment. These advantages include: the Bank health system strengthening capacity, including its potential capacity to disseminate country experience with alternative innovations and reforms; its multisectoral approach to country assistance, which allows it to engage at national and subnational levels with all government agencies (but particularly Ministries of Finance); its capacity for large-scale implementation of projects and programs (including its financial management and procurement systems for extensive operations); its multiple financing instruments and products; its global nature, allowing facilitation of interregional sharing of experience; its core economic and fiscal analysis capacity across all sectors; and its pervasive country focus and presence. The World Bank Group also has significant potential comparative advantages in engaging private health actors through both the Bank (International Bank for Reconstruction and Development, IBRD) and the International Finance Corporation (IFC). Some of these strengths are fully developed at the Bank; some, such as policy and technical advice on regulating private sector and improving public-private collaboration for HNP results, health system strengthening capacity, and intersectoral work for HNP results, need significant reinforcement if the Bank is to give effective support to client countries and the rest of the international community.

Country-Led Lending in HNP

Country focus also means that the Bank will continue to lend, upon country demand, in all areas deemed necessary to improve health status and financial protection for people, especially the poor, in client countries. This includes support for controlling priority diseases because they constitute a large proportion of the burden of disease. However, the Bank will increasingly endeavor to ensure that its priority–disease support will strengthen health systems to solve systemic constraints that impair the effectiveness of country, Bank, and international community financing in achieving HNP results.

Strategic Objectives: What HNP Results?

> The ultimate objective of the World Bank work in HNP and of this new Strategy is to improve the health conditions of the people in client countries, particularly the poor and the vulnerable, in the context of the Bank's overall strategy for poverty alleviation. To achieve this objective, this new Strategy states the vision and actions necessary to strengthen the Bank's capacity to better serve client countries by excelling in areas of Bank comparative advantages and by improving its collaboration with global partners.

To contribute to improving the lives and health conditions of the poor and the vulnerable, the Bank will focus on client–country efforts to achieve results in four areas or Bank Strategic Objectives for HNP:

STRATEGIC OBJECTIVE 1. Improve the level and distribution of key HNP outcomes, outputs, and system performance at country and global levels in order to improve living conditions, particularly for the poor and the vulnerable.

STRATEGIC OBJECTIVE 2. Prevent poverty due to illness (by improving financial protection).

STRATEGIC OBJECTIVE 3. Improve financial sustainability in the HNP sector and its contribution to sound macroeconomic and fiscal policy and to country competitiveness.

STRATEGIC OBJECTIVE 4. Improve governance, accountability, and transparency in the health sector.

These policy objectives represent continuity as well as change as compared with the 1997 HNP Strategy. Improving health outcomes of the poor and the vulnerable, protecting households from the impoverishing effects of illness, and achieving sustainable financing are still central HNP policy objectives. There are, however, three important changes in the new Strategy. First, improving governance and accountability is included as a new policy objective. Second, although focus on strengthening health systems is essential, this strengthening is seen as a crucial means of helping countries achieve HNP results rather than as a policy objective in itself. Third, HNP policy (e.g., regarding financing of health insurance or large scale up for HIV/AIDS) has heavy implications for country fiscal policy and competitiveness. Therefore, linking HNP sectoral policy to these country objectives is essential.

As presented in *World Development Report—2004* (World Bank 2003b), good governance and accountability mechanisms are key determinants of health system performance.

Although demand for advice shows that most countries value results in all four areas, their relative importance varies in different Bank Regions and in LICs and MICs. In LICs, improving outcomes, particularly for the MDGs, may have greater relative importance. In MICs, the priority is increasingly on financial protection and contributions to sound fiscal policy and country competitiveness, although improving health status remains important, particularly to reduce inequities in access to services and financial protection and to address the increasing burden of premature death due to noncommunicable diseases. Governance and transparency are proving critical in all country settings.

Although IDA and IBRD country priorities in health system strengthening present significant similarities (e.g., the challenge of universal health insurance coverage, fiscal sustainability, public-private interface), the specific options for addressing these priorities differ significantly between the two groups of countries. The Bank needs to be able to respond to both and ensure that it generates and disseminates lessons learned and experience among both groups of countries. Improving Bank capacity for health system strengthening will include both IDA and IBRD priorities.

Strategic Directions: How to Support Country Efforts to Achieve Results?

Five new Strategic Directions are specified to improve Bank capacity to assist client countries in achieving the HNP Strategic Objectives in the coming decade:

STRATEGIC DIRECTION 1. Renew Bank focus on HNP results.

STRATEGIC DIRECTION 2. Increase the Bank's contribution to client–country efforts to strengthen and realize well-organized and sustainable health systems for HNP results.

STRATEGIC DIRECTION 3. Ensure synergy between health system strengthening and priority–disease interventions, particularly in LICs.

STRATEGIC DIRECTION 4. Strengthen Bank capacity to advise client countries on an intersectoral approach to HNP results.

STRATEGIC DIRECTION 5. Increase selectivity, improve strategic engagement, and reach agreement with global partners on collaborative division of labor for the benefit of client countries.

STRATEGIC DIRECTION 1: Renew Bank Focus on HNP Results

Focus on HNP outcomes, outputs, and system performance is the key Strategic Direction of the Bank in HNP, to which the rest of the Strategic Directions contribute. The cornerstone of this effort will be the Bank tightening the link between HNP-related lending and nonlending to secure demonstrable HNP results on the ground. Steps in that direction will include: increasing the proportion of output-based HNP lending and implementing up-front investment in monitoring and evaluation for all Bank HNP-related lending; improve quality at entry of new lending portfolio and adjust existing portfolio as needed to improve operations linkage to HNP results; help launch a major effort, in coordination with global partners and global initiatives, to help client countries improve their national public health surveillance and performance-monitoring systems and monitor a core set of indicators at global level; partner with client countries to experiment and learn from innovation provided by country-led reforms and programs supported by the Bank; and set a common global HNP Results Framework for the Bank to guide regional HNP strategies, regional HNP business plans, and overall Bank/global partner monitoring and evaluation activities on HNP results.

STRATEGIC DIRECTION 2: Increase Bank Contribution to Client–Country Efforts to Strengthen and Realize Well-Organized and Sustainable Health Systems for HNP Results

Achieving HNP results requires a well-organized and sustainable country health system to ensure equitable access to effective HNP interventions and a continuum of care. Policy makers in LICs and MICs face difficult challenges to make their health systems work in delivering sustainable health services and protecting people from poverty due to illness. The Bank has important comparative advantages for helping client countries strengthen their health systems, but not for all aspects of it. Collaborative division of labor with global partners is needed to respond to the wide range of demand from client countries (Shakow 2006). The Bank will step up its engagement in health system strengthening, with an unswerving commitment to making it an instrument for achieving concrete results on the ground, appropriate to the specific needs of both MICs and LICs. (For analysis of health system characteristics and challenges, see "New Bank Strategic Directions" and annex F).

STRATEGIC DIRECTION 3: Ensure Synergy between Health System Strengthening and Priority–Disease Interventions, Particularly in LICs

The Bank will make every effort to increase synergy between priority–disease funding and health system strengthening in Bank operations in LICs, and, upon request, will advise client countries on how to achieve this synergy with country and DAH financing. Synergy in this context means addressing priority disease–specific needs simultaneously with the key system constraints to getting the needed results for the priority disease(s) in question, while avoiding or limiting negative spillovers and maximizing positive spillovers.

Bank financing through the International Development Association plays a crucial role in HNP-enhancing interventions to ensure synergy between focus on priority diseases and health system strengthening in LICs. It also helps forestall allocative inefficiency and other distortions that can result from the allocation of large amounts of financing to a few diseases (and neglect of others).

STRATEGIC DIRECTION 4: Strengthen Bank Capacity to Advise Client Countries on an Intersectoral Approach to HNP Results

The HNP sector alone (at country level or internationally) cannot achieve the MDGs (and other priority outcomes) or improve health system performance. These HNP results are seldom determined by any single sector.

Intersectorality is one of the most important comparative advantages of the Bank. It is also one of the most difficult to realize fully due to traditional compartmentalization of sectors in client countries as well as to contradictory incentives within the Bank. The Bank will therefore strengthen its intersectoral work to help client countries and the international communities achieve the best possible HNP results (see "New Bank Strategic Directions" and annex E).

As one of the leading global multilateral organizations in development, the Bank collaborates with many other bilateral and multilateral organizations and global HNP partnerships. Engaging and collaborating with global partners contributes both to Bank capacity to serve client countries and to global partners' own capacity. The volume of the HNP partnership portfolio has increased dramatically over the past five years, mirroring the changes in the global health architecture. As a result, Bank engagement with global partners is fragmented and requires sharper strategic direction. With the implementation of the new Strategy, the Bank will assess its engagement with its partners to ensure effective and sustainable partnerships. For example, the Bank will seek a better balance in its partnerships and its regional work on LIC and MIC priorities, particularly on health systems and will substantially increase its strategic engagement with WHO, the Global Fund, and GAVI in LICs.

In addition to collaborative division of labor in health system strengthening, the Bank will: promote country-level collaboration for alignment and harmonization; direct Bank contributions to promoting global public goods and preventing and mitigating global public "bads" in areas of Bank comparative advantages; and increasingly transition Bank advocacy engagement with partners toward health system strengthening with sharp focus on HNP results and toward synergy between priority–disease financing and system strengthening approaches. In management of trust funds (TFs) and the Development Grant Facility (DGF), the Bank will increasingly concentrate on trust funds and grants that are directly related to the implementation of its HNP Strategic Directions at country level.

Implementing the Bank HNP Strategy

To make full use of its comparative advantages in the new environment in the interests of its client countries, the HNP sector in the Bank needs to make functional and organizational changes and rebalance the skill-mix of its staff and management. Sharpening the regional and Hub HNP units' focus on results, health system strengthening, and intersectoral work will be costly in the short term. Adjustments in skill-mix take time and effort (staff and management training; shifting recruitment toward senior health specialists in systems, economics, and intersectorality skills development of core diagnostic tools). It will also require functional changes in the mission of the HNP Hub so that it becomes more oriented to support Region and country team work. Concomitantly, it will also require revitalization of the role and work of the HNP Sector Board.

A summary Action Plan for implementing key features, leading to the new Strategic Directions and results, is part of this Strategy. It includes: proposals and targets to improve quality at entry of the HNP portfolio; actions to restructure current at-risk portfolio; a design, pilot, and implementation plan for a new tool, the Multisectoral Constraints Assessment for Health Outcomes (MCA); proposals for improving statistical capacity and monitoring core indicators at country and global levels; a results framework to guide regional development of country strategies, and proposals for training and retooling HNP staff and management. It also includes key organizational changes, particularly for the HNP Network (HNPFAM) and the HNP Hub. Finally annex A presents summaries of regional and HNP Hub Action Plans for Strategy implementation.

A Window of Opportunity for Redoubled Support for Countries' HNP Results

The expanded commitment of the international community in health has created an unprecedented window of opportunity for the Bank to further contribute to HNP results globally. Consultations with many global and country leaders in health, including leaders of donor agencies, foundations, Ministries of Health and Finance of client countries, Executive Directors of the World Bank, and management and staff from HNP and other sectors in the Bank have confirmed their expectations of the need for the Bank to rise to these new challenges—and expeditiously. This Strategy offers guidance for the Bank's short- and medium-term response to meet the new challenges.

CHAPTER 2

Opportunities and Challenges in the New International Environment in Health

A New International Environment

Among the many new developments since the 1997 Bank HNP Strategy, particularly important are the: increased prominence of HNP in international development policy; radical changes in the international architecture of development assistance for health and proliferation in the number and influence of global organizations and partnerships; insufficient attention to ensuring results on the ground and installing the monitoring and evaluation systems essential to gauge them; recent revaluation by the international community of the importance of well-organized and sustainable health systems for achieving HNP results; significant increases in efforts to introduce structural changes in the health system, particularly in MICs; proliferation and expansion of single-disease approaches, including vertical program implementation; increasing awareness, without sufficient public policy action, regarding the substantial role of private financing and private sector delivery of health services in client countries; impressive technological development in pharmaceuticals, especially vaccines and antiretroviral drugs (ARVs); and persisting challenges in public health, population, and nutrition.

- *Global attention to health policy and its challenges has burgeoned worldwide* in the last 10 years. Global commitment to the MDGs is one prominent example.

- With the increase in global attention to health policy, *a radical change in the architecture of DAH* has occurred. The number and influence of new multilateral, bilateral, and private initiatives has exploded in the last decade.

The relative importance of Bank financing (in terms of volume) in HNP has decreased since 1997. In 1997, the Bank was the predominant HNP financing organizations. Today it is one of a group of large financiers. In the next five years, annual DAH commitments increased from about US$6 billion in 2000 to almost US$14 billion in 2005 (figure 1.1). However, despite such large increases in DAH, the total is still far from the estimated amount needed to achieve the MDGs (Wagstaff and Claeson 2004).

- Despite the increase in global attention to health, *too little attention has been paid to ensuring results on the ground and establishing the monitoring and evaluation systems so essential for such a focus.* Despite advances in data collection, the HNP sector (globally and within the Bank) is not much better-off today than it was 10 years ago in its capacity to generate basic, reliable, timely information on outcomes, outputs, and inputs, particularly in LICs. This lack is a major obstacle not only for results monitoring but also for countries' own policy formulation and for strengthening causal pathways among inputs, outputs, outcomes, and policy actions.

- At the same time, *client countries have been ahead of the international community in pursuing system strengthening.* Efforts to introduce structural changes in health systems have significantly increased, mainly in MICs but also in LICs. Concomitantly, demand has swelled for sophisticated policy and technical advice on health financing, health insurance, and other health system functions. Client countries want to find out *how* to do it rather than *what* to do.

- In the early 2000s, single priority–disease approaches also coexisted with a *significant underestimation of the importance of well-organized and sustainable health systems for achieving HNP results,* but *the international community has come to realize its full importance.* This realization has brought a sense of urgency about ensuring smoothly functioning health systems, now seen as a prerequisite for obtaining solid HNP results on the ground.

- *Single-disease approaches have proliferated and expanded* during the last decade, hand in hand with single priority–disease approaches and often with a vertical disease-control approach. This trend has created challenges of its own, particularly in low-income countries, and especially in Africa. Multiple donors with different strategic and operational approaches are often an extra burden on policy makers in recipient countries who have to allocate great effort to respond to uncoordinated donor work. In many cases, concern is growing about the equity, effectiveness, and efficiency consequences of vertical implementation of single priority–disease programs nationally.

- *Despite increasing awareness of the large role of private financing and delivery of health services, public policy action has been insufficient in most client countries.* Private providers deliver most ambulatory health services in most LICs, and even the poorest people often seek private care (figures 2.1 and 2.2). Nevertheless, public policy is still not attuned to ensuring public-private complementarity and synergies and effective resource use in the health sector.

- *Technological development in pharmaceuticals has been impressive, especially in vaccines and antiretroviral drugs.* This development has reduced costs and improved the effectiveness of a number of priority–disease treatments (e.g., for HIV/AIDS, malaria). It has also introduced new vaccines (e.g., rotavirus and pneumococcal) with potential for cutting mortality in children under five years of age (U-5) in LICs. This good news for the international community brings with it two important challenges. The first is to develop financing mechanisms (such as the Advance Market Commitment mechanism[34]) to encourage research and development (R&D) and manufacturing for LICs of much-needed technologies for which country fiscal constraints preclude demand. The second is whether and how to mainstream the new vaccines as well as how to sustain them financially in client countries.

Finally, the last three decades have brought impressive achievements in HNP, *but formidable challenges persist:*

- *Actual and potential pandemics and regional epidemics have continuously emerged, and some have expanded* during the last decade (e.g., HIV/AIDS, malaria, drug-resistant TB, SARS, avian flu). There has also been a *significant increase in premature deaths related to traffic accidents and chronic diseases (diabetes, pulmonary diseases, hypertension, and cancer) caused by the tobacco addiction and the obesity pandemics.* The international community has managed such threats in the past, for example, in eradicating smallpox and making deep inroads into the eradication of polio. Significant advances have been made on understanding the determinants of tobacco addiction and obesity. However, HIV/AIDS, malaria, TB, obesity, and new pandemics will continue to challenge client countries in the future.

Figure 2.1: Treatment of Diarrhea

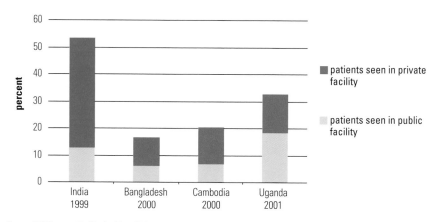

Source: HNP Strategy Facilitation Team 2006. Adapted from World Bank Institute data (A. Yazbeck and Hayashi).
Note: Percentage of patients from the poorest quintile seen in public or private facilities.

Figure 2.2: Who Uses Public or Private Health Facilities for Acute Respiratory Infections?

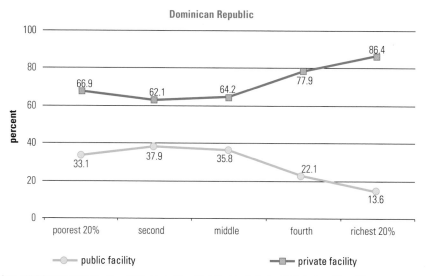

Source: HNP Strategy Facilitation Team 2006. Adapted from World Bank Institute data (A. Yazbeck and Hayashi).
Note: Breakdown by quintile.

Client–country public health surveillance systems must be ready to detect and respond quickly to outbreaks of infectious diseases and promote behavioral changes for obesity and effective policies to reduce tobacco consumption (e.g., tax increases for cigarettes).

- *The world population more than doubled* in the second half of the 20th century. Ninety-five percent of all population growth occurred in developing countries. Since the middle of the last century, fertility and mortality trends almost everywhere have gradually converged toward low fertility and lengthened life expectancy. The exception is the Sub-Saharan Africa Region (east, west, and middle subregions) and many countries in the Middle East and North Africa, where total fertility rates (TFRs) are very high. The persistence of population growth in the absence of economic growth pose significant challenges to developing countries capacity to ensure access to basic services.

- *Malnutrition, now problematic in both poor and rich countries, affects the poorest people most.* Underweight and micronutrient-deficient children and overweight adults live in the same households in both developing and developed countries. Malnutrition, and its negative compounding effect on disease susceptibility, slows economic growth and perpetuates poverty through direct losses in productivity from poor physical status, as well as indirect losses from poor cognitive function and deficits in schooling and direct losses owing to increased health care costs.

The New Architecture for Development Assistance for Health

Over the last 10 years, there have been profound changes in the organizations that play key roles in global health, as large private foundations (e.g., the Bill and Melinda Gates Foundation) and large global funds[35] have entered the scene with substantial amounts of grant money. Other disease-specific initiatives[36] were also founded and have brought new financial resources for specific diseases. Annex C presents an in-depth overview of the new DAH.

Successful advocacy for HNP and increase in DAH is good news. The new global architechture is here to stay, and most likely expand, and has created many opportunities for improving health conditions of the poor in low-income countries. However, it has also created major new challenges for recipient countries. Multiple donors, each with its own strategic and fiduciary approach, have put a weighty managerial and administrative burden on recipient countries. The implementation of the Paris Declaration (OECD/DAC 2005), which is designed to harmonize all donor approaches including the Bank's, is essential to improve effectiveness at the country level.

Determining how, in the new international environment, to make the most of the opportunities opened by increased awareness and financial commitment and minimizing distortions from DAH are essential for Bank effectiveness in HNP in the next decade.

CHAPTER 3

Bank Contribution and Challenges in Implementing the 1997 HNP Strategy

The Bank has substantially contributed to HNP in client countries in the last decade. Since the 1997 HNP Strategy, it has decisively committed to focusing its work on winning health gains for the poor. The Bank has also played a crucial role in advocacy, awareness, and development of new international initiatives. It has contributed substantial financing and policy advice for priority diseases and HNP interventions, with more than 500 projects and programs in more than 100 countries. With total cumulative lending of US$15 billion and about US$12 billion in cumulative disbursements, the Bank has been one of the world's largest international financiers of HNP activities in the last decade. The Bank has also provided substantial policy and technical advice through more than 250 analytical and advisory activities (AAA).

However, the Bank faces important challenges. Despite the good number of excellent projects and programs to its credit in different Regions, the implementation impact of the 1997 Strategy on HNP results on the ground cannot be systematically evaluated, because focus on monitoring and evaluation during the last decade was weak, and impact data are not available. Additionally, the Bank has faced an increased reduction in volume and deterioration in the quality of implementation of its current lending and non-lending portfolio since 2002. The active portfolio has declined about 30 percent since 2001, and the quality of the HNP portfolio has been the lowest performing, below all Bank sectors average for project outcomes. In addition, the focus of AAA on health systems has also been insufficient, less than 35 percent of all AAAs. Although HNP sector operations are inherently complex and high risk as compared with many other sectors, much improvement is needed in the quality at entry and strategic focus of operations to improve HNP portfolio performance.

Bank Contribution to the New DAH Architecture

The Bank has played a significant role in shaping the new DAH architecture. Since 1997, it has participated in the creation and is on the Board of the main global partnerships, including: UNAIDS, Roll Back Malaria, Stop TB, GAVI, Global Fund to Fight AIDS, Tuberculosis and Malaria, Health Metrics Network, the Reproductive Health Supplies Coalition, UNITAID, and others listed in annex G.

In addition to its contribution to these major global initiatives, the Bank has scaled up its engagement with many global partners and partnerships in HNP, mostly through the HNP Hub. Engagement with global partners is part of the Bank mission to better serve client countries by enhancing global public goods and preventing global public "bads." The HNP Hub works in specific areas with more than 55 organizations or initiatives at the global level, including other multilaterals, bilaterals, private foundations, and global partnerships. This extensive engagement also poses internal challenges for the Bank.

Taking Stock of the 1997 HNP Strategy

Since issuing the 1997 HNP Strategy, the Bank has played a major role in HNP globally and has contributed to client–country efforts to improve health conditions of the poor. It has done so mainly through lending and nonlending country support and through contributions to most major global health initiatives. However, taking stock of the ultimate impact of the 1997 HNP Strategy is difficult for two main reasons. First, country-level outcomes and performance results are difficult to attribute directly to Bank financing, which is often relatively small. Second, monitoring and evaluation tools for most HNP-related lending and nonlending support are lacking. The Bank has played a central role in advocacy, awareness, and financing of priority diseases and interventions in HNP in the last decade. Although there are multiple examples of excellent projects, programs, policy advice to client countries, and research, the impact of the 1997 HNP Strategy has not been systematically assessed, nor do the available monitoring data allow it.

The difficulties in obtaining monitoring and evaluation data for HNP projects are not new. In 1999, an evaluation of the effectiveness of HNP projects raised concerns about Bank M&E (World Bank 1999). Addition-ally, the review of all Implementation Completion Reports (ICRs) of HNP projects that closed in FY2004–FY2005 revealed that only 25 percent of all HNP sector–managed projects had a satisfactorily rated M&E (World Bank 2006e). According to the same review, less than half the projects included any outcome-output indicator in the results frameworks, and less than half of those that did measure these indicators did so at least twice. Another review of 118 ICRs in FY2003–FY2005 found that only a few Bank-assisted projects evaluated changes in health services (42 percent), health financing (17 percent), or health status (33 percent). The review also showed that any changes measured were always positive (Subramanian, Peters, and Willis 2006).

Lending Trends since 1997

The Bank is still one of the world's largest single financiers of HNP activi-ties, as measured by cumulative commitments and cumulative disburse-ments. Total Bank active portfolio (projects and programs) amounted to about US$7.0 billion in FY2006, reflecting a steady decrease from US$9.5 billion in FY2001. Average annual disbursements hovered around US$1.1 billion in FY1997–FY2006 (figure 3.1). These numbers include all active lending for health, nutrition, and population (HNP sector and other sec-tors) by both IDA and IBRD.

The Bank has contributed substantially to financing client–country HNP efforts during the implementation of the 1997 HNP Strategy through both lending and projects. World Bank cumulative HNP disbursements for FY1997 through FY2006 stand at about US$12 billion. Since FY1997, more than 500 projects with a health component have been approved.

Bank lending through IBRD, however, has contracted since FY2001. While annual new IBRD lending grew from less than US$0.5 billion in FY2000 to more than US$1.0 billion in FY2004, in the last two years it dropped to around US$0.4 billion in FY2006 (figure 3.2)—in stark contrast to IBRD lending in other sectors. More important, annual commitments have followed the same trend since FY2001. Bank lending through IDA grew from US$0.5 billion in FY2000 to US$0.8 billion in FY2006, in line with international commitments for HNP results in LICs. However, debt relief will shrink the IDA lending envelope for a number of IDA countries

Figure 3.1: All HNP Total Commitments, Disbursements, and New Lending, FY1997–FY2006

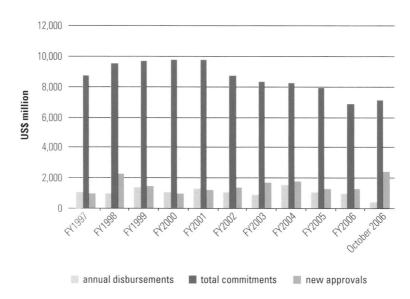

Source: Business Warehouse October 2006.

Note: Includes HNP Sector Board- and other Sector Board-managed lending (allocations to health, noncompulsory health finance, compulsory health finance).

For new lending, FY07 figures are projections—as of October 2006—adjusted with the 0.7 coefficient of realism (ratio of approved new lending over target new lending at the beginning of a fiscal year as deduced by data manipulations from the past years in HNP).

because each dollar of debt relief granted those countries will cut lending proportionately.

A continuation of the cumulative IBRD reduction will have important implications for the Bank business model. No systematic analysis is available on the determinants of the reduction in IBRD lending, but anecdotal evidence suggests that many MICs are changing their engagement. Instead of just borrowing, they are seeking high-level Bank policy advice and knowledge or making such advice a condition for borrowing.

This trend may reflect either better access to favorable borrowing conditions elsewhere or MIC capacity to finance interventions with their own resources. Although this is good news, it also means that the portfolio trends confirm clients' changed expectations of the role of the Bank, as stated in most country consultations. Thus, the quality of Bank policy and technical advice increasingly drives relationships with client countries.

Figure 3.2: Trends in IDA/IBRD Total New Lending for HNP, All Sector Boards Managed, FY1997–FY2006

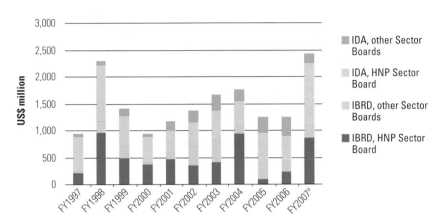

Source: Business Warehouse, HNP Quality Team, October 2006.

Note: Represents new health lending commitment trends, in US$ million, broken down into International Development Agency and International Bank for Reconstruction and Development lending amounts.

a. FY2007 figures are projections adjusted with the 0.7 coefficient of realism (ratio of approved new lending over target new lending at the beginning of a fiscal year as deduced by data manipulations from the past years in HNP).

Need to Rapidly Improve Quality Performance of HNP Portfolio

The overall strategic direction and quality-control mechanism of the HNP portfolio needs reassessment. The performance of the Bank HNP sector portfolio needs major improvement. Portfolio quality, represented by project outcomes as measured by the Bank ("satisfactory" or "unsatisfactory"), has shown the lowest performance among all Bank sectors in the last five years. From FY1997 through October 2006, 423 projects including HNP objectives / activities closed.[37] Of those, 202 were HNP Sector Board–managed projects; 221 were other sector–managed. Of all FY2001–FY2006 closed projects managed by the HNP sector, 66 percent were rated "satisfactory" or better in ICRs (World Bank 2006c), making HNP the worst-performing portfolio among all 19 sectors for the last five years in a row (figure 3.3).

This trend seems to be continuing. According to preliminary Quality Assurance Group (QAG) findings (World Bank *forthcoming* a), only 66 percent of the assessed HNP-managed projects were rated "moderately satisfactory" or better, compared with 90 percent of Bank-wide projects. Key

Figure 3.3: Project Outcomes, by Sector Board, FY2001–FY2006

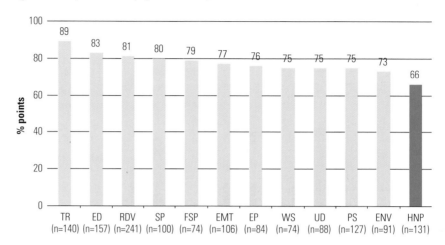

Source: Based on IEG evaluations from *Business Warehouse.*
Note: Definition of acronyms by order of magnitude: Transport, Education, Rural Development, Social Protection, Financial Sector, Energy and Mining, Economic Policy, Water and Sanitation, Urban Development, Public Sector, Environment, and Health, Nutrition, and Population.

determinants of poor portfolio performance in HNP are: quality and readiness of the results framework at entry; adequacy and speed of follow-up actions for nonperforming projects; and attention by management. On the other hand, HNP Sector Board–managed projects seem to perform better in areas of training, capacity building, and effective use of Bank resources.

Projects at risk have increased steadily in the last four years (figure 3.4), with a recent improvement at end-October 2006. In May 2006, 34 percent of the projects and 35 percent of all commitments were at risk in the HNP sector. Despite the improvements noted in October 2006, both the percentage of projects and commitments at risk (20 percent and 23 percent, respectively) remain well above the Bank-wide averages of 14 percent and 12 percent, respectively.

In October 2006, 18 percent of all Bank projects that displayed unsatisfactory implementation progress or were at risk of not achieving their outcomes belonged to the HNP sector. In addition, 60 percent of these projects had important M&E deficiencies, which will make the measurement of results and project impact difficult.

The realism index[38] is 80 percent; the proactivity index[39] is low at 60 percent. Low proactivity needs urgent attention, because it signals that not enough is being done to put nonperforming projects back on track.

Figure 3.4: Trends in Portfolio Riskiness, HNP Sector Board versus Bank Overall, FY1997–FY2006

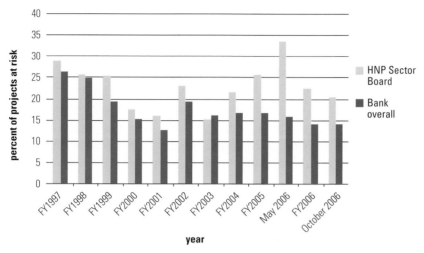

Source: *Business Warehouse* October 2006.
Note: FY1997–FY2006 data are estimates of each fiscal year; end-October 2006.

Within the HNP portfolio, the HIV/AIDS portfolio faces significant challenges. Major steps have been taken to improve HIV/AIDS portfolio performance. As a result, the risk rate has decreased to 18 percent. Actions taken to improve the performance include changes in implementation arrangements to improve performance, establishment of a core quality team for HIV/AIDS projects in Africa, and project support to improve monitoring and evaluation arrangements. Improvement in multisectoral work for HNP results, improved coordination of health system strengthening work within the Bank, and further inclusion of health system strengthening in future operations, including HIV/AIDS, will help improve the HIV/AIDS portfolio performance.

Overall, the HNP sector needs to strengthen its quality control capacity (at entry and during implementation). To do so, the right balance will have to be achieved between the Regions' responsibility for portfolio management and quality control and the responsibility of the HNP Hub and Sector Board for monitoring and assisting Regions in fulfilling their quality control task. The forthcoming evaluation of the HNP portfolio by the Independent Evaluation Group (IEG) will also contribute substantially to informing the process of strengthening portfolio quality.[40]

Need for Sharper Focus of Analytic and Advisory Activities

The Bank has invested significantly in analytic and advisory activities since FY2002. For FY2002–FY2007,[41] 380 economic sector work (ESW) and technical assistance (TA) activities were planned, and 297 have been delivered. Of those 380 ESWs, 274 are ESW products and 106 are TA products addressing health, nutrition, and/or population policy and technical issues.

From FY2002 to FY2005, HNP analytic and advisory activities increased substantially (from 46 to 82 activities), but decreased again, starting in FY2006, to 57 activities. This result is surprising, because AAA services were expected to increase as IBRD lending declined.

The current AAA portfolio shows no particular focus; it includes many aspects of health systems and HNP, but less than 35 percent of the portfolio is concentrated on Bank comparative advantages.

Imbalance in HNP Staff Trends

Since 1997, the number of HNP sector staff has decreased by 15 percent, from 243 to 206 (figure 3.5). This decrease has occurred despite increasing lending and nonlending output and a massive increase in Bank engagement in global partnerships. The proportion of technical specialist staff has risen from 46 percent to 49 percent from 1997 to 2006 (mainly health specialists).

Figure 3.5: Trends in HNP Mapped Staff, FY1997–FY2006

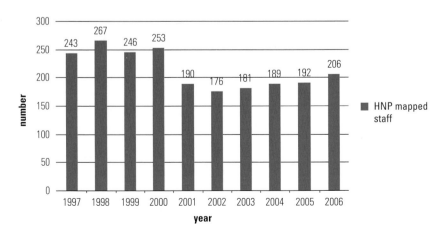

Source: Human Resources October 2006.

Figure 3.6: Health Staff Composition, by Specialty, FY1997

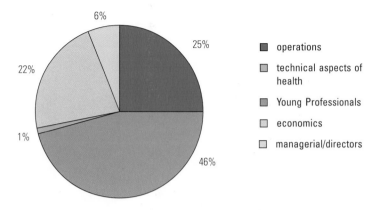

Source: Human Resources October 2006.

The proportion of staff with economics skills has decreased from 22 percent in 1997 to 17 percent in 2006 (figures 3.6 and 3.7).[42] The average age of staff at recruitment has fallen from 48.6 in FY2000 to 39.9 in FY2006 (figure 3.8).

The HNP Hub has undergone a substantial change in staffing since FY2000. Regular or open-ended staff members have decreased in number by 40 percent and have been replaced by Junior Professional Associates (JPAs), Extended Term Consultants (ETCs), and seconded staff, financed mostly by donor Trust Funds in areas of specific donor interest (figure 3.9).

Figure 3.7: Health Staff Composition, by Specialty, FY2006

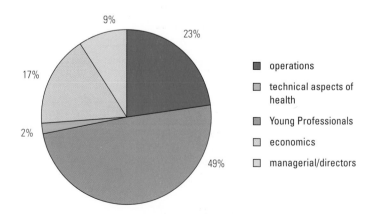

Source: Human Resources October 2006.

Figure 3.8: New HNP Hires, Average Age

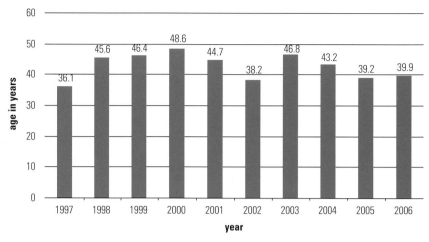

Source: Human Resources October 2006.
Note: Represents average age at hire of staff mapped to HNP.

Figure 3.9: Staff Trends for HNP Hub, by Category, FY1999–FY2006

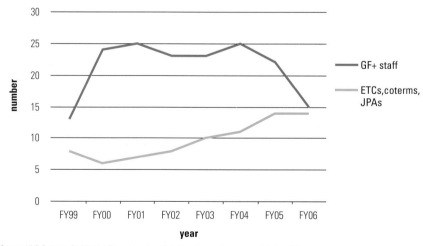

Source: HNP Strategy Facilitation Team, based on data from Human Resources, October 2006.
Note: "ETCs": Extended Term Consultants; "Coterms": Coterminous staff with open-ended or term appointments that are entirely funded from sources other than the Bank Group's administrative budget; "JPAs": Junior Professional Associates; "GF+ staff" represents staff with at least one master degree and 5 years or more of experience.

CHAPTER 4

How Can the Bank Better Serve
Client Countries in the New
Environment? Bank Comparative
Advantages for HNP Results

The new DAH architecture, persisting global challenges, and trends in
Bank portfolio performance consolidate a scenario in which Bank financing,
though still important, is increasingly small, as compared with overall international financing for health, and no longer drives relationships with client
countries. Pressures on policy makers for sound allocation of these
expanded resources have intensified. In this new scenario, the quality of policy dialog and technical advice defines the magnitude of the Bank contribution to country HNP efforts, not only for middle-income countries, but also
for low-aid, low-income countries.[43] Although this is also true for high-aid,
low-income countries,[44] Bank financing is still an important source of revenue for them. In what HNP policy and technical advice areas can the Bank
contribute most in this new scenario? What is the role of Bank HNP-
related financing? According to feedback from client countries and global
partners, Bank comparative advantages lie in addressing "structural and
health system constraints" (particularly health financing, regulation, insurance, and demand-side interventions) to improve outcomes and inputs,
"linkages" of the health sector with macroeconomic, fiscal policy, and labor
markets, and "public sector reform, governance, and fiduciary effectiveness." The Bank is also seen to be in a unique position for identifying and
helping address multiple sectoral constraints to ensure effectiveness on the
ground of the additional international funds. Feedback also indicates that
the Bank has much less (or no) comparative advantages on technical issues
of disease control or micro issues of provider organization such as develop-

ment of training curricula for health personnel, development of new drug technology, or advice on technology and clinical approaches to single-disease treatment, except in contributing to country and global partners' efforts to create the appropriate incentive environment for providers.

Bank Comparative Advantages

Bank comparative advantages in the new scenario include: its health system strengthening and intersectoral approach to country assistance, which allows it to engage in day-to-day dialog at national and subnational levels with all government agencies, but particularly with Ministries of Finance on fiscal and macroeconomic policy; its capacity for large-scale implementation of projects and programs (with its financial management and procurement systems); its multiple financing instruments and products; its global nature, which facilitates interregional sharing of experience; its core economic and fiscal analysis capacity across all sectors; and its substantial country focus and presence. The World Bank Group also has significant potential comparative advantages in engaging private health actors through both the Bank (IBRD) and IFC. Because of its strengths in multisectoral and macro approaches to HNP policy, the Bank is also uniquely positioned to help client countries integrate in their national strategic view the full array of national and international initiatives for improving HNP results on the ground. Bank experience with Poverty Reduction Strategy Papers (PRSPs) is a good example of this integration role.

Bank comparative advantages are distinctive assets for achieving HNP results, but the Bank is not tapping its full potential in some key areas: public policy toward private-public synergies in achieving HNP results at country level, intersectoral approaches to HNP results, and health system strengthening to improve HNP results, particularly for the poor and the vulnerable. In this section, the importance of making full use of these strengths is analyzed. The Bank approach to realizing its full potential in these areas is discussed under "New Bank Strategic Directions."

Knowledge and Policy Advice on Public Policy to Improve Public–Private Synergies for HNP Results

Private service delivery and private funding via household out-of-pocket spending dominate health systems in LICs and in many MICs. Indeed, private ambulatory basic health service provision dominates health systems in LICs (figures 2.1 and 2.2), particularly in Asia. Thus, improving HNP results requires the Bank to provide sound policy advice to client countries on how to ensure effective regulation to enhance equity and efficiency as well as synergy and collaboration between the private and public sectors to improve access to services for the poor.

Bank advisory capacity on health system strengthening needs to be able to provide sound, feasible, and sustainable advice on when and how to invest in in-house public service delivery infrastructure or contract out with the private sector (for-profit and not-for-profit) in LICs and MICs.

The Bank Group has a potential comparative advantage for contributing to client–country development of sound public policy toward the private sector, but the current tendency of the Bank HNP sector to focus on the public sector and of IFC to focus on business development for the private sector has created a vacuum in the Bank Group in terms of supporting client–country development of public policy toward the private health sector. The HNP sector, in collaboration with Private Sector Development (PSD) and IFC, will fill this vacuum in the implementation of the new HNP Strategy. The collaboration will strengthen HNP policy analysis and advisory capacity as well as its engagement with key private actors and policy makers in the areas of public-private collaboration for HNP results. This enhanced capacity aims at generating policy knowledge and lessons learned to advise client countries on options. Ultimately, decisions on specific options are for client countries to make.

Providing Advice and Financing to Strengthen Health Systems for HNP Results

People's understanding of what constitutes a "health system" varies widely, but most specialists agree that it encompasses all country activities, organizations, governance arrangements, and resources (public and private) dedicated primarily to improving, maintaining, or restoring the health of individuals and populations and preventing households from falling into poverty (or becoming further impoverished) as a result of illness (WHO 2000; Kutzin 2000, Baeza and Packard 2006). Annex F presents a basic discussion of what a country health system is and why its smooth functioning is essential to ensure equitable access to effective HNP interventions and a continuum of care to save and improve people's lives—to ensure results.[45] Thus, health systems are not monolithic entities. Interaction among their multiple components results (or not) in sustainable and equitable delivery of public health and medical services to the population. Figure 4.1 depicts the key functions of a well-organized and sustainable health system. These key functions are: health services delivery, resource (input) generation (e.g., human resource training and generation of technological knowledge for disease control, pharmaceuticals, and medical equipment), and system oversight (*stewardship*). Country and sector governance are also key determinants of system performance.

Governments and partners look to the Bank for systemic policy advice on such questions as how to ensure sustainable financing and fiscal space for priority health interventions; how to pay health service providers and set up the right incentives to maximize results on the ground and ensure a presence in

Figure 4.1: Health System Functions and Other Determinants of Good System Performance

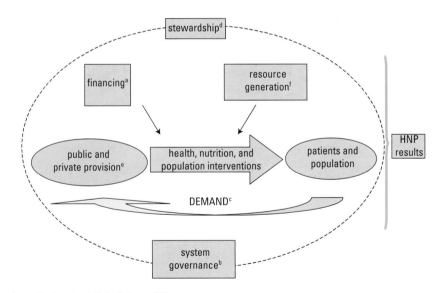

Source: Based on the *World Health Report, 2000.*
a. Includes funding (public, out-of-pocket, and DAH), contributions, pooling, and payment mechanisms.
b. Includes financial management, procurement, and "other" systems.
c. Influenced by preferences, beliefs, and behaviors.
d. Oversight.
e. Service delivery.
f. Includes human resources, pharmaceuticals, and medical equipment.

isolated geographical areas; how to strengthen the sector's fiduciary and financial management systems; how to set the right incentives for multiple branches of government to ensure an intersectoral approach to improving HNP outcomes, outputs, and system performance; how to design and implement health insurance; how to create the appropriate regulatory environment for effective and efficient private-public collaboration and development; how to link increased resources to results without jeopardizing medium-term flexibility in governments' management of funds, both essential for allocative efficiency in public policy; and how to reach the right balance between expanding "own" public health service infrastructure and contracting out with private providers for the needed expansion of health service supply. Both MICs and LICs consider these policy issues critical.

The Bank has a considerable potential comparative advantage in health system development and strengthening, but not in every aspect. Many Bank strengths in health systems stem from its multisectoral nature, its core mandate on sustainable financing, and its fiscal, general economic, and insurance analytical capacity, on regulation, and on demand-side interventions. They also come from its years of experience advising governments and financing broad health sector reforms and infrastructure projects all over the world. Finally, they come from its experienced and motivated staff working in the Regions and the Hubs (Bank technical central units). Consultations with client countries confirm this view of Bank comparative advantages.

However, a large part of health system advice has to do with the micro issues of health service delivery and provider organization, for which the Bank has little comparative advantage. Such issues include the organization of internal hospital or clinic incentives to raise worker productivity and responsiveness; the specifics of medical education appropriate to each country; the development of core public health functions (such as epidemiological surveillance); and the development of specific-disease control knowledge (e.g., which vaccines or drugs to use against diseases in LICs and MICs).

Resolution of these important micro issues, particularly internal organization of providers, though essential for achieving HNP results, lags far behind developments in health financing policy. The international community needs to intensify its efforts to make progress in this aspect of health systems where the Bank has little comparative advantage.

The Bank looks forward to a collaborative division of labor with global partners along each organization's comparative advantages, particularly with the World Health Organization (WHO) and the United Nations Children's

Fund (UNICEF) on leadership, disease control knowledge, and technology, epidemiological surveillance, and program and provider organization; with the United Nations Population Fund (UNFPA) on population, and with the Food and Agriculture Organization (FAO) and the World Food Program (WFP) on nutrition. The Bank also looks forward to close collaboration in the implementation of country-led system strengthening efforts and knowledge generation with global financing partners including bilateral agencies, regional banks, Global Fund, GAVI, GAIN, the Bill and Melinda Gates Foundation, and others.

The following are some of the main health system functions, system activities, and other determinants of system performance. They are listed in descending order of strength of Bank comparative advantage:

- *Health financing.* Funding policy (level, source, fiscal space); risk-pooling organization (health insurance); insurance regulation; health service purchasing and provider payment mechanisms; design of financing incentive framework for efficient allocation of R&D and human resources.

- *Fiduciary, logistical, and financial management arrangements of the system.*

- *System governance.* Accountability arrangements for providers, insurers, and government in health care investments; regulatory framework for private-public collaboration in the health sector; decisions on delegation of decision rights and market exposure for public providers; fiduciary arrangements for fiscal resource management in the public and private sectors; linkage of specific HNP sector reforms to cross-sectoral public sector reforms (e.g., civil service reforms to attract practitioners into rural areas).

- *Positively influencing household demand for effective HNP interventions.* Demand-side interventions (such as conditional cash transfers, girls' education, community-driven development, and voice and choice reforms in health service delivery).

- *Stewardship (sector oversight).* Overall sector leadership; sectoral strategic planning; provider regulation; inputs and health service quality control; epidemiological surveillance; identification of health priorities for setting mandatory basic benefits packages.

- *Organization and management of providers.* How to run a clinic, hospital, or provider network; organizing village volunteers; organizing NGO or private for-profit health service delivery.

- *Technical aspects of disease control.*

- *Human resource training and creation of medical technologies and advances.* Human resources; R&D and manufacturing of drugs and supplies (beyond contributing to global financing and incentives for development and production of orphan drugs); R&D and generation of medical technology.

- *Clinical and field research on disease-control intervention effectiveness and clinical protocols.* Defining effective production functions; testing them in the field.

Drawing on its main comparative advantages in health systems, the Bank will increasingly focus its knowledge creation on health system strengthening mainly in the first five areas, above, and will actively seek advice from, and collaborative division of labor with, global partners in the other areas, particularly WHO, to include their knowledge in Bank priority–disease lending and to coordinate with WHO leadership in global epidemiological surveillance and country preparedness.

Intersectoral Approach for Better HNP Results

Good HNP outcomes and system performance are determined by multiple sectors of the economy. They are strongly influenced by income, education, access to clean water and sanitation, access to clean indoor environments, expedited transportation to facilities and providers, good country governance, and sound macroeconomic policy. Together with basic public health interventions those factors are most likely to play a larger role than health service delivery in low-income/high-mortality country settings (figure 4.2). Therefore, improving HNP outcomes means ensuring an effective intersectoral response to HNP performance and outcomes, both within the Bank and within client countries.

Intersectorality is potentially one of the Bank's most important strengths for contributing to HNP results at country level, both in other sectoral policies that influence HNP results (e.g., environmental policy effect on indoor pollution, water and sanitation) and in its role in health system strengthening.[46] Intersectorality is also the most difficult objective to realize fully, due to both Bank and client–country constraints. Strengthening health systems

Figure 4.2: Multisectoral Determinants of Global Burden of Disease

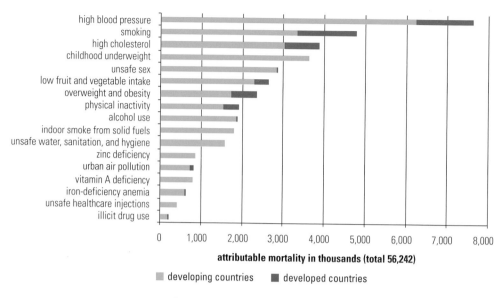

Source: Jamison et al. 2006.

for HNP results, the key contribution of the Bank in the next decade, is a multisectoral endeavor. For example, improving the incentive framework for workers will require a combination of public sector reforms, health financing mechanisms, creation of fiscal space, improved fiduciary systems, and improved sectoral and country governance. For technical, governance, and economic expertise in these areas, the Bank counts on a large group of experienced professional staff (table 4.1).

Table 4.1: IBRD Net Staff By Sector Mapping, June 30, 2006

SECTOR MAPPING	NET STAFF
Environment	255
Rural Development	309
Social Development	165
Financial Sector	147
Education	181
Health, Nutrition, and Population	206
Social Protection	138
Energy and Mining	133
Infrastructure	94
Transport	130
Urban Development	112
Water Supply and Sanitation	124
Financial Management	143
Operation Services	113
Poverty Reduction	171
Economic Policy	349
Poverty	76
Public Sector	101
Public Sector Development	144

Source: Human Resources October 2006.

Note: These data include professional staff grade GF and above. Data do not include support staff (Administrative and Client Services [ACS], Information Solutions Network [ISN], Resource Management [RM]).

CHAPTER 5

New Bank Strategic Objectives: What HNP Results?

To achieve the Bank vision for its HNP role over the next 10 years in the new external environment, making the most of its comparative advantages, the Bank has revised its global HNP policy objectives.

The Bank will focus on contributing to client–country efforts to achieve results in four areas, the Strategic Objectives:

- Improve the level and distribution of key HNP outcomes, outputs, and system performance, at country and global levels to improve living conditions, particularly for the poor and the vulnerable.

- Prevent poverty due to illness (by improving financial protection).

- Improve financial sustainability in the HNP sector and its contribution to sound macroeconomic and fiscal policy and to country competitiveness.

- Improve governance, accountability, and transparency in the health sector.

The revised Bank HNP policy objectives are both a continuation of and a departure from the 1997 HNP Strategy objectives (World Bank 1997). Three of the four Strategic Directions of the 1997 Strategy are still valid: to improve HNP outcomes for the poor; to protect households from the impoverishing effects of illness; and to work with countries to ensure sustainable financing. As a result of lessons learned in the last 10 years, however, the new policy objectives differ in two respects. First, they include improving sector governance as a key strategic objective. Second, they do not include health system strengthening as an objective, but rather as a means for Bank country assistance to achieve all of them.

Strengthening health systems is a tool for achieving the HNP strategic policy objectives. The 1997 Strategy reflected knowledge of the HNP sector that was current at that time. Since then, the Bank and the international community have learned that strengthening health systems is meaningless without demonstrable improvements in outcome results, outputs, and system performance.[47] The Bank will ramp up its engagement in health system strengthening, but with an unswerving commitment to results on the ground.

Strategic Objective 1: Improve the Level and Distribution of Key HNP Outcomes, Outputs, and System Performance at Country and Global Levels to Improve Living Conditions, Particularly for the Poor and the Vulnerable

Despite important gains in reducing avoidable mortality and the prevalence and incidence of disease in the last 10 years, the world still faces enormous challenges. Achieving the MDGs by 2015 is at risk due to a combination of insufficient financing and inefficient health systems. Health indicators are worsening in fragile states. The poor—households and countries—suffer most from avoidable mortality, morbidity, and malnutrition. Sub-Saharan Africa is the epicenter of challenges ahead, falling well short of achieving most of the MDGs. In MICs, the challenge is low efficiency, poor performance, and financial difficulties.

Health, nutrition, and population improvements in all Regions were a striking achievement for human welfare in the 20th century (figure 5.1), but as discussed above, formidable challenges still persist.

Evidence-based, cost-effective interventions could drastically improve health outcomes. For example, controlling tobacco use (e.g., through taxation) has proven effective in most client countries and is the single most important intervention for reducing premature mortality due to noncommunicable diseases (UN Millennium Development Project 2005). It is also one of the few interventions that directly increase fiscal revenue in the short term. Similarly, at a cost of only US$0.02 per dose, administering a vitamin "A" supplement every day to poor children would substantially reduce U-5 mortality in low-income/high-mortality countries.

The Bank is committed to supporting efforts to reduce avoidable mortality and morbidity and improve the distribution of good health within individual countries and internationally. It will do so along the lines of its comparative advantages and Strategic Directions. The international community knows the most cost-effective interventions for saving millions of

Figure 5.1: Trends in Infant Mortality, by World Bank Region, 1980, 1990, 2004

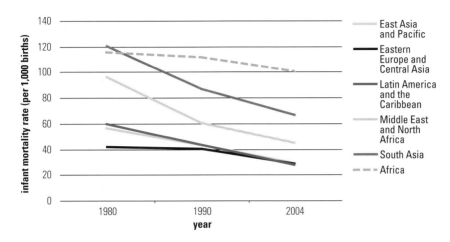

Source: World Bank 2001b, 2005h.

lives, for example, access to safe water and sanitation. But everyone is still struggling to find the best ways of reaching the poor with these proven interventions in low-income countries, especially in Sub-Saharan Africa. A well-functioning health system is essential if these interventions are to reach the poor. Success will owe much to increased financial commitments by the international community, but money alone cannot guarantee a well-functioning health system. Bank experience in this realm, one of its comparative advantages, can contribute to solving this problem.

Specific areas for reduction of mortality and morbidity are summarized in the Bank HNP Results Framework (annex D). The Framework serves as guidance for the Regions and country teams setting priority targets in the context of results-based CASs, when appropriate, and for all HNP programs and projects in their respective countries. The Bank is committed to supporting client countries' efforts to achieve the MDGs.

Strategic Objective 2: Prevent Poverty Due to Illness (by Improving Financial Protection)

Health shocks—illness, accidents, even normal life-cycle events such as pregnancy and old age—can throw a household into poverty or become an obstacle to overcoming it. Illness is a determinant of poverty due to both excess health expenditures and loss of income resulting from nonparticipation in the labor market (or reduced productivity). Protection against the impoverishing effects of health shocks is an important challenge in both LICs and MICs. Figure 5.2 presents findings in Peru, where households report health shocks as a main cause of economic distress, second only to unemployment of the breadwinner. Figure 5.3, recent findings in four Latin American countries (Argentina, Chile, Ecuador, and Honduras) (Baeza and Packard 2006), shows that health shocks plunge between 1 percent and 10 percent of the population into poverty every year. Similar findings have been reported for China, Vietnam, and Thailand (Eggleston et al. 2006).

Household out-of-pocket private funding dominates health financing in LICs and in many MICs. Indeed, except in a few client countries, out-of-pocket expenditures account for most health expenditures in LICs, even in countries receiving large amounts of DAH (tables 5.1, 5.2, and 5.3). Thus, improving financial protection requires the Bank to provide sound policy advice to client countries not only about the best use of DAH but also about how to pool household out-of-pocket expenditures for the nonpoor so that household demand and insurers (public and/or private) offer better pooling

Figure 5.2: Most Frequent Shocks Causing Household Financial Stress, Peru

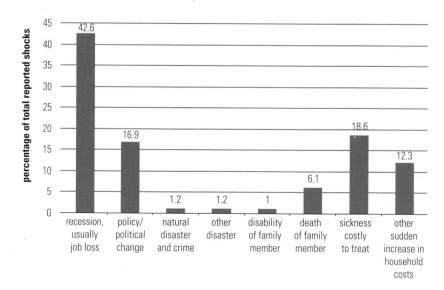

Source: Baeza and Packard 2006.

Note: Responses to survey question, "In the past three years, has your household experienced an event that has caused a significant loss of income?"

Figure 5.3: People Fall into Poverty due to Health Expenses

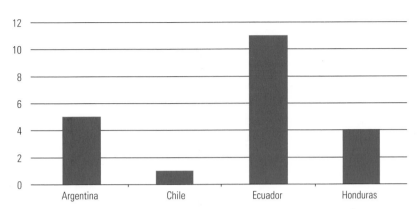

■ percent of total nonpoor population that falls below the poverty line and/or
indigence line due to out-of-pocket health expenditures

Source: Baeza and Packard 2006.
Note: Percentage of nonpoor population forced into poverty or indigence by out-of-pocket health expenses.

of financial risk. In the same context, user fees have a role to play as copay-
ment when there is evidence of excess demand. Protecting the poor from
further impoverishment from out-of-pocket financing will require
increased fiscal capacity, fiscal space, and, in LICs, financial support from
the international community.

Upon client–country demand, the Bank stands ready to support countries
that want to remove user fees from public facilities *if:* the lost revenue from
user fees can be replaced with resources that reach the facilities in a timely

Table 5.1: Time Series Trends in Health Expenditures, Low-Income Countries, FY1999–FY2003

ALL LICS	FY1999–FY2003		FY1999–FY2003	
	FISCAL EXPENDITURE	PRIVATE EXPENDITURE	EXTERNAL EXPENDITURE	OUT-OF-POCKET EXPENDITURE
1999	44.35	55.65	17.66	48.95
2000	45.07	54.93	19.70	47.77
2001	45.36	54.64	18.31	47.49
2002	46.37	53.63	16.48	46.84
2003	46.05	53.95	17.53	47.07

Sources: WHO 2006b; World Bank 2005h.
Note: Total health expenditure is the sum of fiscal and private health expenditures. External resources for health are allocated to
both public and private sources, but the proportion allocated to each is unknown. Out-of-pocket expenditures are one type of private expenditure, but in many low-income countries out-of-pocket spending accounts for most of private spending.

Table 5.2: Time Series Trends in External Expenditures for Health as Percent of Total Health
Expenditures, FY1997–FY2003

	EXTERNAL[a]						
	1997	1998	1999	2000	2001	2002	2003
Income							
Low-income countries	6.4	7.6	7.0	8.1	7.1	7.9	7.1
Lower-middle income countries	0.8	1.2	1.4	1.2	0.8	0.7	0.6
Upper-middle income countries	0.4	0.6	0.7	0.5	0.5	0.4	0.3
High-income countries	0.0	0.0	0.0	0.0	0.0	0.0	0.0
Regions							
East Asia and Pacific	1.2	1.7	1.8	1.6	1.1	0.7	0.9
Eastern Europe and Central Asia	0.8	1.0	1.5	1.6	1.4	1.6	1.3
Latin America and the Caribbean	1.5	1.6	1.7	1.6	1.5	1.4	1.1
Middle East and North Africa	1.2	1.2	1.1	1.2	1.2	1.1	1.1
South Asia	3.3	3.9	2.5	3.2	2.3	2.5	2.9
Sub-Saharan Africa	12.6	16.0	16.3	18.3	17.1	17.8	14.8

Sources: WHO 2006b; World Bank 2005h.

Note: The data in this table are population-weighted.

a. External resources for health are funds or services in kind that are provided by entities not part of the country in question. The
resources may come from international organizations, other countries through bilateral arrangements, or foreign nongovernmental
organizations. These resources are part of total health expenditures and are spent on both public and privately provided services.

Table 5.3: Time Series Trends in External Expenditures for Health as Percent of Fiscal Health
Expenditures, FY1997–FY2003

	EXTERNAL[a]						
	1997	1998	1999	2000	2001	2002	2003
Income							
Low-income countries	20.4	24.8	22.2	25.6	20.8	21.6	20.2
Lower-middle income countries	2.3	3.7	3.9	3.6	2.1	1.8	1.5
Upper-middle income countries	0.7	1.3	1.4	1.1	1.0	0.9	0.6
High-income countries	0.0	0.0	0.0	0.0	0.0	0.0	0.0
Regions							
East Asia and Pacific	4.2	5.8	6.0	5.5	3.2	1.9	2.7
Eastern Europe and Central Asia	1.3	2.4	3.2	3.7	3.7	3.8	3.7
Latin America and the Caribbean	3.1	3.5	3.9	3.7	3.4	3.1	2.5
Middle East and North Africa	3.3	3.5	3.1	3.2	3.1	3.0	2.8
South Asia	15.9	13.7	9.6	13.6	8.7	10.1	10.5
Sub-Saharan Africa	27.9	48.5	45.8	49.9	44.3	44.8	37.9

Sources: WHO 2006b; World Bank 2005h.

Note: The data in this table are population-weighted.

a. External resources for health are funds or in-kind services that are provided by entities not part of the country in question. The
resources may come from international organizations, other countries through bilateral arrangements, or foreign nongovernmental
organizations. These resources are part of total health expenditures and are spent on both public and privately provided services.

and fiscally sustainable manner over the long-term; effective public financial management systems ensure that such financial transfer replacements will effectively reach the health facilities that need them the most and in the context of the appropriate incentive framework for the provision of services to the poor; and resource replacements will be used to pay for the delivery of effective quality services for the poor, provided at the health facilities.

A well-organized and sustainable health system is essential to achieve financial protection by preventing the impoverishing effects of health shocks (e.g., through health insurance) and mitigating their effects. An efficient public financing and pro-poor subsidy policy in the health sector, access to effective financial risk-pooling mechanisms (e.g., health insurance), and household access to borrowing through better financial market environments are among the interventions that can help improve financial protection. Client countries face options in organizing risk pooling, including general tax-based systems, social insurance systems (financed out of payroll-tax contributions), and/or private health insurance arrangements, including not-for-profit community health insurance.

Fragmentation[48] of health systems hampers systemic capacity to provide effective access to services and financial protection (WHO 2000; Gottret and Schieber 2006; Baeza and Packard 2006). Unfortunately, health system fragmentation is extensive in most client countries. The Bank will strengthen its capacity to support country efforts to improve health systems integration and reduce fragmentation. Countries have options to improve integration, including setting a common regulatory framework for public-private collaboration; giving incentives for aggregating existing pools to efficient pool sizes and improve the interactions among them; transitioning toward single risk pools (or very few of them), and/or transitioning to universal, general tax–financed risk-pooling arrangements. The Bank will provide technical and policy advice for countries to identify options; support fiscal, technical, and financial feasibility assessments; and advise on pros and cons of these different options for the specific country context and preferences. Ultimately, the choice of a path to transition toward health system integration is the country's decision.

Widespread (and growing) labor informality (and its substantial overlap with poverty) as well as rural population dispersal (overlapping with both informality and poverty) pose a significant challenge to improving risk pooling. Extending risk pooling to the informal and the rural population will be a key priority of both the research agenda and the operational strategic focus of HNP in health systems in the implementation of this Strategy.

So far, judging by the evidence, there is no "silver-bullet" for organizing risk pooling, reducing excess out-of-pocket expenditures on health care, and extending risk pooling to the informal and rural poor. Therefore, the Bank is committed to advising client countries to increase risk pooling, but it does not promote any one-size-fits-all blueprint for organizing risk pooling across countries. Decisions on risk-pooling arrangements are country specific, often based on historical events and cultural preferences. However, risk-pooling decisions need to be guided by solid evidence, which is unfortunately lacking so far, particularly for LICs. The Bank has a significant opportunity to learn from close monitoring and evaluation of Bank-supported initiatives and programs. It also needs to assist countries in monitoring results of their initiatives to verify whether chosen arrangements actually improve financial protection for everyone, but particularly for the poor and near-poor.

The Bank will expand its knowledge creation and policy advice on improving financial protection. It will do so intersectorally, addressing the growing challenge of extending health insurance to the informal sector.

The Results Framework presented in annex D summarizes the main outcomes on financial protection. Measuring, monitoring, and evaluating financial protection outcomes is a relatively recent field. A major challenge for Bank HNP work in this field is to facilitate collaboration for research with partners and experts in this field to develop, test, and scale up monitoring of financial protection indicators. Developing such indicators and facilitating consensus on them among the international community will be a major early activity of Strategy implementation in this field.

Strategic Objective 3: Improve Financial Sustainability in the HNP Sector and Its Contribution to Sound Macroeconomic and Fiscal Policy and Country Competitiveness

For governments to ensure their people's access to essential services and financial protection, countries need to raise stable, sufficient, long-term public and private financial resources, predictably, equitably, efficiently, and in a way that minimizes economic distortions. Health sector financing policy should also contribute to sound fiscal management, create necessary fiscal space, and foster productivity, employment, and growth. On the spending side, individuals need access to affordable basic services and financial protection; spending should maximize health outcomes and ensure equitable access and technically efficient production; cross-sectoral linkages should be explicitly addressed through planning and budget processes; and spending should be cushioned as much as possible against economic shocks in ways consistent with sound economic management.

Financial sustainability has different implications for LICs and MICs. For LICs, it means: developing sound policy to leverage private household financing to expand participation in risk pooling (public and/or private);[49] solving the DAH volatility problem, a major challenge in LICs (figures 5.4 and 5.5); and ensuring sufficient economic growth to sustain and increase pro-poor fiscal policy. MICs face two main challenges: fiscal sustainability linked to systemic efficiency and potential challenges from past decisions linking social health insurance financing to labor status. The insurance-labor link can distort labor markets and labor costs through the use of payroll taxes as the main revenue-raising mechanism for social health insurance.

The World Bank is in a unique position to promote these objectives through its macroeconomic management, cross-sectoral purviews, and roles as a development institution, financial institution, and multisectoral knowledge-dissemination agency. The Bank's underlying charter as a development agency and bank uniquely qualify it to advise client countries on this complex menu of sectoral, fiscal space, macroeconomic policy, growth, and sustainable financing issues.

Figure 5.4: External Expenditures on Health, Selected Countries, 1999–2003

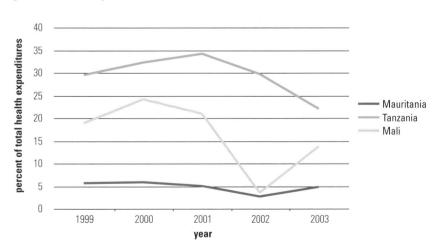

Source: WHO 2006b.

Figure 5.5: External Expenditures on Health, Selected Countries, 1999–2003

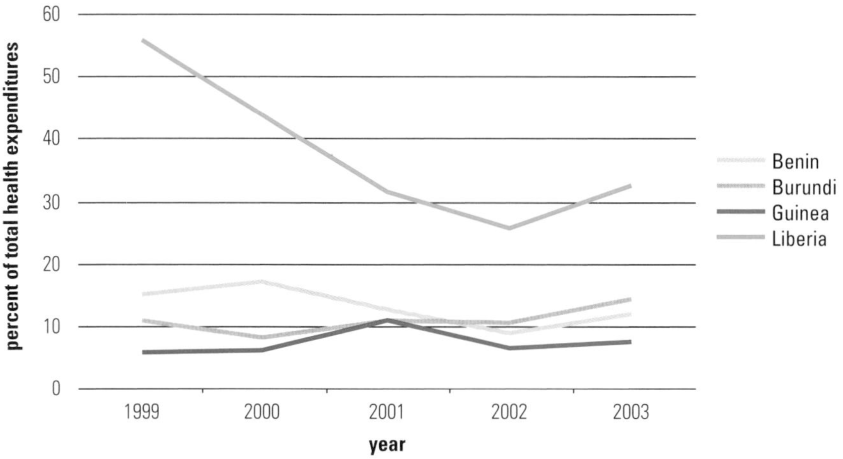

Source: WHO 2006b.

The Bank (HNP in working with PREM, Development Economics [DEC], and others) in collaboration with the IMF and other global partners will seek to develop, test, and support country monitoring of indicators for health sector/program fiscal sustainability, fiscal space, effects of health financing on labor markets, and other sustainability and potentially health sector–related country competitiveness determinants.

Strategic Objective 4: Improve Governance, Accountability, and Transparency in the Health Sector

Evidence shows that development assistance works—but mostly in countries with good governance and little corruption. Kaufman and Kraay (2003) define *good governance* as "the traditions and institutions by which authority in a country is exercised." For the health sector, this definition means the set of relationships that hold health service providers, insurers, and governments accountable to their clients and citizens for HNP results—health outcomes, income protection, and social inclusion (World Bank 2003b, figure 5.6). Bardham (1997) defines *corruption* as the "use of public office for private gains."

Poor governance in health care delivery does not necessarily mean corruption (box 5.1). "Poor governance" can describe anything from haphaz-

Figure 5.6: Creating Accountability in Health

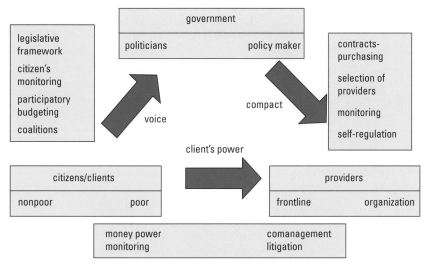

Source: Adapted from World Bank 2003b.

ard management to outright dishonesty. These indicators, to cite just a few, encompass: mismanagement; staff absenteeism and low productivity; leakage of funds, drugs, and supplies; lax procurement and oversight practices; informal payments from patients; mistreatment of the poor by service providers; and patently corrupt practices ranging from petty theft to kickbacks to selling public office. Some of these events result from failure of clients' power—patients too poor or socially deprived to claim their entitlement to services from providers, frontline professionals, and staff. Voice failures also occur, when the state simply does not care about providing services—or provides the bare minimum. There are also compact failures, in which the state fails to set incentives for public and private providers, to delineate their responsibilities, or to enforce accountability. An increasing concern in partner countries is the high transaction and administration costs of DAH governance on the ground in a very fragmented environment.

Good governance and accountability, the enforcers of honesty, are key determinants of health system performance. Building accountability for health is not easy, due to the great asymmetry of information between users and providers and the difficulty of attributing most final outcomes to a particular service provider. It is hard, for example, for patients to know whether the medical treatment they received was effective and appropriate for their

---

Box 5.1: What Are Governance and Corruption in the Health Sector?

Health care provision depends on efficiency and honesty in combining financial resources, human resources, and supplies and on delivery of services, in a timely fashion, distributed equitably and spatially throughout a country. This requires a "system" that mobilizes and distributes resources, processes and acts upon information, and motivates appropriate behavior by individual providers, health care workers, and administrators. Good governance is a critical factor in making such a system work.

Governance and accountability can be improved through actions including:

- *Management and performance.* Incentives for sound behavior by health professionals, including performance-based pay; drug distribution to ensure that demand and supply align; databases for tracking staff, supplies, and drugs; and local oversight of medical staff.
- *Anticorruption measures.* National anticorruption initiatives; clear rules for and audits by enforcement agencies; community oversight; and drug procurement reform.
- *Affordability improvements.* Charging formal fees with exemptions; reorganizing staffing and performance with reward systems; and seeking alternative financing options.
- *Accountability tightening.* Embedding accountability at every level of the system, combined with clear and transparent expectations; contracting out services and overseeing performance; calibrating performance through consumer satisfaction surveys and citizen report cards.

Accountability is the single most important element to ensure good governance—accountability to ministries, local governments, managers, and citizens. It leads to better performance on other measures but is a difficult goal to meet in any setting. Increasing choice and alternatives for publicly subsidized health services increases empowerment of the poor vis-à-vis health service providers.

Source: Lewis 2006.

---

condition. To monitor health care outcomes, OECD countries have developed a rich combination of direct control over users, governmental regulatory instruments, and professional self-regulation. Yet, most LICs and many MICs are still developing their own instruments and institutional arrangements. Self-regulation is particularly underdeveloped in MICs and LICs, and many bureaucratic failures are still insufficiently addressed. The Bank will work intersectorally to strengthen governance and accountability relationships within countries, support accountability-fostering instruments and institutions, and promote strong fiduciary systems.

CHAPTER 6

New Bank Strategic Directions: How Should the Bank Support Client–Country Efforts?

The new Strategic Directions will guide Bank efforts to help client countries achieve the strategic HNP results over the next 10 years. To implement these new directions, this Strategy presents an Action Plan (last section) outlining key organizational changes and incentives, new analytical tools, and a rebalancing of the skill-mix of Bank management and staff. The new Strategic Directions for Bank HNP results are:

- Renew Bank focus on HNP results.

- Increase the Bank contribution to client–country efforts to strengthen health systems for HNP results.

- Ensure synergy between health system strengthening and priority-disease interventions, particularly in LICs.

- Strengthen Bank capacity to advise client countries on an intersectoral approach to HNP results.

- Increase selectivity, improve strategic engagement, and reach agreement with global partners on collaborative division of labor for the benefit of client countries.

Strategic Direction 1: Renew Bank Focus on HNP Results

Renewing Bank focus on HNP results is the primary Strategic Direction for the Bank. All the others are based on it. As the cornerstone, the Bank will tighten the direct link between HNP-related lending and nonlending support and outcomes, outputs, and system performance. The Bank is amassing promising experience with output-based investment lending for HNP.

A results focus poses some short-term challenges for the Bank, despite internal consensus on the need and willingness to move toward accountability for outcomes. First, monitoring and evaluation systems have to be improved. Until recently, neither the Bank nor many client countries or global partners have systematically measured outcomes with sufficient precision, frequency, and disaggregation to be useful for M&E. Second, achieving results (final and intermediary outcomes) on the ground depends on many actors (different levels of government, service providers, citizens, donors) and on a variety of exogenous factors. Assessing the contributions of each actor and attributing results to their individual actions is often elusive, if not impossible. Furthermore, the Bank can affect outcomes only indirectly—using its lending and nonlending services to influence domestic actors, particularly governments.

The Bank will substantially increase both its analytical work on health systems and its monitoring and evaluation capacity to ensure that the renewed commitment to HNP is actually rendering results on the ground. It is essential that this increased capacity and commitment to M&E also be effectively linked to and inform policy design and policy management in the health sector.

Support the Shift toward Linking Finance to HNP Results

The Bank will: partner with client countries to identify opportunities to experiment and learn from innovation in results-based lending; support the launch, in coordination with existing global initiatives, of a major effort to help client countries improve their national public health surveillance and performance-monitoring systems; set a common global HNP Results Framework for the Bank (annex D) to guide regional HNP strategies, regional HNP implementation plans, and overall Bank monitoring and evaluation of HNP results; and commit to monitoring a core group of indicators presented in the framework.

Link Lending to HNP Results

Financing inputs does not guarantee improvements in HNP conditions for the poor. Achieving the MDGs in lower-income countries requires sustaining and further scaling up of DAH. To achieve both—bringing lending close to results and scaling up in LICs—the Bank needs to increase output-based or performance-based investment lending and development-policy lending for policy action, mixed according to country needs and context. Some movement in this direction is occurring in HNP and vaccine "buy-downs" (box 6.1) and in direct payment of outcomes and outputs in maternal and child health, but it is not enough. Linking financing to results carries some risks, due mostly to bias in surveillance and monitoring reporting, introduced by perverse incentives, as well as risks due to systemic and governance fragility in many client countries. This is one reason the Bank teams up with client countries and global partners—to experiment and learn from innovation in results-based lending.

Launch a Major Effort to Improve National Public Health Surveillance and Health System Performance Monitoring

The Bank will work in close collaboration with global partners to persuade client countries, and support their efforts and those of global partners, to launch a build-up of public health surveillance and health system performance-monitoring systems at country level. Launching this build-up will be one of the contributions of the Bank to HNP results in the first three years of the new HNP Strategy. A focus on results is not possible without reliable data. This contribution will be the foundation for a renewed culture, centered on the impact of HNP results within the Bank and in Bank relations with client countries. Close coordination with other institutions such as the Health Metrics Network and other global initiatives will be important.

Set a Common Global HNP Results Framework

The Results Framework (annex D) will guide the Bank in developing regional HNP strategies and strengthening surveillance and monitoring. The Framework covers health MDGs, other priority HNP outcomes, financial protection indicators, governance, and financial sustainability indicators. It is intended to guide Bank development of HNP knowledge creation and management, to direct the surveillance and monitoring initiative, and to provide general guidance to the Regions for the preparation (or update) of their own HNP strategies and implementation plans. Developing some of the proposed outputs and outcomes will require an important

Box 6.1: Promising New Mechanism Linked to Results: Loan Buy-Downs for Polio Eradication Results in Pakistan

The Concept

Results-based investment credits and loans are linked to the achievement of specified outputs, particularly where significant externalities or public good characteristics result in underinvestment. As an incentive, grant money from foundations and bilaterals "buy down" the loan or credit if the agreed results are achieved. There are three parts to buy-downs: setting an appropriate target goal, tying performance (targets) to the financial buy-down, and monitoring actions and evaluating outputs.

The Pilot

The buy-down mechanism was piloted in several polio eradication projects in Pakistan and Nigeria approved by the Board between 2003 and 2005. Polio eradication was selected for the pilot because of its obvious global public good characteristics. Financial support was provided by the Bill and Melinda Gates Foundation, United Nations Foundation, Rotary International, and U.S. Centers for Disease Control and Prevention (CDC). The Bank is now moving forward with a modest expansion of the pilot to meet a broader range of client needs and to capitalize on country and donor interest.

How does it work?

The government and the Bank identify the outputs and targets that would trigger the buy-down of the IDA credit into a grant. In the polio eradication projects, the targets are timely receipt of polio vaccine and polio coverage.

A financial incentive to achieve the targets is provided in tandem with the IDA credit. Donor funds are set aside to pay the credit fees and buy down the credit to a grant if the targets are reached. The first project is coming to a close, and an independent performance audit will occur in early FY2007 to verify results. If the project's intended benefits do not materialize, the funding remains an IDA credit, and no donor funds are awarded.

The Future

The initial pilot for polio projects was expanded by management to cover up to six health projects, and IBRD buy-downs are being explored. For buy-downs, projects must meet the following eligibility criteria:

- *Significant cross-border externalities.* The primary selection criterion is that eligible projects or project components must have significant positive cross-border externalities linked to the achievement of the MDGs.
- *Measurable outcomes.* Projects or components must have measurable and feasible outcomes that can be achieved through policy actions by the government so that the trigger-point for buying down the credit will be transparent and objective. Countries must also have adequate monitoring systems to measure these outcomes.
- *Standard Bank appraisal requirements.* Projects must meet appraisal requirements and standards applied to all projects. In particular, investment in a project using a credit buy-down must be supported by a strong political commitment by the government and be used for activities that are cost-effective, fiscally sound, and equity enhancing.

effort early in the Strategy implementation (e.g. financial protection, fiscal sustainability, and governance).

The Bank portfolio is already focused largely on most of the proposed outcomes and outputs but has given insufficient attention to monitoring program performance and evaluating the implications of Bank and client–country trends for results. Most LICs and MICs are committed to health MDG outcomes, and the IDA-14 replenishment confirmed Bank and donor commitment to the MDGs and other priority HNP outcomes. The same is reflected in most regional and Hub Vice-Presidential Unit Strategic Performance Contracts.

Most Bank operations already focus on health-related MDGs, improving sexual and reproductive health and child nutrition, as seen in the review of 116 Implementation Completion Reports for IDA and IBRD projects closed in FY2001–FY2005 and the review of current active portfolio project development objectives (PDOs) (Subramanian, Peters, and Willis 2006). These reviews reflect the emergence of common outcome and system performance objectives in client countries across all Bank Regions. The performance objectives include addressing and reducing the noncommunicable disease epidemic, improving financial protection, improving governance and reducing corruption, and improving health sector financial sustainability in general and donor assistance and fiscal sustainability in particular. HNP outcomes included in the Results Framework potentially account for 60 percent of the total avoidable burden of disease in LICs and MICs combined.

The global HNP Results Framework is presented to guide the Regions in elaborating their regional strategies and identifying constraints to improving in-country performance. Its country-driven application and adaptation must be ensured, and the framework should not be understood as a prescriptive, limiting instrument. The key to making a country-led approach and the Results Framework compatible is the systematic intersectoral identification of constraints to improving HNP outcomes at country level and the subsequent design and implementation of effective sectoral interventions to overcome these constraints—tailored to individual country contexts. For example, the CAS and HNP portfolios of both Argentina and Rwanda emphasize reducing U-5 mortality, but each country has to take a different path. To reduce infant and neonatal mortality, Argentina is concentrating on improving provider incentives to expand access and quality of health service delivery for poor mothers and children (box 6.2), particularly for neonatal care. In contrast, reducing U-5 mortality in Rwanda requires a much broader intersectoral approach, entailing, for example, expanding basic vaccine coverage, increasing access to basic perinatal health services, raising educational levels, expanding access to safe water and sanitation, improving access to key micronutrients, and increasing birth space (closely linked to women's participation in the labor market).

Box 6.2: Argentina *Plan Nacer*—Health System Strengthening Built into Results-Based Lending for MCH

Plan Nacer is a two-phase Adaptable Program Loan of about US$440 million that supports the implementation of Argentina's public national maternal and child health program. The program ensures synergies between priority diseases and health system strengthening. It does so by directly (out of loan proceeds) paying for results (outputs and outcomes) for maternal and child health of the poorest population. Structural changes and health system strengthening interventions are deeply embedded in program implementation design. The program is intended to:

- Increase access to basic health services for uninsured mothers and children (up to six years old), contributing to decrease infant and maternal mortality.
- Strengthen the health system and introduce structural changes in the incentive framework for the national-provincial and provincial-provider relationships, linking project financing with results (mainly output—health services delivered to target population—but also intermediary outcomes).

Most (85 percent) of program proceeds finance a conditional matching grant from the federal government to provinces to pay half the average per capita cost of providing a package of basic health services to uninsured mothers and children. The package covers 70 services addressing the main causes of child and maternal mortality. This capitation grant is the equivalent of financing a health insurance premium for the uninsured. Disbursements are made in two installments, if target results are met. By November 2006, more than half the originally targeted population had been enrolled (more than a half million mothers and children); and more than 2 million consultations and 20,000 deliveries had been financed by the program. Infant mortality in the target provinces has dropped.

In addition to increasing access to services, the program has had significant health system strengthening effects. To be able to achieve the targets and ensure appropriate use of funds, provinces have introduced output-based payment for providers, contracting (public and/or private sector) mechanisms, health service purchaser agencies, independent concurrent auditors, incentives to high-performing personnel, significant upgrades in monitoring and information systems, and demand-boosting actions such as linking *Plan Nacer* with conditional cash transfer programs already existing in the country.

The first two years of program implementation have been so successful that it is being expanded from the original nine provinces to the entire country, with a total beneficiary population of more than 2.2 million uninsured mothers and children.

Source: World Bank 2006k.

Strategic Direction 2: Increase the Bank Contribution to Client–Country Efforts to Strengthen Health Systems for HNP Results

Despite the Bank's potential comparative advantages, its health system capacity has not escaped the consequences of global trends in vertical and single-disease approaches. Though still strong, current capacity in health systems is scattered throughout the Bank. To realize its full potential and to respond to growing demand from the international community, the Bank needs to raise its health system strengthening contributions to client–country efforts for HNP results in areas in which the Bank has comparative advantages.

Client countries have been ahead of the international community debate on health systems. In the last decade, many health system reforms have begun throughout the world. In these reforms, governments attempt to address such basic health system questions as: how to ensure equitable access to effective, quality health services that respond to the needs of the community? what is the right balance between investments in the HNP sector and other sectors to achieve both HNP results and much-needed economic growth? what specific policies/actions are required to ensure synergy between priority–disease and system strengthening approaches? what type of provider governance, contracting, financial management, procurement, and provider-payment mechanisms are necessary to ensure efficient and equitable results? how should government engage and regulate a predominantly private delivery sector in LICs to improve equity, ensure consumer protection, and improve public-private collaboration to achieve HNP results? how can government ensure sustainable financing and improve fiscal space for priority diseases? what are the public and private sector roles in the quest to expand health insurance coverage and supply of priority health services? how can policy makers extend health insurance (public and/or private) to the large informal and self-employed sectors? and how can they leverage, for that purpose, most client–country high, private household (out-of-pocket) expenditures among the nonpoor? These are some of the key health system challenges common to most Bank client countries.

Middle-income countries face additional challenges derived mostly from past decisions on health system financing and organization (Baeza and Packard 2006). Among these new challenges are to: address gathering concerns about the effects of payroll-tax financing of social health insurance on labor markets; regulate competing private health insurance; and navigate the transition in the public sector from historical input financing to production-based (output-based) provider financing ("money follows the patient").

A central objective of the implementation of this new HNP Strategy is to improve Bank capacity to help client countries find the most appropriate answer to these questions for their country context to get concrete HNP results on the ground.

Strengthening health systems by setting the right incentives for efficiency will substantially contribute to broadening access to services. However, improving efficiency will be insufficient in LICs; strengthening systemic delivery capacity will also entail expanding the supply of cost-effective health services, fiscal space, and international financing, commitment permitting.

Expanding health service supply capacity is particularly challenging in rural areas where high degrees of informality and poverty, usually compounded by geographical isolation, determine low levels of demand, making public investments costly and lacking incentives for private provision of services.

The Bank remains committed to supporting country efforts to strengthen health system infrastructure (e.g., clinics, hospitals, and medical equipment purchases). The Bank has comparative advantages in large infrastructure investments. However, client countries and country teams need to decide, case by case, Bank investments in health service delivery infrastructure in the context of allocative efficiency of country resources, in-depth analysis of all alternatives to increase service supply, and in line with the implementation of an adequate incentive framework for any new infrastructure so that HNP results on the ground are actually delivered. Investments in the absence of adequate incentive frameworks too often result in empty buildings.

The Bank stands ready to support client–country efforts to expand health services to the poor. To do so, an in-depth assessment of health systems policy and investment gaps is needed, to identify needs and options and set up the appropriate strategy to extend supply capacity. No country strategy to improve access to health services to its people, particularly to the poor, is complete without considering all potential alternatives to expand supply, including decisions assessing the appropriateness of investments on public sector capacity and/or expansion through publicly financed private sector provision of health service to the poor and/or private provision of privately financed services. IFC and the Bank will further enhance their collaboration to help client countries identify best options, and, upon country request, provide financial support to implement them.

To realize its full potential in health systems, the HNP sector will rearticulate its health system capacity, now scattered throughout the Bank. It will strengthen its capacity in health financing (including fiscal management, health insurance, and health service purchasing)—and in system governance. It will seek more effective intersectoral collaboration with PREM (on fiscal space and management and on public sector governance) and with Financial Services and Social Protection (on health insurance). To this effect, the HNP sector will assemble a health system policy advice team, which will allow it to respond rapidly to the need for health system strengthening to obtain solid HNP results on the ground. Details on team mission, work scope, and organization are provided under the HNP Hub Action Plan (annex A).

Strategic Direction 3: Ensure Synergy between Health System Strengthening and Priority–Disease Interventions, Particularly in LICs

Upon country demand, the Bank will continue lending for priority diseases and programs. But when doing so, it must stay sharply focused on solving systemic constraints to improving HNP results on the ground and on ensuring synergy in priority–disease treatment and system strengthening. Preliminary lessons from Argentina's maternal and child health program (box 6.2) suggest that this synergy can be better achieved by: packaging the main priority diseases in one program/project; and embedding in the project/program implementation design actions for health system strengthening (e.g., provider payment per child vaccinated or malaria patient treated). Doing so will most likely require the implementation of multiple system strengthening activities.

Bank financing through IDA plays a crucial role in HNP-enhancing interventions to ensure priority–disease and system strengthening synergy in LICs. It also helps forestall allocative inefficiency and other distortions that can result from the allocation of large amounts of financing to a few diseases (and neglect others) and to system strengthening in LICs. Technical advice and AAA can play a crucial role in strengthening health systems to remove country-identified bottlenecks that prevent increased financing from achieving its maximum impact.

Strategic Direction 4: Strengthen Bank Capacity to Advise Client Countries on an Intersectoral Approach to HNP Results

It is universally acknowledged that reducing mortality, morbidity, fertility, and malnutrition requires intersectoral inputs and actions. However, little in-country systematic analysis has been done to document the bottlenecks in different critical sectors, set out a framework for prioritizing actions, or assess institutional constraints. Nor has this research been done within Bank lending operations. Preliminary evidence (World Bank 2006b) suggests that intersectoral approaches can greatly enhance results on the ground.

Effective core diagnostic tools are needed to identify intersectoral constraints to achieving HNP results. The Bank will develop, test, and implement a core diagnostic tool for systematic assessment of these multisectoral constraints at country level. The results of this process will feed into CAS preparation. The main purpose of the process will be to identify the priority HNP outcome(s), output, and performance improvements for the specific country, the binding constraints to improving that outcome and performance at national and/or subnational levels, and the key feasible multiple-sector interventions (technical, investment, policy actions) critical to overcoming these constraints. This "Multisectoral Constraints Assessment (MCA) for Health Outcomes" will be referred to as "MCA" in the remainder of this Strategy. Annex E outlines the rationale and objectives of MCA, which will be developed and pilot tested in four client countries by FY2009. Country teams have no such process or tool today. Significant inputs for developing this core diagnostic tool will come from the methodological discussions in the *PRSP Sourcebook* (World Bank 2002a) on identification of constraints to improving specific outcomes, the experience of the Africa Region with the Marginal Budgeting for Bottlenecks tool,[50] the experience of the multisectoral economic sector work (ESW) for Orissa state in India,[51] and the experience of the *Recurso Peru* ESW in LCR.[52]

Intersectoral identification of constraints should not be confused with a call for multisectoral investment projects across the board. One does not automatically lead to the other. In improving intersectoral work, the Bank needs to take into account the complexity that client countries face in improving their own intersectoral approach to HNP results. Given the much greater complexity and the often-difficult political economy of reform at country level, increasing intersectoral work will focus first on ensuring intersectoral identification of different sectors' lending and nonlending activities required to improve HNP outcomes and system performance at country level. Identifying those activities to inform CAS preparation would be an important contribution to a results-based CAS and to policy dialog with client countries when defining the strategic directions of the CAS.

It will be up to the country team, based on context and needs, to decide whether to go for multisectoral projects/programs or for multiple parallel but coordinated sectoral projects or programs. In fact, considering the difficulties client countries have implementing multisectoral projects, the effectiveness of such projects should not be taken for granted and should be pursued only when the approach promises good HNP results at the country level. Identifying and coordinating HNP-related programs and projects intersectorally in a new CAS would be a big step toward the multisectoral determinants of HNP results.

Strategic Direction 5: Increase Selectivity, Improve Strategic Engagement, and Reach Agreement with Global Partners on Collaborative Division of Labor for the Benefit of Client Countries

As one of the leading multilateral organizations in development, the Bank collaborates with many bilateral and multilateral organizations and global HNP partnerships. This collaboration can facilitate harmonization of development partner efforts and can reduce transaction costs for client countries in their pursuit of improving HNP results. The volume of the HNP partnership portfolio has increased dramatically over the past five years, mirroring the changes in the global health architecture. As a result Bank engagement with global partners is fragmented and needs sharper strategic direction. With the implementation of the new Strategy, the Bank will assess its engagement with its partners to ensure effective and sustainable partnerships. For example, the Bank will seek a better balance in its partnerships and its regional work on LIC and MIC priorities, particularly on health systems, and will substantially increase its strategic engagement with WHO, Global Fund, and GAVI, particularly in LICs.

Engaging with global partners and partnerships has two main objectives for Bank work in HNP: to complement Bank work in areas in which it has no comparative advantages or to complement other partners needing Bank expertise, all in direct benefit of client countries on the ground; and to contribute to international community support of global public goods and prevention of global public "bads." Good examples of this type of collaboration are Bank involvement in donor harmonization, efforts to address the avian flu livestock crisis and scale up preparedness in the case of a human health pandemic, and the design and launching of global financing instruments such as the Advance Market Commitment.

For areas in which the Bank has comparative advantages (e.g., health system finance, intersectorality, governance, demand-side interventions), the Bank will: collaborate with partners that share all or part of these comparative advantages (e.g., IMF, regional banks, International Labour Organisation Actuarial and Financial Services) to further develop and disseminate knowledge; and collaborate with other financing partners and technical agencies (annex G) to share Bank expertise and to coordinate further development of knowledge in areas in which Bank expertise might be needed. A good example of global partnership collaboration in knowledge creation is the analytical work contributed by the Bank to the OECD High-Level Forum (World Bank 2006a).

For areas of expertise and knowledge in which the Bank has no comparative advantages, the Bank will seek out effective collaboration mechanisms and pursue collaborative division of labor at the country level and with other development organizations in their respective areas of comparative advantage as discussed, for example, in disease-control knowledge as well as micro-organizational aspects of provision and the need for collaborative division of labor with the WHO. This will ensure mainstreaming of partners' knowledge in Bank operations.

Different areas of expertise offer opportunities for division of labor and collaboration among global partners. However, because the failure of any of the nine key functions may compromise overall health system performance, partners need to closely monitor collaboration at the country level.

Many successful global advocacy organizations and partnerships have emerged in the last decade. Partnerships have potential for strengthening Bank effectiveness, but they can also "pull" the Bank policy function in directions that are not in line with its policy objectives, Strategic Directions, or comparative advantages. Engaging partners that best complement its own comparative advantages poses a great challenge to the Bank. Having contributed to the emergence, consolidation, and success of many of these advocacy organizations and partnerships, but confronted with the need for greater selectivity, the Bank will increasingly concentrate advocacy in HNP on sound intersectoral and health system strengthening policies.

The Bank is increasingly involved in managing a multiplicity of Trust Funds (provided by bilateral agencies or private foundations). Many of them provide substantial support for Bank country-level operations. However, the Bank is managing more and more such funds with narrow objectives that may or may not fit into its overall comparative advantages, strategic policy objectives, and country work. Managing these funds has an opportunity cost for operational and policy focus. Some of these funds have the potential to de facto steer the operational and policy priority focus of the Bank, particularly the HNP Hub. The Bank will review current and future management of Trust Funds and be selective in managing only those directly linked to its strategic objectives and comparative advantages to support country-level work.

CHAPTER 7

Implications for Priority Health, Nutrition, and Population Programs and Interventions

The new environment, Strategic Objectives, and Strategic Directions discussed here apply to all HNP program areas for which the Bank provides technical and financial support, including nutrition, population, and HIV/AIDS. Some of the core policy implications of this Strategy in nutrition, population, and on HNP's contribution to combating HIV/AIDS are examined in this section.

Upon country demand, the Bank will continue to support through lending and policy advice, all health, nutrition, and population activities necessary to improve HNP outcomes, especially for the poor and the vulnerable. The Bank will increasingly ensure that Bank operational support and policy advice for priority areas in health will strengthen country health systems. Strengthening health systems will lead to removing systemic constraints and thus improve the effectiveness of country, Bank, and international community financing to achieve HNP results. Through policy analysis and policy dialog, the Bank can also assist countries in realizing levels of investment in HNP sector and rational allocations within the sector consistent with accelerated progress toward MDGs 1, 4, 5, and 6, and with other international commitments to achieving better health outcomes and greater health equity.

A Strong Commitment to Population, Sexual and Reproductive Health, and Maternal and Child Policy

The term "population" covers a variety of topics. Within the HNP sector two broad areas are most commonly referred to as population:

- Reproductive, maternal, and sexual health issues, and the health services that are concerned with addressing them.

- Levels and trends in births, deaths, and migration that determine population growth and age structure, and frequently have an impact on economic growth, poverty, labor markets, and other sectors.

The Bank commitment to population issues is embedded in the Programme of Action of the International Conference on Population and Development (UNFPA 2004) and identifies a number of entry points for the Bank to engage in population issues from within and outside the health sector. The Bank endorsed the Cairo Consensus in 1994 and continues to do so (box 7.1).

The ICPD called for achieving broader development goals through empowering women and meeting their needs for education and health, especially safe motherhood and sexual and reproductive health. It recommends that health systems provide a package of services, including family planning, prevention of unwanted pregnancy, and prevention of unsafe abortion and dealing with its health impact, safe pregnancy and delivery, postnatal care, as well as the prevention and treatment of reproductive-tract infections and sexually transmitted diseases, including HIV/AIDS.

Background and Context to Today's Population Issues

In the second half of the 20th century, the world population more than doubled, reaching 6.4 billion by mid-2004. According to current projections, 95 percent of all population growth will occur in developing countries (United Nations 2003). Since the middle of the last century, fertility and mortality trends almost everywhere have gradually started to converge toward low fertility and lengthened life expectancy. The exception is the Sub-Saharan Africa Region, where total fertility rates are still high: nearly 6 children per woman, compared with an average TFR of 2.6 in other low- and middle-income Regions (figure 7.1). About 200 million women who either want to space or limit their childbearing lack access to effective contraceptives. Intermediate fertility countries in South Asia and elsewhere, some with total fertility rates of 3 or 4, also continue to face challenges as they proceed through the demographic transition.

Africa will be the fastest growing Region, but most of the people born into the world between 2005 and 2050 will be Asians, due to the huge pop-

---

Box 7.1: The World Bank Commitment to Reproductive Rights and Reproductive Health

---

The ICPD Programme of Action includes the following:

- Improving knowledge and information on reproductive health services.
- Providing access to quality services particularly for the poor and vulnerable groups (i.e., migrants, adolescents, etc.).
- Including youth in sexual and reproductive health programs, outreach, and services (including provision of birth spacing methods).
- Preventing sexually transmitted diseases, including HIV.
- Promoting gender equality with particular attention to preventing violence against women.
- Ensuring that decisions concerning reproductive health be free of discrimination, coercion, and violence.

The ICPD Programme of Action states: "Reproductive health is a state of complete physical, mental and social well-being and not merely the absence of disease or infirmity, in all matters relating to the reproductive system and to its functions and processes." (ICPD, Section 7.2)

"Reproductive health therefore implies that people are able to have a satisfying and safe sex life and that they have the capability to reproduce and the freedom to decide if, when, and how often to do so. Implicit in this last condition are the right of men and women to be informed and to have access to safe, effective, affordable and acceptable methods of family planning of their choice, as well as other methods of their choice for regulation of fertility which are not against the law, and the right of access to appropriate health care services that will enable women to go safely through pregnancy and childbirth and provide couples with the best chance of having a healthy infant. In line with the above definition of reproductive health, reproductive health care is defined as the constellation of methods, techniques and services that contribute to reproductive health and well-being by preventing and solving reproductive health problems. It also includes sexual health, the purpose of which is the enhancement of life and personal relations, and not merely counseling and care related to reproduction and sexually transmitted diseases." (ICPD, Section 7.2)

"While the International Conference on Population and Development does not create any new international human rights, it affirms the application of universally recognized human rights standards to all aspects of population programs. It also represents the last opportunity in the twentieth century for the international community to collectively address the critical challenges and interrelationships between population and development. The Programme of Action will require the establishment of common ground, with full respect for the various religious and ethical values and cultural backgrounds. The impact of this Conference will be measured by the strength of the specific commitments made here and the consequent actions to fulfill them, as part of a new global partnership among all the world's countries and peoples, based on a sense of shared but differentiated responsibility for each other and for our planetary home." (ICPD, Section 1.15)

Source: UNFPA 2004.

Figure 7.1: Fertility Trends, by Geographic Region, 1950–2005

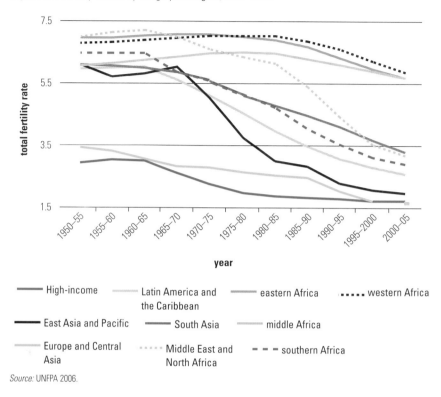

Source: UNFPA 2006.

ulation size of Asia (60 percent of the world's population in 2005) and the associated population momentum. Concurrently, most countries in Europe and Central Asia are expected to grow little, and a decline in population is projected in a few. Population aging is also a concern in many countries.

Countries can be grouped into three categories with broadly similar population issues (table 7.1): countries with high fertility rates (TFR over 5.0), often showing little change in fertility over time; countries with intermediate fertility rates (TFR ranging from 2.5 to 5.0); and countries with fertility rates near replacement level and below. Individual country-level analyses of population trends will be required to identify specific constraints and remedies for policy formulation. Countries in various stages of fertility transitions face diverse challenges in the areas of sexual and reproductive health.

Many aspects of effective reproductive and sexual health service delivery depend on overall health system strengthening, including planning, human resources, financing, regulation, information systems, management, and

Table 7.1: Some Characteristics of Countries According to Fertility Levels

	TOTAL FERTILITY RATE		
INDICATOR	GREATER THAN 5 [RANGE]	BETWEEN 5 AND 2.5 [RANGE]	LESS THAN 2.5 [RANGE]
Gross national income (GNI per capita, US$)	344	1,110	10,502
	[90–950]	[250–17,360]	[540–56,380]
Life expectancy at birth (years)	46	63	74
	[38–61]	[36–79]	[61–82]
Under-5 mortality rate per 1,000	175	75	25
	[59–283]	[6–156]	[3–106]
Primary completion rate, total	52	93	98
(% of relevant age group)	[25–89]	[29–107]	[75–114]
Population age over 65 years (% total)	3	4	11
	[2–3]	[2–10]	[1–20]

Sources: UN 2005; World Bank 2005h.

commodity procurement and logistics. There is now a robust body of evidence and experience to guide the design, delivery, and assessment of sexual and reproductive health programs. However, the determinants and consequences of demographic change need urgent study, specifically on policies and interventions affecting fertility, family planning, population aging, and utilization of other sexual and reproductive health care. Trends resulting from demographic processes—large birth cohorts in high-fertility countries, changes in the age structure resulting in large youth populations and rapidly growing elderly cohorts—all have profound implications for HNP, education, labor markets, pensions, poverty reduction, and environment.

Countries with High Unmet Needs in Sexual and Reproductive Health as a Priority

Despite the dramatic decline in global fertility rates, 35 countries, mostly in Sub-Saharan Africa, and a few countries in other Regions (Timor Leste, Afghanistan, West Bank-Gaza, and Yemen) still have fertility rates above 5 (United Nations 2003). Fertility rates in a number of these countries have not declined for several decades (figure 7.2), demonstrating their high unmet needs in sexual and reproductive health and maternal mortality reduction.

The rationale for Bank focus on these countries, along the lines of Bank comparative advantages, is clear from an economic growth/poverty reduc-

Figure 7.2: Fertility Trends, Selected High-Fertility Countries, 1950–2005

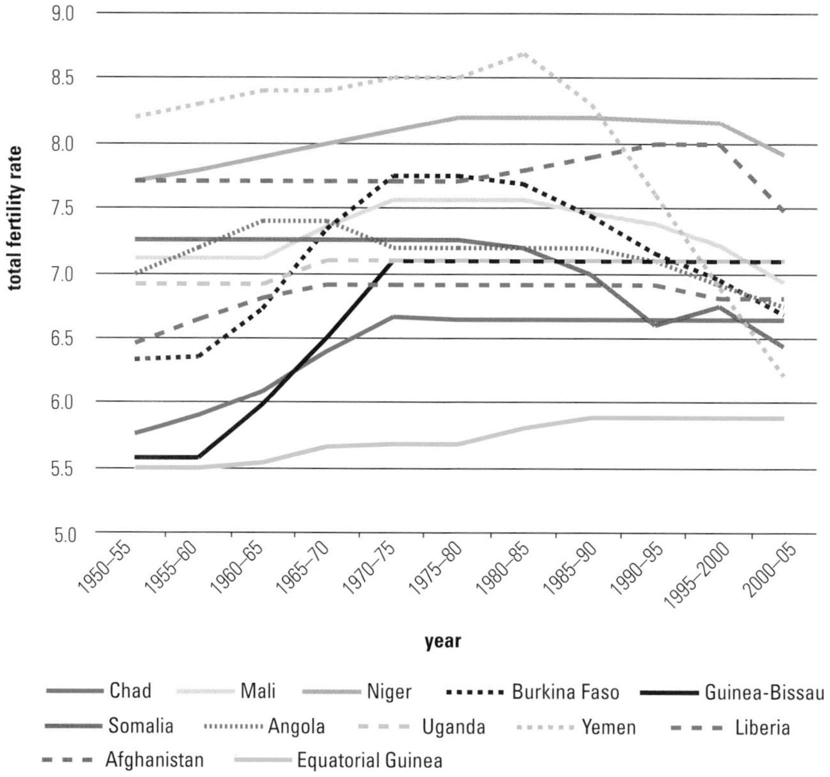
9.0
8.5
8.0
7.5
7.0
6.5
6.0
5.5
5.0
total fertility rate
1950–55
1955–60
1960–65
1965–70
1970–75
1975–80
1980–85
1985–90
1990–95
1995–2000
2000–05
year
Chad
Mali
Niger
Burkina Faso
Guinea-Bissau
Somalia
Angola
Uganda
Yemen
Liberia
Afghanistan
Equatorial Guinea

Source: UNFPA 2006.

tion perspective as well as from equity considerations. The consensus today is that rapid population growth constrains countries at low levels of socioeconomic development (Kelley 1988; Birdsall, Kelley, and Sinding 2001). It raises demand for public services and financial resources in countries that cannot create the fiscal space to provide either. Women endure a disproportionate burden of poor sexual and reproductive health. Their full and equal participation in development is therefore contingent on accessing essential sexual and reproductive health care, including the ability to make voluntary and informed decisions about fertility.

Notwithstanding, global attention to population issues has been declining (PATH/UNFPA 2006). The earlier success in reducing global fertility rates, the rise of competing priorities, the unintended loss of focus on family planning services within the broader ICPD agenda, and the changing environment have all contributed to persistently high fertility rates in some countries and declining funding for family planning (figure 7.3). Repositioning family planning within the ICPD agenda and, in collaboration with development partners, strengthening its visibility, are important. Harmonization and aid alignment at the country level is necessary to make sure that sexual and reproductive health services are funded adequately in national budgets. A comprehensive operational and systems strengthening response is required from the Bank and its partners.

Future Directions for the Bank

The Bank commitment to population issues is embedded in the ICPD Programme of Action (ICPD 1994).[53] The Bank recognizes that UNFPA and WHO are the main agencies working on the technical aspects of reproductive health issues. The Bank will work on population issues on the basis of its comparative advantages. Upon country demand, the Bank will focus its contributions in countries with high unmet needs in sexual and reproductive health in the following areas:

Figure 7.3: Population Activities Expenditures as Share of Total Population Assistance, 1995–2004

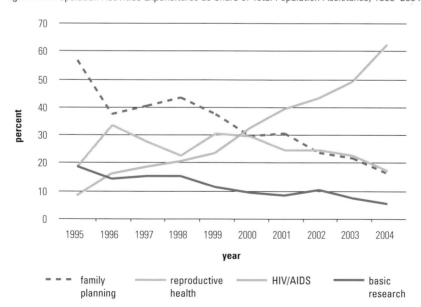

Source: UNFPA 2006.

- Assessing multisectoral constraints to reducing fertility, determining impacts of population changes on health systems and other sectors, and assisting countries in strengthening population policies.

- Providing financial support and policy advice for comprehensive sexual and reproductive health services, including family planning, and maternal and newborn health.

- Generating demand for reproductive health information and services, including improving girls' education and women's economic opportunities, and reducing gender disparities.

- Raising the economic and poverty dimensions of high fertility in strategic documents that inform policy dialog (such as CASs, CEMs, and country-led PRSPs).

Opportunities for Sustaining, and Challenges to Improving, HNP Contributions to Combating HIV/AIDS

The Bank Reaffirms Its Commitment to Assist Client Countries and the International Community in Combating the HIV/AIDS Pandemic

This effort is a worldwide health priority, as articulated in 2005 through its Global HIV/AIDS Program of Action (GHAPA) for supporting the global, regional, and national AIDS response (World Bank 2006g). The pandemic jeopardizes economic development in many countries, particularly in Africa. Here, too, recent financial and political commitments for combating HIV/AIDS present new opportunities, but also new challenges. Much of the new funding is dedicated to expanding access to antiretroviral therapy (ART). By end-2005, the number of people on ART in low- and middle-income countries amounted to 1.3 million, only an estimated 20 percent of the number needing treatment (UNAIDS 2006). Annex H summarizes the Bank vision on the HNP sector contribution to combating the HIV/AIDS pandemic.

Scaling Up and Sustaining Prevention and Treatment

Sustainable scaling up of HIV/AIDS prevention and treatment depends on health systems that can: overcome increasingly worrisome health financing constraints and set the right provider incentive framework for results; and solve supply bottlenecks through efficiency improvements and supply expansion, particularly in LICs. It also depends on the ability of the international community to fulfill its promises. The Bank remains committed to financing HIV/AIDS interventions, upon country demand and in concert with integrated health system strengthening projects, programs, and analytic and advisory services.

Health Financing Constraints

Some characteristics of development assistance for health that are relevant to HIV/AIDS cause increasing concern: the volatility and predominance of short-term commitments by the international community; increasing funding distortions; allocative inefficiencies; and the need to find effective ways of creating fiscal space for HNP in general and HIV/AIDS in particular.

- *Volatility and predominance of short-term commitments.* The amount of DAH funds countries receive varies greatly from year to year. This makes long-term planning difficult for Ministries of Health and Finance.

- *Funding distortions.* Fragmentation of donor assistance to health distorts funding, making it difficult for governments to finance systemic requirements for staff, supervision, training, management and maintenance, and expansion of access to ART.

- *Allocative inefficiencies.* With the large influx of funding for HIV/AIDS, the question arises of whether the money is being used to its maximum net benefit. Funding for prevention has not been similarly expanded. ART appears to help prevent, as well as treat, HIV infection; but preventive interventions could do more to limit new HIV infections and are more cost-effective (Hogan et al. 2005; Salomon et al. 2005; Bertozzi et al 2006). Might some funds be better and more equitably spent on prevention?

- *Need to find effective ways to create fiscal space.* Large increases in public spending on HIV/AIDS or health initiatives that create future spending commitments must be considered in the context of governments' ability to provide resources from current and future revenues. This is a serious constraint in low-income countries. The problem is compounded if large expenditures are financed by borrowing, which requires additional revenue to service the debt and could impair overall economic growth.

Improve Efficiency and, When Necessary, Expand Supply Capacity

The Bank will contribute to:

- *Efficiency improvements.* More funding is not enough; additional funding must be linked to improving health system efficiency, as discussed throughout this Strategy.

- *Supply capacity.* The Bank remains committed to supporting country efforts to strengthen health system supply through infrastructure investments (e.g., clinics, hospitals, and medical equipment purchases), when necessary.

Bank Contributions to HIV/AIDS Financing

The Bank will contribute to financing HIV/AIDS programs and health systems in a several ways:

- *Supporting increased, long-term, predictable funding.* Upon country demand, the Bank is committed to leveraging global partner funding and/or providing increased and predictable long-term financing for the health sector and HIV/AIDS.

- *Creating fiscal space and reducing distortions.* The Bank will work intersectorally with client countries, the IMF, and global partners to help countries develop ways of enhancing capacity to absorb and reduce the adverse effects of fiscal shocks and create fiscal space for necessary HNP interventions, including HIV/AIDS prevention and treatment.

- *Enhancing accountability.* The Bank will promote budgetary and financial reporting processes that accommodate and respond to the views of critical stakeholders within the country. The Bank will support client–country efforts to sustain specific efforts to protect the interests of poor, vulnerable, and marginalized groups, including people living with HIV/AIDS, in order to increase accountability and enhance people's voices.

- *New types of financing.* The Bank will provide financial, technical, and convening capacity to countries requesting help with development of health financing systems that promote accountability, efficiency, and financial protection. This work forms the framework for financing

HIV/AIDS prevention, care, and treatment at country level. Upon country request, the Bank will also test new country-led and country-owned approaches to its own financing of HNP and HIV/AIDS.

Strengthening health systems is critical for scaling up and improving the effectiveness of HNP interventions, including HIV/AIDS treatment and prevention. As discussed throughout this Strategy, the Bank is committed to sharpening its focus and improving its capacity to support client countries in strengthening health systems, along the lines of Bank comparative advantages. It will seek to improve system capacity to deliver services for the entire range of disease interventions prioritized by client countries. HIV/AIDS, malaria, tuberculosis, maternal and child health, reproductive and sexual health, and micronutrient interventions are prominent in the agendas of most client countries, particularly LICs.

Repositioning Nutrition to a Central Place in Development[54]

Malnutrition, and its negative compounding effect in disease susceptibility, slows economic growth and perpetuates poverty via three routes: direct losses in productivity from poor physical status, indirect losses from poor cognitive function and deficits in schooling, and losses owing to increased health care costs. Malnutrition's economic costs are substantial: individual productivity losses estimated at more than 10 percent of lifetime earnings and gross domestic product forgone as high as 2 to 3 percent. Improving nutrition is therefore at least as much an economic issue as one of welfare, social protection, and human rights.

Investing in nutrition in early childhood lays the foundation for lifelong health and development. A well-nourished child, for example, is less likely to suffer from disease and more likely to achieve better educational attainment and labor productivity as an adult. Moreover, improving children's health has longer-lasting gains that may be discerned in the next generation of healthier and more productive people.

Reducing undernutrition and micronutrient malnutrition also multiplies the effectiveness of health prevention and curative interventions and directly reduces *poverty*, broadly defined to include human development and human capital formation. Undernutrition is closely connected to income poverty. Malnutrition is often two, three, or more times more prevalent among the poorest income groups than among the highest. This means that improving nutrition is a pro-poor strategy: it disproportionately increases the income-earning potential of the poor.

The returns on investing in nutrition are high. The Copenhagen Consensus ranked returns on nutrition interventions among the highest of 17 potential development investments (table 7.2). Improving nutrition is essential to reduce extreme poverty. The first MDG, for eradicating extreme poverty and hunger, recognizes this requirement.

The key indicator for measuring progress on the nonincome poverty goal is the prevalence of underweight U-5 children. Yet most assessments of progress toward the MDGs have dwelled mainly on the income poverty target and have found most countries on track. However, of 143 countries, only 34 (24 percent) are on track to achieve the nonincome target (nutrition MDG) (table 7.3). No country in South Asia, where undernutrition is highest, will achieve the MDG—although Bangladesh will come close, and Asia as a whole will achieve it. More alarmingly, nutritional status is deteriorating in 26 countries, many of them in Africa where the nexus between HIV and undernutrition is strong and mutually reinforcing. And in 57 countries, no data are available to evaluate progress. A renewed focus on the nonincome poverty target, including nutrition, is central to any poverty reduction efforts.

Table 7.2: Nutrition Provision Rated a Top Investment by Copenhagen Consensus

RATING		CHALLENGE	OPPORTUNITY
Very good	1.	Diseases	Controlling HIV/AIDS
	2.	Malnutrition and hunger	Providing Micronutrients
	3.	Subsidies and trade	Liberalizing trade
	4.	Diseases	Controlling malaria
Good	5.	Malnutrition and hunger	Developing new agricultural technologies
	6.	Sanitation and water	Developing small-scale water technologies
	7.	Sanitation and water	Implementing community-managed systems
	8.	Sanitation and water	Conducting research in water and agriculture
	9.	Government	Lowering costs of new business
Fair	10.	Migration	Lowering barriers to migration
	11.	Malnutrition and hunger	Improving infant and child malnutrition
	12.	Diseases	Scaling up basic health services
	13.	Malnutrition and hunger	Reducing the prevalence of low birth weight
Poor	14–17.	Climate/migration	Various

Source: Bhagwati, Fogel et al. 2004.

Table 7.3: Progress toward Nonincome Poverty Target

ON TRACK (24%)			DETERIORATING STATUS (18%)		
AFR (7)	**ECA (6)**	**MENA (5)**	**AFR (13)**	**ECA (4)**	
Angola	Armenia	Algeria	Niger	Albania	
Benin	Croatia	Egypt, Arab.	Burkina Faso	Azerbaijan	
Botswana	Kazakhstan	Rep. of	Cameroon	Russian Federation	
Chad	Kyrgyz Rep.	Iran	Comoros	Serbia and Montenegro	
Gambia, The	Romania	Jordan	Ethiopia		
Mauritania	Turkey	Tunisia	Guinea	**LCR (3)**	
Zimbabwe			Lesotho	Argentina	
			Mali	Costa Rica	
EAP (5)	**LCR (10)**	**SAR (0)**	Senegal*	Panama	
China	Bolivia		Sudan		
Indonesia	Chile		Tanzania	**MENA (2)**	
Malaysia	Colombia		Togo	Iraq	
Thailand	Dominican Republic		Zambia	Yemen, Republic of	
Vietnam	Guyana				
Haiti		**EAP (2)**	**SAR (2)**		
Jamaica		Mongolia	Maldives		
Mexico		Myanmar	Nepal		
Peru					
Venezuela, R. B. de					
SOME IMPROVEMENT, BUT NOT ON TRACK (18%)			NO TREND DATA AVAILABLE (40%)		
AFR (14)	**EAP (3)**	**MENA (1)**	**AFR (14)**	**ECA (17)**	**LCR (12)**
CAR	Cambodia	Morocco	Burundi	Belarus	Belize
Congo, Dem. Rep. of	Lao, PDR		Cape Verde	Bosnia and Herz.	Brazil
Côte d'Ivoire	Philippines	**SAR (4)**	Congo, Rep. of	Bulgaria	Dominica
Eritrea		Bangladesh*	Eq. Guinea	Czech Republic	Ecuador
Gabon		India	Guinea	Estonia	Grenada
Ghana		Pakistan	Guinea-Bissau	Georgia	Paraguay
Kenya		Sri Lanka	Liberia	Hungary	St. Kitts and Nevis
Madagascar	**ECA (0)**		Mauritius	Latvia	St. Lucia
Malawi			Namibia	Lithuania	St. Vincent
Mozambique	**LCR (4)**		São Tomé and Principe	Macedonia	Suriname
Nigeria	El Salvador		Seychelles	Moldova	Trinidad and Tobago
Rwanda	Guatemala		Somalia	Poland	Uruguay
Sierra Leone	Honduras		South Africa	Slovak Republic	
Uganda	Nicaragua		Swaziland	Tajikistan	
				Turkmenistan	
			EAP (11)	Ukraine	**MENA (2)**
			Fiji	Uzbekistan	Djibouti
			Kiribati		Lebanon
			Marshall Is.		
			Micronesia		**SAR (2)**
			Palau		Afghanistan
			Papua N. G.		Bhutan
			Samoa		
			Solomon Is.		
			Timor-Leste		
			Tonga		
			Vanuatu		

Sources: Author's calculations based on data in World Bank 2006l; WHO Global Database on Child Growth and Malnutrition.

Note: All calculations are based on 1990-2002 trend data from WHO Global Database on Child Growth and Malnutrition (as of April 2005). Countries indicated by an asterisk subsequently released preliminary Demographic and Health Survey (DHS) data that suggest improvement and therefore may be reclassified when their data are officially released.

The Alarming Shape and Scale of Malnutrition

Malnutrition is now problematic in both poor and rich countries, but it affects the poorest people most. In developed countries, obesity is growing fast, especially among poorer people. An epidemic of diet-related NCDs such as diabetes and heart disease is raising health care costs and reducing productivity. In developing countries, obesity is also fast emerging as a problem, on top of widespread undernutrition and micronutrient deficiencies. Underweight children and overweight adults often live in the same households in both developing and developed countries.

Malnutrition also occurs in many nonpoor families. People do not always know what foods are best for them or their children, and the untrained eye does not usually notice abnormally slow growth or associate it with micronutrient deficiencies. Education can play a major role in correcting malnutrition stemming from ignorance.

Effective interventions exist, so what is missing? Nutrition investments have been low priority for both governments and development partners for three reasons. First, there is little demand for nutrition services from communities because malnutrition is often invisible; families and communities are unaware that even moderate and mild malnutrition contributes substantially to death, disease, and low educational attainment; most malnourished families are poor and hence have little voice. Second, governments still do not recognize how high malnutrition's economic costs are; that malnutrition holds back progress toward all the MDGs, not just the nutrition MDG; and that plenty of experience has been acquired with implementing cost-effective, affordable nutrition programs on a large scale. Third, there are multiple organizational stakeholders in nutrition. Because most country financing is allocated by sectors or ministries, malnutrition can fall between the cracks in both national programs and global assistance.

The Bank Contribution to Reposition Nutrition in Development

Bank increased knowledge and policy development work on nutrition is summarized in *Repositioning Nutrition as Central to Development* (World Bank 2006l). In the area of nutrition, the Bank will further contribute by: expanding its capacity to generate country-specific policy knowledge and advice to identify the magnitude of malnutrition as an outcome and as a constraint to other outcomes; improving its capacity to identify structural issues (e.g., failures in agricultural, taxation, rural development, water supply and sanitation, social protection, education, community-driven development, and other policies and devising multisectoral policies to help countries beset by malnutrition address it; upon country demand, supporting integration of appropriately designed and balanced nutrition policies and interventions in CASs and in client country–led PRSPs; improving Bank monitoring and evaluation capacity of nutrition-enhancing interventions to ensure evidence-based learning and policy adjustments; and including nutrition as one of the multisectoral parameters in the MCA tool. Beyond structural and systemic issues, the Bank will seek advice from specialized global partners for Bank in-country operations on the technical aspects of appropriate nutrition interventions.

CHAPTER 8

Implementing New Bank HNP Strategic Directions

To make full use of its comparative advantages in the new environment in the service of client countries, the Bank HNP sector needs to make functional and organizational changes and rebalance the skill-mix composition of its staff and management. Strengthening Bank capacity (regional and Hub) to sharpen focus on HNP results, health system strengthening, health economics, and intersectoral work is costly in the short term. The requisite skill-mix adjustment will take time and effort (through staff and management training, reorientation of recruitment toward expertise in health financing/systems/economics/intersectorality skills, development of core diagnostic tools). The adjustment will also require functional changes in the mission of the HNP Hub toward one more oriented to support Region and country team needs. Concomitantly, it will require revitalizing the role and work of the HNP Sector Board.

This section includes a summary Action Plan to implement key features of the HNP Strategy that lead to the new Strategic Directions and results. It includes: proposals and targets to improve quality at entry of the HNP portfolio; actions to restructure the current at-risk portfolio; a design, pilot, and implementation plan for MCA; proposals for improving statistical capacity and monitoring of core indicators at client–country and global levels; a Results Framework to guide regional development of country strategies; and proposals for training and retooling HNP staff and management. It also includes key organizational changes, particularly for the HNP Network (HNPFAM) and the HNP Hub.

Annex D presents the Bank HNP Results Framework, which summarizes the main outcomes and outputs for the Bank in HNP. The framework is intended as guidance for country teams for developing country-specific and detailed results frameworks for Bank operations and programs. The Results

Framework links the main outcomes and outputs for the Bank with the Action Plan for Strategy implementation.

The Action Plan also includes transition proposals to implement a rapid Bank response in the areas of health system strengthening. Constraints on budgets and on the availability of health system experts would preclude short-term strengthening of every Region's capacity for health system advice. Thus, the Action Plan proposes creating and locating a health system policy team in the HNP Hub to support the HNP Sector Board (to take advantage of initial economies of scale) to: support Regions in their health system capacity strengthening process; provide support to Regions in their policy advice to client countries through their lending and AAA work during this transitional period (initially with IDA country focus); and advise the Bank and international community on next steps for developing and implementing the health system strengthening agenda. It also will include a moderate increase in senior health system experts at regional level. The Hub health systems team is envisioned as being fully functional 12 to 18 months after approval of the new Strategy, contingent on availability of transition funding.

Action Plan for Implementing Strategic Directions

Sharpening the focus on results will require intensifying both client–country efforts to identify, monitor, and evaluate government programs and Bank capacity to evaluate Bank-supported programs using country systems. It will also require innovation in linking lending to results to such output. Finally, it will require a significant effort to restructure nonperforming projects in the HNP portfolio to improve Bank-assessed results of closing projects. Table 8.1 summarizes actions to be taken by the HNP sector to sharpen its focus on results.

Strengthening the Bank health system capacity and synergy among systems and priority diseases will require hiring of additional health system staff for the Regions and the creation of a health systems policy team to take advantage of economies of scale and facilitate regional cross-fertilization. This team will give country teams immediate health system analytical and operations advice support in identifying actual constraints and provide recommendations on Bank, donor, and government funding needed to achieve HNP results and to help Regions refine and develop their own health system capacity in the medium term. Table 8.2 summarizes actions to be taken by the HNP sector to improve Bank capacity on health system strengthening.

Table 8.1: Five-Year Action Plan—Renewing Focus on Results

WHAT?	BASELINE	HOW MUCH AND BY WHEN?	BY WHOM?
1. *Build statistical capacity* for client countries on priority HNP outcome indicators (disaggregated by gender and age) directly through Bank operations and/or supporting global partner's country support (e.g., MDGs). This includes the development of country-based frameworks for the collection of essential household HNP and multisectoral indicators.	Less than 10% of CASs targeting HNP results	At least 40% of new CASs targeting HNP results to be discussed with the Board in 2009 and thereafter will identify capacity and systems building activities (Bank and/or coordinated with global partners) for, monitoring, and evaluating HNP results in government programs.	Regional HNP Sector Manager and HNP country team and Country Directors with technical support from HNP Hub and Development Economics (DEC), as needed
2. *Pilot and evaluate impact of output-based and performance-based financing* for HNP-related projects/programs.	4 active projects in FY2006	By FY2010, at least 14 active projects with most loan proceeds allocated on output-based financing. Impact evaluation plans in place for 60% of these projects or more upon approval.	Regional HNP Sector Manager and HNP Sector Board with technical support from HNP Hub, as needed
3. *Develop Bank Global Results Monitoring Framework* for key outcomes, outputs, and system performance indicators to be monitored by the Bank globally. This will include indicators on gender disparities in health.	Presented with this new HNP Strategy	Strategy for global monitoring arrangement designed (in collaboration with global partners) by end-FY2008. Implementation launched by end-FY2009.	HNP Hub with support of HNP Sector Board, DEC, and others
4. *Introduce results frameworks* for all projects targeting HNP outcomes, outputs, and system performance, including baseline data and output targets.	Less than 25% of active projects with satisfactory results frameworks as of FY2006	At least 70% of new projects/programs approved by the Board in FY2008 and thereafter.	Regional HNP Sector Manager and country team, with technical support from HNP Hub
5. *Periodic data collection and updates* (as appropriate to specific indicators) for at least 70% of the indicators included in project results framework and updated periodically in Implementation Status Reports (ISRs).	Less than 15% of active projects as of FY2006	At least 65% (annually) of all projects/programs approved by Board in FY2008 and thereafter.	Regional HNP Sector Manager and country team, with technical support from HNP Hub
6. *Develop indicators (including gender-based indicators) for priority HNP outcomes* for which no agreed indicators exist (e.g., financial protection, governance in the health sector, and financial and fiscal sustainability).	Does not exist	Develop indicators by end-FY2008.	*Identification of indicator needed:* HNP country team and Regional HNP Sector Manager *Development:* HNP Hub in collaboration with PREM, DEC, and country teams

(Continues on the following page)

Table 8.1: Five-Year Action Plan—Renewing Focus on Results (continued)

WHAT?	BASELINE	HOW MUCH AND BY WHEN?	BY WHOM?
7. *Improve results in existing portfolio.* Review and restructure existing HNP portfolio (project design and/or project development objective, PDO) to achieve satisfactory PDO or higher outcome at project closing.	Annual average of 66% of projects closing with satisfactory PDO or higher result (FY2005 and FY2006)	75% for FY2009 and thereafter (each Region and total HNP portfolio).	Regional HNP Sector Manager with support from HNP Sector Board HNP Hub, IEG, DEC and Operations, Policy, and Country Services (OPCS)
8. *Concurrent monitoring of overall active Bank portfolio performance and PDO indicators on HNP results.* Develop and implement central database with HNP project results based on ISR and project results framework data online for monitoring portfolio results and quality.	Does not exist	Develop by end-FY2008; implement by end-FY2009.	*Develop:* HNP Hub in collaboration with results team in OPCS/DEC and with Information Solutions Group *Implement:* HNP Sector Board *Manage:* HNP Hub and HNP Sector Board

Table 8.2: Five-Year Action Plan—Strengthening Health Systems and Ensuring Synergy between Health System Strengthening and Priority–Disease Interventions

WHAT?	BASELINE	HOW MUCH AND BY WHEN?	BY WHOM?
9. Increase support to Bank country teams to *identify health system constraints (including gender-specific constraints) to achieving HNP results* and mainstream system strengthening actions to overcome constraints in all new HNP operations (or other sectoral or global partner operations), including priority-disease interventions.	Less than 25% identify health system constraints. Less than 45% include health system strengthening in areas of Bank comparative advantages.	Develop operations toolkit for rapid assessment of health system constraints for better outcomes (completed by end- FY2008). Complete identification of 7 countries by December 2007. Launch on-demand support in four countries by June 2008. Put on-demand support in place to Bank country teams in 7 countries by June 2009. At least 60% of projects approved in FY2009 and thereafter will include assessment of health system constraints to reaching HNP results. At least 70% of those identifying constraints will include appropriate policy actions/investments to overcome them.	*Identify countries:* Regional HNP Sector Managers with support from HNP Hub. *Provide support to country teams:* Health System Policy Team (HSPT). *Support client countries in designing system strengthening interventions:* Country teams with on-demand support from HSPT. *Support country teams in assessing health system constraints:* HNP Hub.

(*Continues on the following page*)

Table 8.2: Five-Year Action Plan—Strengthening Health Systems and Ensuring Synergy between Health System Strengthening and Priority–Disease Interventions (continued)

WHAT?	BASELINE	HOW MUCH AND BY WHEN?	BY WHOM?
10. *Assemble Health Systems Policy Team (HSPT) and hire additional health system staff for the Regions.* (Contingent to Budget Availability).	Does not exist	Write TORs and launch recruitment process by December 2007. Complete recruitment by June 2008. Put team in place and working by December 2008.	HNP Hub in coordination with HD Council and HNP Sector Board. Team would be located in restructured HNP Hub. Regional staff in regions.
11. *Put in place arrangements for collaborative division of labor* on health systems with global partners at global and country levels.	Does not exist	Dialog in place for global arrangements by December 2007. Launch collaborative division of labor arrangements for at least 10 countries where projects/programs include interventions requiring expertise other than Bank comparative advantages (by December 2008).	*Global arrangements:* HNP Network Director with support from HD Vice President, HD Council, HNP Sector Board, and HSPT. *Country-level arrangements:* Country teams with support of Regional Sector Manager and HSPT.
12. *Focus knowledge creation and policy advice (AAA) on Bank comparative advantage.* Increase proportion of country- and regional-level AAA, appropriate to requirements of LICs and MICs, focused on Bank comparative advantages.	Less than 35% so focused	By end-FY2008, 50% and by end-FY2009 70% of new HNP sector AAA will be focused on areas of Bank comparative advantage in specific areas appropriate for LICs' and/or MICs' requirements, e.g., health system financing, demand-side determinants of results, intersectoral contribution to HNP results, private-public collaboration.	Regional HNP Sector Manager with support from HSPT.
13. Develop and implement a training and accreditation program for Bank staff on *technical and operational aspects of health system strengthening.*	Does not exist	In place by end-FY2008; 30% of HNP staff accredited by end-FY2009; 60% of HNP staff accredited by end-FY2010.	HNP Sector Board with support from HNP Hub, WBI, and DEC.

Intersectoral work for HNP results will be strengthened in two phases. First, the Bank will develop necessary tools to identify intersectoral constraints to achieving HNP results. The tools will be used to identify potential operations (whose primary objective is achieving HNP results), or identify potential actions/components (in operations whose primary objective is not HNP results) and to suggest the AAA work required to overcome the constraints. For that, the Bank will develop the Multisectoral Constraints Assessment tool. Second, the Bank, upon country demand, will further experiment with multisectoral operations when the country context lends itself to it. Table 8.3 summarizes actions to be taken by the HNP sector to improve intersectoral work for HNP results.

Table 8.3: Five-Year Action Plan—Strengthening Bank Intersectoral Advisory Capacity

WHAT?	BASELINE	HOW MUCH AND BY WHEN?	BY WHOM?
14. Develop, pilot test, and implement *Multisectoral Constraints Assessment (MCA)* tool and process. Pilot test in a number of LICs and MICs.	Does not exist	First tool will be developed by end-FY2008 and pilot tested in 2 MICs and 2 LICs by end-FY2009.	*Development:* Intersectoral thematic group (all sectors concerned through respective Hub Sector Managers, led by HNP Hub Sector Manager). Ad hoc technical team to design instrument. *Selection of country pilots:* Virtual intersectoral thematic group and Country Directors. *Implementation of pilots:* Ad hoc TTL from country team and Regional Sector Manager, under oversight of intersectoral thematic group.
15. *Identify lending and AAA in CAS.* MCA-identified HNP-related Bank projects/programs/components in CAS.	Does not exist	MCA will be used to identify 40% of projects/programs with HNP results included in at least 50% of new CASs discussed with Board by FY2010 and thereafter.	Regional HNP and other Sector Managers involved with support from HNP Hub and intersectoral thematic group.
16. Develop, implement, and manage an *intersectoral coordination thematic group* for HNP results.	Does not exist	Functioning by December 2007.	The thematic group would be composed of interested sectors through their respective sector Hub Managers. *Development:* HNP and other sector Hub Managers. *Management:* HNP Hub Director.

To increase selectivity and achieve complementarity with global partners, the HNP sector will seek agreements with them on collaborative division of labor. The Bank will concentrate its knowledge creation and policy advice activities on its areas of comparative advantage. It will seek its partners' advice on areas in which it has limited or no comparative advantage. Table 8.4 summarizes specific actions to be taken by the HNP sector to improve selectivity and collaborative division of labor with global partners.

HNP Hub Mission and Organizational Changes

The HNP hub will facilitate HNP network implementation of the new Strategy. In order to adequately play its role, the Hub will adjust its organizational structure and functioning in four work teams as follows:

Table 8.4: Five-Year Action Plan—Increasing Selectivity, Strategic Engagement, and Collaborative Division of Labor

WHAT?	BASELINE	HOW MUCH AND BY WHEN?	BY WHOM?
17. *Increase use of harmonization and alignment* principles for Bank projects in at country level.		By FY2011, at least 81% of projects approved by Board will be based on country fiduciary systems or will have common fiduciary arrangements/rules for all participating donors.	Country teams with support of Regional Sector Manager, Regional Fiduciary Teams, and on-demand support from HSPT.
18. *Develop overall HNP fiscal space assessment in priority countries*	Does not exist	Develop and pilot fiscal space assessment methodology (completed by end of FY2008). Full fiscal space assessment in 7 priority countries in coordination with Global Partners.	HNP Hub in collaboration with DEC and PREM and with regional HD Departments. Country teams with support from HNP Hub.
19. *Review and reorient Bank grants (DGF)* in HNP toward areas of Bank comparative advantages.	Currently less than 1% of DGF grant financing is allocated to partners working on issues related to Bank comparative advantages.	By end-FY2008, 5%, by end-FY2009 30%, and by end- FY2010 50% of DGF grant financing will be allocated in partnerships related to Bank comparative advantages.	HNP Sector Board with support of HNP Hub.
20. Realign secondments and Trust Fund management in HNP sector with Bank comparative advantages.	Currently 60% of secondments in HNP sector are in areas in which Bank has little comparative advantage.	By end-FY2009, 80% of secondments to Bank and 80% of total Trust Fund financing managed by HNP sector will be in areas of Bank comparative advantages.	

Performance Monitoring and Action Team

This team will be responsible for the maintenance of a data base of HNP indicators; the maintenance of a data base of health financing indicators; contributions to institutional reports (Global Monitoring Report [GMR], Country Performance and Institutional Assessment [CPIA], World Development Report [WDR], etc.); portfolio monitoring and quality enhancement; monitoring and evaluation capacity building (staff and clients); and regular updating of progress on the HNP Results Framework, including support to country teams on results framework development.

Global Health Coordination and Partnerships Team

The following functions will be covered: coordinate work with global partnerships and initiatives; facilitate selective fund raising and TF management for the HNP network; DGF management support; selective joint ventures around themes of convergence (comparative advantages); and harmonization and alignment.

Health Systems Policy Team

The preparation of the Strategy has identified a gap in high-level health system policy skills to guide the implementation of the Bank agenda and an unmet demand from the Regions to receive timely support in their country dialog. It has also identified the need for practical and concrete advice to country teams and partners on how to overcome health system constraints to DAH effectiveness for results. This will become even more pressing with the new policy drivers of the HNP strategy. The team will: provide country teams with overall policy, technical, and operational advice on health systems; manage knowledge creation on health systems, develop and manage technical assistance for the Multisector Constraints Assessment tool; respond to country team demands on ensuring synergy between priority–disease and system strengthening approaches; and advise global partners on the health system aspects for which the Bank has comparative advantages. About 50 percent of their time will be allocated to country-team support and field work.

The team will focus closely on the following themes identified as priorities by client countries and global partners: health financing and economics, including health insurance; linkage to macroeconomic and fiscal policy; health service purchasing; health system governance; and facilitating synergy between priority–disease and system strengthening in Bank operations.

Technical Aspects of Public Health, Nutrition, and Population

The team will support the Regions on technical aspects of core public health functions, disease control, nutrition, and population, supporting with existing in-house expertise but, more important, helping country teams establish the necessary working collaboration arrangements at country level with technical agencies such as the WHO, UNICEF, UNFPA, and others.

Rebalancing Staff Skill-Mix

The staff is the single most important asset of the Bank and its most important comparative advantage. Bank personnel working on HNP results represent a wealth of multisectoral experience and knowledge from almost every country. Managing and strengthening this asset is crucial for good Bank performance on HNP results.

The skill-mix of the HNP sector staff has undergone important changes. Focusing on Bank comparative advantages will require rebalancing the skill-mix of staff and management in two directions through new hiring and retooling/training of staff and management: increasing the proportion of economics and health systems skills and, more important, increasing the proportion of staff with recognized seniority in hands-on health system experience and sufficient breadth of knowledge to encourage and lead intersectoral work for HNP results (the horizontal part of the HR "T" skills) in high-level policy dialog with government counterparts. The HNP Sector Board and HD Council will ensure that future recruitment seeks out those skills for both staff and management appointments, to reach a balance between health specialist and economics/senior systems specialist.

Preliminary Estimates of Strategy Implementation Costs

The Board and management are currently discussing the budget allocations for FY2008 and beyond as part of the four-point engagement on the budget previously agreed. In this context, management and staff are undertaking a more detailed task-based budgeting exercise as part of the normal budget cycle. The resource requirements for implementing the HNP strategy will be a function of the pace of implementation of the Strategy (pace of change), the demand from countries, and the availability of resources in an environment of zero growth in the overall Bank budget. It is expected that the cost of implementing the new HNP Strategy will involve a modest increase in the base budget for the HD network over the FY2007 base budget, after taking into account one-off transitional adjustments. An extraordinary allocation to the HD network above the regular base budget will be utilized to finance these transition expenses, as justified.

ANNEX A

HNP Hub Action Plan and Regional Action Plans

HNP Hub Action Plan

The Health, Nutrition, and Population (HNP) Hub will facilitate HNP Network implementation of the new Strategy. In order to adequately play its role, the Hub will adjust its organizational structure and functioning in four work teams as follows:

Performance Monitoring and Action Team

This team will be responsible for the maintenance of a database of HNP indicators, the maintenance of a database of health financing indicators, contributions to institutional reports (e.g., GMR, CPIA, WDR); portfolio monitoring and quality enhancement, monitoring and evaluation (M&E) capacity building (staff and clients); and the regular updating of progress on the HNP Results Framework, including support to country teams on results framework development.

Global Health Coordination and Partnerships Team

The following functions will be covered: coordinate work with global partnerships and initiatives; facilitate selective fund raising and Trust Fund (TF) management for the HNP Network, Development Grant Facility (DGF) management support; selective joint ventures around themes of convergence (comparative advantages), and harmonization and alignment.

Health Systems Policy Team

The preparation of the strategy has identified a gap in high-level health system policy skills to guide the implementation of the Bank agenda and an unmet demand from the Regions to receive timely support in their country dialog. It has also identified the need for practical and concrete advice to country teams and partners on how to overcome health system constraints to development assistance for health (DAH) effectiveness for results. This will become even more pressing with the new policy drivers of the HNP Strategy. The team will: provide country teams with overall policy, technical, and operational advice on health systems; manage knowledge creation on health systems, develop and manage technical assistance for the Multi-sectoral Constraints Assessment (MCA) tool, and respond to country-team demands on ensuring synergy between priority disease and system strengthening; advise global partners on the health system aspects for which the Bank has comparative advantages. About 50 percent of the team's time will be allocated to country-team support and field work.

The team will focus closely on the following themes identified as priorities by client countries and global partners: health financing and economics, including health insurance; linkage to macroeconomic and fiscal policy; health service purchasing; health system governance; and synergy facilitation between priority disease and system strengthening in Bank operations.

Technical Aspects of Public Health, Nutrition, and Population

The team will support the Regions on technical aspects of disease control, nutrition, and population, drawing on in-house expertise but, more important, helping country teams establish the necessary working collaboration arrangements at country level with technical agencies such as the WHO, UNICEF, UNFPA, and others.

Regional Action Plans

Africa Region

Health outcomes in the Africa Region are not progressing fast enough to achieve economic growth and reduce poverty (table A.1), and the Region is unlikely to meet the health Millennium Development Goals (MDGs).

Laboring under geographical, environmental, cultural, and political challenges, the HIV/AIDS crisis puts a heavier burden on Africa than on any other part of the world. What should be the Africa Region's response to the situation?

Table A.1: Health Indicators in the Africa Region

INCOME GROUP/ COUNTRY	GNI PER CAPITA, 2005 (US$)	HEALTH EXPENDITURE, 2004 (% OF GDP)	EXTERNAL ASSISTANCE, 2004 (% OF TOTAL)	U-5 MORTALITY, 2005 (PER 1,000 LIVE BIRTHS)	MATERNAL MORTALITY RATE (MMR) MODELED ESTIMATES, 2000 (PER 100,000 LIVE BIRTHS)	PREVALENCE OF CHILD MALNUTRITION 2000-06 (% OF UNDERWEIGHT U-5 CHILDREN)	HIV PREVALENCE, 2005 (% OF TOTAL POPULATION, AGES 15–49)
Low income							
Benin	510	4.9	10.2	150	850	30	1.8
Burkina Faso	400	6.1	26.8	191	1000	38	2.0
Burundi	100	6.7	28.5	190	1000	45	3.3
Central African Republic	350	4.1	47.7	193	1100	24	10.7
Chad	400	4.2	7.0	208	1100	37	3.5
Comoros	640	2.8	18.3	71	480	25	0.1
Congo, Dem. Rep. of	120	4.0	19.1	205	990	31	3.2
Côte d'Ivoire	840	3.8	5.0	195	690	17	7.1
Eritrea	220	4.5	59.6	78	630	40	2.4
Ethiopia	160	5.3	35.2	127	850	38	1.4
Gambia, The	290	6.8	23.0	137	540	17	2.4
Ghana	450	6.7	29.9	112	540	22	2.3
Guinea	370	5.3	9.5	160	740	33	1.5
Guinea-Bissau	180	4.8	31.6	200	1100	25	3.8
Kenya	530	4.1	18.3	120	1000	20	6.1
Liberia	130	5.6	37.8	235	760	27	n.a.
Madagascar	290	3.0	45.5	119	550	42	0.5
Malawi	160	12.9	59.4	125	1800	22	14.1
Mali	380	6.6	13.8	218	1200	33	1.7
Mauritania	560	2.9	20.2	125	1000	32	0.7
Mozambique	310	4.0	55.9	145	1000	24	16.1
Niger	240	4.2	21.3	256	1600	40	1.1
Nigeria	560	4.6	5.6	194	800	29	3.7
Rwanda	230	7.5	37.1	203	1400	23	3.0
São Tomé and Principe	390	11.5	53.3	118	n.a.	13	n.a.
Senegal	710	5.9	12.8	119	690	23	0.9
Sierra Leone	220	3.3	35.4	282	2000	27	1.6
Somalia	n.a.	n.a.	n.a.	225	1,100	33	0.9
Sudan	640	4.1	5.1	90	590	41	1.6

(Continues on the following page)

Table A.1: Health Indicators in the Africa Region (continued)

INCOME GROUP/ COUNTRY	GNI PER CAPITA, 2005 (US$)	HEALTH EXPENDITURE, 2004 (% OF GDP)	EXTERNAL ASSISTANCE, 2004 (% OF TOTAL)	U-5 MORTALITY, 2005 (PER 1,000 LIVE BIRTHS)	MATERNAL MORTALITY RATE (MMR) MODELED ESTIMATES, 2000 (PER 100,000 LIVE BIRTHS)	PREVALENCE OF CHILD MALNUTRITION 2000-06 (% OF UNDERWEIGHT U-5 CHILDREN)	HIV PREVALENCE, 2005 (% OF TOTAL POPULATION, AGES 15–49)
Tanzania	340	4.0	27.1	122	1,500	22	6.5
Togo	350	5.5	8.9	139	570	n.a.	3.2
Uganda	280	7.6	25.2	136	880	23	6.4
Zambia	490	6.3	36.3	182	750	23	17.0
Zimbabwe	340	7.5	13.1	132	1,100	n.a.	20.1
Middle income							
Angola	1,350	1.9	9.1	260	1,700	31	3.7
Botswana	5,180	6.4	2.5	120	100	13	24.1
Cameroon	1,010	5.2	5.3	149	730	18	5.4
Cape Verde	1,870	5.2	20.7	35	150	n.a.	n.a.
Congo, Rep. of	950	2.5	3.6	108	510	n.a.	5.3
Equatorial Guinea	n.a.	1.6	3.8	205	880	19	3.2
Gabon	5,010	4.5	1.3	91	420	12	7.9
Lesotho	960	6.5	8.7	132	550	18	23.2
Mauritius	5,260	4.3	1.4	15	24	n.a.	0.6
Mayotte	n.a.	n.a.	n.a.	n.a.	n.a.	n.a.	n.a.
Namibia	2,990	6.8	16.9	62	300	24	19.6
Seychelles	8,290	6.1	2.4	13	n.a.	n.a.	n.a.
South Africa	4,960	8.6	0.5	68	230	n.a.	18.8
Swaziland	2,280	6.3	9.5	160	370	10	33.4

Source: World Bank 2006o.

Strategic Directions: How Should the Bank Support Country Efforts?

Opportunities exist for the Africa Region to help clients improve HNP outcomes through a specific focus on fiscal and economic policy.

RENEW BANK FOCUS ON HNP RESULTS. The Africa Region staff *work closely with central ministries on designing Poverty Reduction Strategy Papers* (PRSPs), and assist with *public sector reform* initiatives. Achieving *more efficient and equitable spending and allocation of resources* will entail evidence-based planning to target resources where they will do the most to improve outcomes and *reduce disparities between regions and groups.* Because absent or weak accountability mechanisms undermine HNP strategies, the Bank, tapping *its expertise in public sector governance, will assist country efforts to strengthen national and subnational accountability mechanisms.*

STRENGTHEN HEALTH SYSTEMS FOR HNP RESULTS. The World Bank will emphasize health systems as a key vehicle for improving HNP outcomes and protecting people from the impoverishing impact of illness. The Africa Region will draw on the Bank's global knowledge base and experience to help strengthen systems and institutional capacity, focusing on: health workforce limitations; access to, and management of, pharmaceuticals; institutional frameworks, including planning and budgeting capacity for pro-poor service delivery; and expanding household demand for services.

MULTISECTORAL ACTION TO IMPROVE HNP OUTCOMES. Because many determinants of health lie outside the health sector, the World Bank has a unique opportunity to foster multisectoral action in the Africa Region. From the Bank's decision to emphasize multisectoral action for HIV/AIDS, lessons applicable to other diseases have begun to emerge. Areas where *collaboration will increase synergy* include: *education, agriculture and food security, water and sanitation, road safety, energy, telecommunications, and environmental actions.*

SUSTAINABLE FINANCING OF HNP INTERVENTIONS. Total health expenditures in Sub-Saharan Africa (SSA) average 6 percent of gross domestic product (GDP) and US$13 per capita per year, compared with 5.6 percent and US$71 per capita per year in other developing countries. The poorest 18 African countries spend much less, an average of only US$2.10 per capita in 2000. Debt relief and DAH have helped lighten the health care load, and governments are trying out a variety of strategies to manage health financing. Classical health insurance is not an option in most SSA countries because formal employment is low and perceptions and practice of corruption fragment the solidarity and confidence on which insurance must be founded. However, a number of countries have started to experiment with community financing such as health funds, mutual health organizations, rural health insurance, revolving drug funds, and prepayment initiatives.

Payment remains a major obstacle to use of health services among Africa's poor, and user payments still account for up to half of health expenditures in some SSA countries. In 2000, private expenditure represented between US$0.50 and US$21 per capita per year in the 38 poorest African countries. This is an issue that the Africa Region is following.

The Africa Region can help countries address efficiency and equity issues by finding the right mix of public expenditures and international financing over the medium term. The marginal budgeting for bottlenecks (MBB) instrument has been introduced in at least 10 countries. Work is also being done on contracting for services, including capitation-based payments. Deriving and disseminating lessons on public and private expenditures for health will be a priority for the Africa Region.

Implications for Operations in the Africa Region

In line with the Africa Action Plan of April 2005, the Africa Region HNP operations aim to achieve sustainable improvements on MDG-related indicators with high-impact interventions:

- Helping countries build outcome-oriented and evidence-based national strategies, plans, and budgets, building on global knowledge and experience.

- Strengthening the capacity of client countries' health systems to implement these strategies.

- Integrating the scaling up of support to malaria control and HIV/AIDS and interventions to combat malnutrition and child and maternal mortality.

- Helping clients mobilize domestic resources and international financing.

- Monitoring and evaluating (M&E) the impact of country strategies on health outcomes and helping countries develop their own M&E systems.

In line with the Paris Declaration on Harmonization and Aid Effectiveness, the Africa Region will support country-level negotiations to reach agreement between the government and development partners on improving aid alignment and effectiveness.

The Region will continue to promote sectorwide approaches to help ensure that strengthened public and private health care systems are mutually reinforced by disease-specific programs. To that effect, project implementation units should be avoided and common implementation procedures should be an objective. Africa Region staff must ensure that clients receive the best possible technical support and refer them to other partners, as necessary.

HNP activities will be financed through both investment projects and Development Policy Lending (DPL). The Africa Region's approach to the transfer of resources is shifting from free-standing projects toward programmatic lending. Adaptable Program Loans/Credits (APLs) would support long-term commitment to sector programs. Poverty Reduction Support

Credits (PRSCs) or Sector Adjustment Loans/Credits would be preferred if the government has the proper systems and procedures in place. In some settings such as post-conflict African countries, strengthening the Bank's presence in the sector through more targeted subsectoral operations may be required before engaging the country in discussions of a sectorwide approach.

East Asia and Pacific Region

As one of the most diverse regions in the world, the East Asia and Pacific (EAP) Region encompasses some of the world's least-developed countries (e.g., Cambodia, Timor Leste) and some of the most rapidly emerging economies (e.g., China, Vietnam). Countries in the Region also differ along other dimensions—size, epidemiological profile (table A.2), vulnerability to natural disasters, and political stability. Yet some regional trends and patterns are discernable. Overall, the Region has seen rapid growth, both a cause and a consequence of increasing migration and urbanization, but inequalities have also widened—across individuals, urban and rural areas, and regions within countries. All these changes create both opportunities and challenges in the HNP sector.

Most countries in the Region face a double burden of disease, with noncommunicable diseases becoming increasingly important, while infectious diseases persist and new and reemerging diseases strain scarce health resources further. Moreover, the nutrition and population agendas remain important in many countries. At system level, decentralization, rising inequalities, expanding needs and expectations, and a large private sector role in both financing and service delivery have brought health system issues to the fore. While the need for health system reform is increasingly recognized, the consequences of pandemics have also become apparent following the SARS epidemic, AHI outbreaks, and the ever-present threat of HIV/AIDS. As a result, public health surveillance and outbreak control have gained importance in many countries in the EAP Region.

Strategic Directions: How Should the Bank Support Country Efforts?

OVERVIEW. The HNP Strategy in the World Bank's EAP Region calls for a focus on improved health outcomes for the poor, enhancing the performance of health care systems, and securing sustainable health care financing.

Table A.2: Health Indicators in East Asia and Pacific Region

INCOME GROUP/ COUNTRY	GNI PER CAPITA, 2004 (US$)	HEALTH EXPENDITURE, 2004 (% OF GDP)	EXTERNAL ASSISTANCE, 2004 (% OF TOTAL)	U-5 MORTALITY, 2005 (PER 1,000 LIVE BIRTHS)	MMR MODELED ESTIMATES, 2000 (PER 100,000 LIVE BIRTHS)	PREVALENCE OF CHILD MALNUTRITION 2000-05 (% OF UNDERWEIGHT U-5 CHILDREN)	HIV PREVALENCE, 2005 (% OF TOTAL POPULATION, AGES 15–49)
Low income							
Cambodia	350	6.7	28.5	87	450	36	1.6
Korea, Democratic People's Republic of	n.a.	5.6	0.0	55	67	24	n.a.
Lao PDR	390	3.9	10.2	79	650	40	0.1
Mongolia	600	6.0	4.6	49	110	13	0.1
Myanmar	n.a.	2.2	13.1	105	360	32	1.3
Papua New Guinea	560	3.6	26.5	74	300	n.a.	1.8
Vietnam	540	5.5	2.0	19	130	28	0.5
Middle income							
China	1,500	4.7	0.1	27	56	8	0.1
Indonesia	1,140	2.8	1.3	36	230	28	0.1
Malaysia	4,520	3.8	0.1	12	41	11	0.5
Philippines	1,170	3.4	3.6	33	200	28	0.1
Thailand	2,490	3.5	0.3	21	44	n.a.	1.4

Source: World Bank 2006o.

Within that framework, each country team has developed a strategy for HNP that is consistent with the Country Assistant Strategy (CAS) and which responds to both demands from client countries and Bank capacity. The country-specific strategy also takes into account the role and activities of other development partners.

In a region as diverse as EAP and with a strong MIC presence, *a strong country focus is essential and will be maintained as the Bank moves forward, emphasizing* HNP outcomes and results.

- *In middle-income countries, the focus is on using various tools for innovation, learning, and addressing reform issues.* Lending is expected to continue, but it will be centered on health system strengthening and supported by a strong program of analytic work. Analytic work and lending on disease-specific issues will continue where there is demand and a strategic role for the World Bank.

- *In low-income countries, external financing from the World Bank and other development partners will play an important role relative to domestic resources.*

Donor coordination is critical. As in middle-income countries, support of health system strengthening through both analytic work and lending will be important, but improved donor coordination and multisectoral work to address broader determinants of health outcomes are also critical elements of success. Where governance and fiduciary systems permit, development policy lending will gain importance, but investment lending is likely to remain a relevant instrument.

RENEW BANK FOCUS ON HNP RESULTS. Focus on HNP outcomes and results is an integral part of both the ongoing portfolio and pipeline activities. This includes:

- *Outcome-based country strategies.* As in other Regions, country strategies provide the basis for the HNP work program. Drawing on the regional strategy and the global HNP Strategy, country teams in the EAP Region prepare country strategy notes for the HNP sector. These strategy notes seek to identify key constraints to improving HNP outcomes, as well as strategic areas for Bank support to address these constraints, serve as the basis for dialog with government and key partners at the country level.

- *Strong results framework in programs and AAA work.* Some of the success stories include the Timor health program (Bustreo et al. 2005), the HIV/AIDS prevention project in Vietnam that supported the development of a monitoring and evaluation framework, the National Sector Support for Health Reform Project in the Philippines that has piloted performance-based contracts between central and local government, and the Health Eight Project in China that has demonstrated results that have helped influence policy of rural health delivery programs in China.

- *Impact evaluation of selected programs.* The Region has invested, and will continue to invest, in selected impact evaluation efforts. These are integral to the overall knowledge generation and sharing efforts of the Bank to help inform broader policy dialog and program design.

STRENGTHEN HEALTH SYSTEMS FOR HNP RESULTS. Many countries in the Region are exploring ways to make health financing more equitable, increase access to health care, improve the performance of both public and private health care providers, strengthen pharmaceutical systems, and address imbalances in the health workforce. Reforms in these areas are particularly challenging as they are often being implemented in contexts where governance arrangements, intergovernmental fiscal relations, and social security systems are changing at the same time. Given these challenges, client demand for support on health system strengthening, and on related governance and public sector management issues, has seen significant growth. Ongoing and planned activities include both lending and analytic work, often with strong complementarities.

ENSURE SYNERGY BETWEEN HEALTH SYSTEM STRENGTHENING AND PRIORITY–DISEASE INTERVENTIONS. The limited number of disease-specific programs in the Region reflect client demand and regional issues. Nevertheless, emphasis should be put on systemic issues and linkages to broader health sector reform.

MULTISECTORAL ACTION TO IMPROVE HNP OUTCOMES. Cross-sectoral collaboration is an essential element of outcome-based strategies. These collaborations can take several forms: policy alignments with other sectors, joint sectoral programs to achieve desired impacts on health outcomes, and working with other sectors to achieve desired HNP outcomes. However, it is important to identify which cross-sectoral tasks are likely to produce the desired impacts on HNP outcomes.

STRATEGIC PARTNERSHIPS. Strategic partnerships are fundamental to the EAP Strategy and are important for both analytic work and lending operations. The key for such partnerships is how they work at the country level and leverage the overall agenda. Several business models developed through the various partnerships provide the flexibility needed to respond to client and donor needs.

DIVERSE PRODUCT LINES. The EAP Region has been expanding its product line to respond to various demands and improve results. The Comprehensive Development Partnership model in Thailand (an excellent approach to work in partnership with MIC clients), the DFID-Bank partnership in China, the different partnership models and stand-alone trust-funded operations, and the various lending instruments used for cross-sectoral work all reflect the wide range of AAA, lending, and partnership products being used. Impact evaluation is also seen as another stand-alone product line. Making sure that the different products come together at the country level is now critical to achieve the desired HNP outcomes and results.

Eastern Europe and Central Asia Region

In the ECA Region, the new World Bank HNP Strategy will have to reflect real and growing differences (table A.3) between countries and subregions. Implementation approaches will have to be custom-made to fit specific country and/or subregional situations. A large part of ECA HNP staff is based in the field, which increases the ability to be responsive to counterpart needs.

Table A.3: Health Indicators in the Eastern Europe and Central Asia Region

INCOME GROUP/ COUNTRY	GNI PER CAPITA, 2005 (US$)	HEALTH EXPENDITURE, 2004 (% OF GDP)	EXTERNAL ASSISTANCE, 2004 (% OF TOTAL)	U-5 MORTALITY, 2005 (PER 1,000 LIVE BIRTHS)	MMR MODELED ESTIMATES, 2000 (PER 100,000 LIVE BIRTHS)	PREVALENCE OF CHILD MALNUTRITION 2000-05 (% OF UNDERWEIGHT U-5 CHILDREN)	HIV PREVALENCE, 2005 (% OF TOTAL POPULATION, AGES 15–49)
Low income							
Kyrgyz Republic	440	5.6	15.1	67	110	7	0.1
Tajikistan	330	4.4	9.1	71	100	n.a.	0.1
Uzbekistan	510	5.1	3.9	68	24	8	0.2
Middle income							
Albania	2,580	6.7	2.4	18	55	14	n.a.
Armenia	1,470	5.4	7.2	29	55	3	0.1
Azerbaijan	1,240	3.6	1.6	89	94	7	0.1
Belarus	2,760	6.2	n.a.	12	35	n.a.	0.3
Bosnia and Herzegovina	2,440	8.3	1.3	15	31	4	0.1
Bulgaria	3,450	8.0	1.0	15	32	n.a.	0.1
Croatia	8,060	7.7	0.4	7	8	n.a.	0.1
Czech Republic	10,710	7.3	0.0	4	9	n.a.	0.1
Estonia	9,100	5.3	0.5	7	63	n.a.	1.3
Georgia	1,350	5.3	9.8	45	32	n.a.	0.2
Hungary	10,030	7.9	0.4	8	16	n.a.	0.1
Kazakhstan	2,930	3.8	0.9	73	210	n.a.	0.1
Latvia	6,760	7.1	0.3	11	42	n.a.	0.8
Lithuania	7,050	6.5	3.1	9	13	n.a.	0.2
Macedonia, FYR	2,830	8.0	1.4	17	23	n.a.	0.1
Moldova	880	7.4	4.8	16	36	4	1.1
Poland	7,110	6.2	0.1	7	13	n.a.	0.1
Romania	3,830	5.1	25.0	19	49	3	0.1
Russian Federation	4,460	6.0	0.1	18	67	6	1.1
Serbia and Montenegro	3,280	10.1	0.5	15	11	2	0.2
Slovak Republic	7,950	7.2	0.0	8	3	n.a.	0.1
Turkey	4,710	7.7	0.0	29	70	4	n.a.
Turkmenistan	n.a.	4.8	0.4	104	31	12	0.1
Ukraine	1,520	6.5	0.7	17	35	1	1.4

Source: World Bank 2006o.

Strategic Directions: How Should the Bank Support Country Efforts?

RENEW BANK FOCUS ON HNP RESULTS. The evolving issues across the ECA Region, together with the priorities reflected in the new HNP Strategy, have resulted in a focused and quantifiable set of results-based indicators:

- HIV/TB rates in line with MDG targets.

- Nutritional MDG targets achieved in Central Asia and Caucasus.

- Premature death and disability from noncommunicable diseases reduced by 20 percent.

- Increased sector transparency and improved governance, as measured by reduction in informal payments and transparent drug procurement.

- Inequalities in access to necessary services reduced by 25 percent—particular focus on minorities.

- Health care infrastructure at sustainable levels, providing continuum of services at high-quality health and cost-effectiveness.

- Increase patient satisfaction with service quality by 25 percent.

- ECA countries to introduce risk-pooling arrangements, guaranteeing minimum protection and risk mitigation for poor.

- ECA countries to develop plans for demographic transition, including long-term care financing and service provision.

- Improved understanding, among decision makers, of public health and cross-sectoral dimension of health determinants (e.g., transport, water, infrastructure, education).

STRENGTHEN HEALTH SYSTEMS FOR HNP RESULTS. Improved results must also be achieved on health system issues such as transparency, governance, informal payments, access to health services, and measurement of results. The largely unfinished agenda of ensuring appropriate health infrastructure, including necessary intersectoral linkages to other types of social services, will also need priority attention. This will become increasingly important as more and more of the Soviet-era infrastructure wears out.

ECA HNP sees an increasing emphasis from counterparts on health financing and fiscal sustainability (e.g., provider payments, benefits packages, informal payments), as well as capacity building, including policy development, human resources management, health services planning (including with respect to rationalization of health facilities and services), health care management, quality improvement, national health accounts, and improved monitoring and evaluation systems. This reflects an ongoing shift from "rowing" to "steering" in the counterpart Ministries of Health, and the concomitant need for adaptation by other parts of the health system. Other evolving issues center on medical education and regulatory/governance functions (training/retraining, continuous medical education, licensing, and accreditation).

MULTISECTORAL ACTION TO IMPROVE HNP OUTCOMES. The *upgrading of public health/surveillance capability* is an important issue in many countries, underscored by recent developments regarding avian flu. In light of the changing demographics and rapid aging in many ECA countries, *appropriate provision and financing of long-term care* is another emerging issue with significant multisectoral implications, especially as related to the social protection system. Many countries are interested in *private health insurance* as a way of relieving pressure on government programs, but good examples are scarce. Similarly, a number of countries have expressed interest *in health savings accounts* and have asked for World Bank assistance in exploring this issue.

The unfinished health infrastructure agenda will require *increased interaction with the energy and infrastructure sectors,* to ensure that proposed approaches are the most cost-effective available. Gains from energy efficiency investments alone could yield significant payoffs in terms of freeing up resources for direct service delivery.

STRATEGIC PARTNERSHIPS. Key technical partners in ECA include the WHO-EURO, CDC, the European Center for Disease Prevention and Control, OECD, and the IMF. Strategic partners would include the European Commission, the European Investment Bank, and IFC (potentially in the area of public-private partnerships). A critical partnership is the ongoing collaboration with the European Observatory on Health Systems and Policies, which is supported by the World Bank (through the Development Grant Facility).

Implications for Operations in the ECA Region

Overall, it is expected that there will be *less emphasis on direct financing of health infrastructure and equipment, and an increased need for developing capac-*

ity for health technology assessment and attention on developing facility rationali-zation strategies, a large, unfinished agenda in most ECA countries.

Ensuring *high-quality portfolio performance* is important as an accountabil-ity indicator, but also as evidence of the Bank's comparative advantage. There will also be a growing need to continue *exploring a widened range of instruments for supporting client countries*, including reimbursable TA, jointly funded programs, and subnational lending (in some countries).

Both *budget and staffing issues* are interlinked constraints to achieving these results. In the face of declining Bank budgets (resulting from reduced lending activity), maintaining policy dialog with countries across the Region becomes increasingly difficult (box A.1). Perhaps even more important, *continuity and relationship management issues* must be addressed if the Bank is going to be suc-cessful. The skill set needed will include direct hands-on experience in health system reform and management, health financing, and other key areas, as well as the ability to identify needs, coherently engage in discussions with counter-parts, and quickly arrange for these needs to be addressed in a substantive way. This will be a critical element for maximizing both the Bank's ongoing engage-ment as well as new business opportunities: improving the capacity of staff to choose the right approach to meeting counterpart needs in terms of lending instruments, nonlending support, technical assistance, and policy dialog.

Box A.1: HNP and the MIC Agenda

The Bank, in its relations with middle-income client countries, will seek to:

- Become reestablished as the partner of choice in development knowledge and finance, for its reservoir of global expertise, range of products and services, attractive financial terms, and ability to catalyze support from other partners.
- Maintain and, where possible, increase the quality of lending and other services to meet increased demand.
- Strengthen the ability of its staff to respond to the specific needs of the diverse group of MIC countries.

These principles encourage MICs to continue or resume borrowing, by removing impedi-ments and providing other "value-added" benefits, such as policy advice and technical assis-tance. But what about countries that either no longer need or want to borrow? The lack of sustained engagement, in the absence of lending, weakens business development efforts and client relations generally, thus reducing further the prospects for new lending business. This is perhaps a more critical issue in HNP, where in-depth knowledge of the sector takes time and ongoing involvement.

Source: World Bank 2006p.

Latin America and the Caribbean Region

Following a wave of health sector reforms, countries in the Latin America and the Caribbean Region (LCR) have made great strides in the way they finance, regulate, and deliver health care. Overall, impressive gains have been made in health outcomes and services in the past 15 years, but generalizations are difficult in so widely diverse an area. Some groups have benefited far more than others from these advances, and results have been insufficient in some key areas such as malnutrition and maternal mortality (table A.4).

Table A.4: Health Indicators in the Latin America and the Caribbean Region

INCOME GROUP/ COUNTRY	GNI PER CAPITA, 2005 (US$)	HEALTH EXPENDITURE, 2004 (% OF GDP)	EXTERNAL ASSISTANCE, 2004 (% OF TOTAL)	U-5 MORTALITY, 2005 (PER 1,000 LIVE BIRTHS)	MMR MODELED ESTIMATES, 2000 (PER 100,000 LIVE BIRTHS)	PREVALENCE OF CHILD MALNUTRITION 2000-06 (% OF UNDERWEIGHT U-5 CHILDREN)	HIV PREVALENCE, 2005 (% OF TOTAL POPULATION, AGES 15–49)
Low income							
Haiti	450	7.6	14.2	120	680	17	3.8
Middle income							
Argentina	4,470	9.6	0.2	18	82	4	0.6
Barbados	..	7.1	2.0	12	95	n.a.	1.5
Belize	3,500	5.1	5.3	17	140	n.a.	2.5
Bolivia	1,010	6.8	9.1	65	420	8	0.1
Brazil	3,460	8.8	0.0	33	260	n.a.	0.5
Chile	5,870	6.1	0.1	10	31	1	0.3
Colombia	2,290	7.8	0.1	21	130	7	0.6
Costa Rica	4,590	6.6	0.8	12	43	n.a.	0.3
Dominica	3,,790	5.9	3.0	15	n.a.	n.a.	..
Dominican Republic	2,370	6.0	1.5	31	150	5	1.1
Ecuador	2,630	5.5	0.8	25	130	12	0.3
El Salvador	2,450	7.9	1.2	27	150	10	0.9
Grenada	3,920	6.9	1.5	21	n.a.	n.a.	..
Guatemala	2,400	5.7	2.3	43	240	23	0.9
Guyana	1,010	5.3	8.2	63	170	14	2.4
Honduras	1,190	7.2	8.7	40	110	17	1.5
Jamaica	3,400	5.2	1.4	20	87	4	1.5
Mexico	7,310	6.5	0.3	27	83	n.a.	0.3
Nicaragua	910	8.2	11.3	37	230	10	0.2
Panama	4,630	7.7	0.2	24	160	n.a.	0.9
Paraguay	1,280	7.7	1.9	23	170	5	0.4
Peru	2,610	4.1	1.3	27	410	7	0.6

(Continues on the following page.)

Table A.4: Health Indicators in the Latin America and the Caribbean Region (continued)

INCOME GROUP/ COUNTRY	GNI PER CAPITA, 2005 (US$)	HEALTH EXPENDITURE, 2004 (% OF GDP)	EXTERNAL ASSISTANCE, 2004 (% OF TOTAL)	U-5 MORTALITY, 2005 (PER 1,000 LIVE BIRTHS)	MMR MODELED ESTIMATES, 2000 (PER 100,000 LIVE BIRTHS)	PREVALENCE OF CHILD MALNUTRITION 2000-06 (% OF UNDERWEIGHT U-5 CHILDREN)	HIV PREVALENCE, 2005 (% OF TOTAL POPULATION, AGES 15–49)
St. Kitts and Nevis	8,210	5.2	1.8	20	n.a.	n.a.	n.a.
St. Lucia	4,800	5.0	0.7	14	n.a.	n.a.	n.a.
St. Vincent and the Grenadines	3,590	6.1	0.1	20	n.a.	n.a.	n.a.
Suriname	2,540	7.8	9.7	39	110	13	1.9
Trinidad and Tobago	10,440	3.5	0.2	19	160	6	2.6
Uruguay	4,360	8.2	0.3	15	27	n.a.	0.5
Venezuela, R. B. de	4,810	4.7	0.0	21	96	4	0.7

Source: World Bank 2006o.

Note: n.a. = not available.

Strategic Objectives: What HNP Results?

Given the heterogeneity of the Region, the scope of Bank activities is necessarily broad. Consistent with its new HNP Strategy and in line with its comparative advantages, the Bank will continue to help countries pursue four broad Strategic Objectives: improve focus on the poor to reduce inequity; strengthen government attention to public goods; improve health financing for greater equity, efficiency, and sustainability; and improve health system stewardship and governance.

Strategic Directions: How Should the Bank Support Country Efforts?

RENEW BANK FOCUS ON HNP RESULTS. LCR has used the Bank's comparative advantage to help countries improve results in health and nutrition, with an emphasis on reducing inequalities by targeting the poor and most-vulnerable population groups.

The Bank supported Argentina in developing and implementing a new maternal and child health insurance program (*Plan Nacer*), targeting poor and indigenous women and children living in urban and rural parts of the nine poorest provinces. Twenty months after the project went into effect, half of the eligible population (400,000 beneficiaries) was enrolled in the program. Ten months after the federal government negotiated targets with provincial health authorities, an average of 7 out of 10 indicators had been achieved or surpassed. Similar results-based models are being employed in Ecuador, Nicaragua, and Paraguay in Bank-supported projects.

STRENGTHEN HEALTH SYSTEMS FOR HNP RESULTS. In high-middle-income and several low-middle-income LCR countries where most of the population has access to basic health care services, governments are expanding social protection in health. Other low-middle-income countries where the provision of basic services is still an important challenge are focusing on strengthening health systems to expand the supply of these services.

The Bank has supported countries' efforts to strengthen health systems by developing new organizational and institutional arrangements to extend social protection in health, with a focus on basic health care services for poor mothers and children. In *Bolivia*, the Bank for the first time conditioned disbursements on the achievements of outputs and intermediate indicators to provide health insurance to poor mothers and children. Other similar efforts include the *Argentina* Maternal and Child Health Insurance, the Health Sector Reform in *Bahia, Brazil*, the PROCEDES Project in *Mexico*, and Maternal and Child Basic Health Insurance in *Paraguay*. The regional study *Beyond Survival: Protecting Households from Health Shocks in Latin America* (2006) has launched a regional dialog on this urgent topic.

In *Brazil*, health sector projects such as Family Health Extension and the Second Disease Surveillance and Control Projects introduced performance-based financing in the federal Health Ministry (MOH). Based on a pooled-financing SWAp, these projects mingle loan financing with MOH grants to states and municipalities. Participating subnational entities sign contracts that specify activities and corresponding performance indicators. Achievement of performance benchmarks determines future levels of financing.

In *Nicaragua*, the Bank has worked with other development partners (UNFPA, IADB, and the governments of Austria, Holland, Finland, and Sweden) in supporting the government's national strategy and action plan to strengthen the health system to improve access to basic health care services. In *Peru*, the first Health Reform APL supported development of insurance for nearly three million mothers and children. In both countries, good results have been confirmed in coverage and equity.

During *Argentina's* socioeconomic and political crisis that reached its peak in 2002, the Bank helped the government maintain the health system's capacity to deliver basic health services and goods to the poor and the uninsured. The Health Emergency Project was part of a multisectoral strategy and supported the government's effort to transform this major challenge into an opportunity to strengthen the health system.

ENSURE SYNERGY BETWEEN HEALTH SYSTEM AND PRIORITY–DISEASE INTERVENTIONS. The Bank works closely with governments in IDA-eligible or IBRD/IDA-mixed countries to balance single-disease and targeted programs with health system strengthening. In *Honduras* and *Nicaragua*, for example programs that prioritize mother and child health interventions are fully integrated within the national strategies and action plans to improve national health care systems. In 10 *Caribbean countries and Central America*, the Bank is supporting HIV/AIDS programs that foster complementarities between health care systems and other important actors.

MULTISECTORAL ACTION TO IMPROVE HNP OUTCOMES. The HNP team in LCR works actively with other sectors and departments on a broad range of analytical and operational work initiatives. Recent examples include a multisectoral analysis combining HNP, the chief economist of the Bank, Social Protection, PREM, and the government of *Mexico*, reviewing options for improving social protection in Mexico. The last Institutional and Governance Review of *Bolivia*, led by PREM with the active involvement of HNP, analyzed policy options for an inclusive decentralization process. In the *Dominican Republic* HNP and PREM coordinated action on public sector reform to improve human resource policy effectiveness and national health procurement accountability. A new basic services and employment project is being prepared in *Brazil*, where HNP worked with teams from the Water Supply and Sanitation and the Sustainable Development Sectors to design a project to improve quality of life and reduce poverty.

Malnutrition is a serious intersectoral problem that hinders economic growth and improvement of population well-being in several LCR countries. The design and implementation of conditional cash transfer (CCT) projects offered HNP an opportunity to work with Social Protection, Education, and PREM to improve health and nutritional outcomes among poor mothers and children in *El Salvador* and *Ecuador*. Nutrition work is also underway in *Guatemala* and *Peru*.

STRATEGIC PARTNERSHIPS. The LCR Region will continue to engage in strategic partnerships such as the multiorganizational review of HIV/AIDS projects in the Caribbean in 2006, conducted in collaboration with the Global Fund,

UNAIDS, DFID, and Pan American Health Organization (PAHO)/WHO. In coordination with UNFPA, the Bank Maternal and Child Health Care Project in Argentina supported the launch of a new reproductive health program and procurement of inputs, giving poor women, for the first time, access to preventive and family planning services.

Implications for Operations in the LCR Region

The chief constraint on LCR health work is the declining budget, which is beginning to erode the Region's capacity. The diminishing personnel budget has already imposed a small contraction on the Region, which, even by Bank standards, already carries a very heavy workload. This constrains analytic work and may become a growing business impediment in a Region where the clients are technically sophisticated and expect state-of-the-art advice from the Bank.

Middle East and North Africa Region

The Middle East and North Africa (MENA) Region has made significant improvements in the health status of its people (table A.5). However, high rates of infant and maternal mortality, malnutrition, and micronutrient deficiencies persist in the low-income countries and among certain population groups in middle-income countries. With growing prosperity, the prevalence of lifestyle-related noncommunicable diseases is rising.

Strategic Objectives: What HNP Results?

The MENA HNP Strategic Objectives reflect the varying needs of four categories of countries at different stages of economic development:

- *Yemen and Djibouti*, the two IDA countries in the Region, face the greatest challenges and are at risk of not meeting the HNP-related MDGs. In Djibouti, the HIV/AIDS epidemic is taxing the country's economic resources.

- *Middle-income countries* (Algeria, Egypt, Iran, Jordan, Lebanon, Libya, Morocco, Syria, and Tunisia) are generally on track for achieving the health MDGs but rural/urban disparities in health outcomes and gaps in health coverage persist.

Table A.5: Health Indicators in the Middle East and North Africa Region

INCOME GROUP/ COUNTRY	GNI PER CAPITA, 2004 (US$)	HEALTH EXPENDITURE, 2004 (% OF GDP)	EXTERNAL ASSISTANCE, 2004 (% OF TOTAL)	U-5 MORTALITY, 2005 (PER 1,000 LIVE BIRTHS)	MMR MODELED ESTIMATES, 2000 (PER 100,000 LIVE BIRTHS)	PREVALENCE OF CHILD MALNUTRITION 2000-05 (% OF UNDERWEIGHT U-5 CHILDREN)	HIV PREVALENCE, 2005 (% OF TOTAL POPULATION, AGES 15–49)
Low income							
Yemen	570	5.0	15.0	102	570	46	n.a.
Djibouti	960	6.3	34.0	133	730	27	3.1
Middle income							
Algeria	2,270	3.6	0.0	39	140	10	0.1
Egypt, Arab Rep. of	1,250	5.9	n.a.	33	84	9	0.1
Iran, Islamic Rep. of	2,330	6.6	0.2	36	76	n.a.	0.2
Iraq	n.a.	5.3	2.5	125	250	16	n.a.
Jordan	2,260	9.8	7.1	26	41	4	n.a.
Lebanon	6,040	11.6	1.7	30	150	4	0.1
Morocco	1,570	5.1	0.9	40	227	10	0.1
Syria	1,270	4.7	0.2	15	160	7	n.a.
Tunisia	2,650	n.a.	n.a.	24	120	4	0.1
West Bank and Gaza	n.a.	n.a.	n.a.	23	100	5	n.a.
Gulf Cooperation Council							
Bahrain	14,370	4.0	0.0	11	28	n.a.	n.a.
Kuwait	24,040	2.8	0.0	11	5	n.a.	n.a.
Oman	9,070	3.0	0.0	12	87	n.a.	n.a.
Qatar	n.a.	2.4	0.0	21	23	n.a.	n.a.
Saudi Arabia	10,170	3.3	n.a.	26	23	n.a.	n.a.
United Arab Emirates	23,770	2.9	0.0	9	54	n.a.	n.a.

Source: World Bank 2006o.

- *Members of the Gulf Cooperation Council* (GCC), assisted by high oil revenues, have achieved universal access to health services and good health outcomes, but still have room for efficiency and quality improvements.

- *Conflict-affected countries* are suffering significant reversals in health status and deterioration of their health systems (West Bank and Gaza, Iraq, and Lebanon).

Strategic Objectives: What HNP Results?

The HNP business strategy for the MENA Region will need to find an appropriate balance in responding to growing demand for knowledge products and to emer-

gency and reconstruction operations. Due to the availability of alternative financing, the Bank is not seen as a primary source. The HNP team will *capitalize on the Bank's extensive international knowledge base* and analytical capacity in health systems.

Strategic Directions: How Should the Bank Support Country Efforts?

RENEWING THE FOCUS ON HNP RESULTS. A regional HNP Strategy Report (ESW) is proposed for FY2008 to develop a conceptual framework for defining the HNP Results Framework for the MENA Region. In parallel, the HNP team will review the portfolio to identify potential synergies and gaps in AAA and lending and to ensure timely application of the framework in upstream work on Country Assistance Strategy. A major investment will be needed to develop effective monitoring and evaluation tools for measuring HNP Results.

STRENGTHENING HEALTH SYSTEMS FOR HNP RESULTS. Across the MENA Region, demand is growing for health system modernization. The challenge is to define the areas in which the Bank has a comparative advantage. The following priority areas are identified: health finance reforms to improve financial protection and access to health care; improving the performance of health service delivery systems; and enhancing the governance and stewardship role of the state in the health sector.

Many governments in the MENA Region are seeking alternatives to their centralized government-managed health system, toward a more pluralistic system that includes active private sector participation. Demand is growing in the Region for technical advice on design and implementation of effective governance and regulatory functions, particularly accountability, where the Bank has a comparative advantage.

MULTISECTORAL ACTION TO IMPROVE HNP OUTCOMES. Within the MNSHD department, the introduction of an HD coordinator function has contributed to a more integrated approach to Human Development (Education, Social Protection [SP], and HNP) at country level. Under this framework, *HNP and SP teams collaborate closely* in the areas of social security administration and health insurance. MENA Region programs on youth and early childhood development include a significant health component and offer a basis for strengthening collaboration between the *HNP and Education teams.*

Other opportunities for collaboration are being explored in the *Water and Sanitation* and the *Urban and Transport Sectors*. With the PREM group, the MENA HNP team will be collaborating on two priority regional themes: *gender, and governance and anticorruption*. Finally, the MENA HNP team has been seeking active partnership *with IFC and the Private Sector Unit* in MENA to promote private-public partnership in health.

STRATEGIC PARTNERSHIPS. As part of the MENA Regional Strategy, the HNP team will expand its collaboration with *key regional partners* and continue to work with bilateral, multilateral, and private donors in partnership with the IBRD and IDA countries receiving funding from these sources. To enhance the ability of policy makers and health care managers to evaluate the impact of HNP policies and programs, the Bank is collaborating with *international organizations, nongovernmental organizations, and academic institutions* to establish a *Middle East and North Africa Health Policy Forum*, modeled on the European Observatory on Health Systems and Policies.

ADDRESSING THE NEEDS OF FRAGILE STATES AND CONFLICT-AFFECTED COUNTRIES. An increasing share of Bank resources and HNP staff time is being directed toward mobilizing and coordinating contributions from the donor community during reconstruction in Iraq, Lebanon, and West Bank and Gaza. In this, MENA HNP team will work closely with the new Fragile States Unit (FSU) and Conflict Prevention and Reconstruction Unit (CPRU). The Bank could play an important role in bridging the gap between short-term humanitarian operations and longer-term development activities and in ensuring adequate attention to investments in human capital in recovering countries.

REIMBURSABLE TECHNICAL ASSISTANCE. Reimbursable programs in the MENA Region increased from US$6 million in FY2004 to US$10 million in FY2006, some 12 percent of the MENA FY2006 budget. Most of the growth occurred under reimbursable technical assistance (RTA), now comprising about US$7 million. RTA will continue to be a growing and important component of the MENA regional program, provided that the Bank can translate its international experience and knowledge into practical, country-tailored implementation actions. This will require access to a network of international expertise and continuous upgrading of knowledge about new developments in health system reform.

South Asia Region

The South Asia Region (SAR) encompasses only eight countries (Afghanistan, Bangladesh, Bhutan, India, Maldives, Nepal, Pakistan, and Sri Lanka), but it is home to a quarter of the world's population. The countries vary widely in size, wealth, and health problems (table A.6), and dependence on international assistance. For all these reasons, the SAR HNP needs a differentiated strategic focus:

- *India, Pakistan, Bangladesh:* MDGs; focus on disadvantaged; new approaches to noncommunicable diseases (NCDs); financial risk protection.

- *Afghanistan, Nepal:* (the poorest countries) focus almost entirely on achieving MDGs.

- *Sri Lanka, Maldives, Bhutan:* more focus on NCDs; financial protection; macro-financing for the HNP sector.

Strategic Objectives: What HNP Results?

The Strategy focuses on two outcomes: improved health status particularly for the poor and reducing health-related impoverishment through

Table A.6: Health Indicators in the South Asia Region

INCOME GROUP/ COUNTRY	GNI PER CAPITA, 2005 (US$)	HEALTH EXPENDITURE, 2004 (% OF GDP)	EXTERNAL ASSISTANCE, 2004 (% OF TOTAL)	U-5 MORTALITY, 2005 (PER 1,000 LIVE BIRTHS)	MMR MODELED ESTIMATES, 2000 (PER 100,000 LIVE BIRTHS)	PREVALENCE OF CHILD MALNUTRITION 2000-06 (% OF UNDERWEIGHT U-5 CHILDREN)	HIV PREVALENCE, 2005 (% OF TOTAL POPULATION, AGES 15–49)
Low income							
Afghanistan	n.a.	4.4	6.1	257	n.a.	39	0.1
Bangladesh	470	3.1	15.1	73	380	48	0.1
Bhutan	870	4.6	14.5	75	420	n.a.	0.1
India	720	5.0	0.5	74	540	n.a.	0.9
Nepal	270	5.6	17.6	74	740	45	0.5
Pakistan	690	2.2	2.5	99	500	38	0.1
Middle income							
Maldives	2,390	7.7	1.6	42	110	30	n.a.
Sri Lanka	1,160	4.3	1.2	14	92	29	0.1

Source: World Bank 2006o.

improved financial risk protection. Implementation of the new Strategy would lead to an HNP portfolio "make over" by 2011, resulting in more outcome-focused operations, inventive approaches aimed at strengthening health systems, probably fewer but larger operations that use innovative lending instruments, and a substantial Bank role in encouraging, analyzing, and evaluating novel approaches. The portfolio will have more sectorwide programming and will help strengthen the monitoring and evaluation systems in client countries to bolster the results culture.

Strategic Directions: How Should the Bank Support Country Efforts?

RENEWING THE FOCUS ON HNP RESULTS. The SAR HNP business plan is based on a results framework that links outcomes with specific strategies (figure A.1). At the regional level, the strategic priorities guide analysis of how to focus the instruments available to the Bank to get results and what resources and actions need to be developed in the Region.

These approaches/strategies have been formulated to address the following priority areas:

- Political economy: To increase attention and commitment to HNP outcomes;

- Financing for adequate resources: Many SAR countries are very low investors in public health; essential inputs are lacking;

- Public health functions: Government has a critical stewardship role to play in the sector in terms of regulation, setting and enforcing standards, surveillance and information. Government also has an important role to address market failures and create demand for the right services;

- System innovations: Service delivery suffers widely from poor access, quality, and efficiency;

- Improved accountability and governance capacities: Accountability is a key tool for improving service performance and improved governance is essential for implementation of any plan;

- Measurement: Measuring results is a necessary element to create a process of continual, evidence-based improvement.

Recent operations of the SAR HNP unit already include several of the features mentioned, such as sectorwide approaches, strengthening of public

Figure A.1: Results Framework: An Innovations Agenda

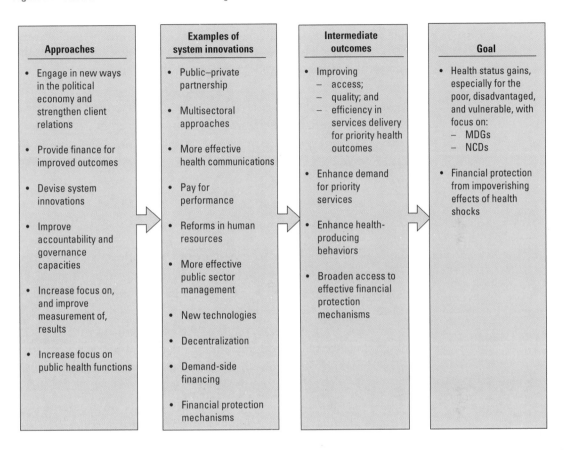

health functions, health insurance, etc. The unit's portfolio will gradually better reflect these reforms over the coming years.

STRENGTHEN HEALTH SYSTEMS FOR HNP RESULTS. The Strategy recognizes several causes for the poor performance of health systems in the Region. These include (in no specific order): insufficient drive for improving health outcomes from government and civil society leaders; overcentralized systems in which not enough resources reach the periphery; public sector service delivery that suffers from a poor incentive structure, weak management, rigid organization, and lack of accountability, and has few reasons for improving human resources that suffer from inadequate supply, overconcentration in urban areas, weak management, and limited incentives; insufficient engagement with the nongovernmental sector, which already provides most curative services, even for the poor; high out-of-pocket costs for all, especially the poor, even in the public sector, and lack of organized financial risk protection; few effective efforts to improve health-promoting behaviors; and little effective targeting to reduce health status disparities by income, gender, or geographical location.

INTERSECTORAL APPROACH TO HNP OUTCOMES. A team led by an HNP lead specialist and comprised of a mix of Country Directors, Sector Directors, Sector Managers, and sector specialists will explore opportunities for operations focused on the specific role of various sectors working together to achieve HNP-related MDGs.

Implications for Bank Operations in the SAR Region

The South Asia Region Human Development Department (SASHD) HNP business plan creates space for innovation wherever possible, using all the instruments at its disposal. New staff skills and financial resources will be needed to support this innovations agenda, both from traditional trust fund sources as well as from new global and regional development partners, such as private foundations. The continuation of a dedicated M&E team (with a specific budget) will assist in improving M&E designs and staff knowledge.

LENDING. Where possible, the *lending program* will move toward more programmatic financing, sectorwide support, or multisectoral lending in close cooperation with other development partners. The programmatic lending could take the format of development policy lending or be more broadly defined as output-based lending. In general, lending will shift away from traditional items of buildings and equipment and toward areas such as health financing linked to results/performance, financial protection, public health functions of government, and cross-cutting systems issues such as human resources. Priority would be given to MDG-related interventions.

AAA. The *analytical and advisory work* of SASHD HNP will focus on strengthening the analytical basis for innovative approaches to service delivery and on disseminating evidence and analysis to decision makers through partnerships with WBI, other development partners, in-country institutions, and civil society organizations. Health financing will remain central, and increased attention will be given to governance and accountability.

ANNEX B

Acknowledgments

This Bank HNP Strategy was prepared by a team led by Cristian C. Baeza (Lead Health Policy Specialist, LCSHH /Acting Director, HDNHE) and composed of Nicole Klingen (Senior Health Specialist, HDNHE), Enis Baris (Senior Public Health Specialist, ECSHD), Abdo S. Yazbeck (Lead Economist, Health, WBIHD), David Peters (Senior Public Health Specialist, HDNHE), Eduard Bos (Lead Population Specialist, HDNHE), Sadia Chowdhury (Senior Health Specialist (HDNHE), Pablo Gottret (Lead Economist, HDNHE), Phillip Jeremy Hay (Communications Adviser, HDNOP), Meera Shekar (Senior Nutrition Specialist, HDNHE), Kathleen Lynch (Consultant), Eni Bakallbashi (Junior Professional Associate, HDNHE), Lisa Fleisher (Junior Professional Associate, HDNHE), Jessica St. John (Junior Professional Associate, HDNHE), Elisabeth Sandor (Health Specialist, HDNHE), Andrianina Rafamatanantsoa (Program Assistant, HDNHE), and Victoriano Arias (Program Assistant, HDNHE), *with contributions from* Rama Lakshminarayanan (Coordinator, HDNHE), Ariel Fiszbein (Adviser, DECVP), Maureen Lewis (Acting Chief Economist, HDNVP), Susan Stout (Manager, OPCRX), Paul Gertler (former Chief Economist, HDNVP), John Newman (Country Manager, LCCPE), Jed Friedman (Economist, DECRG), Alison Buttenheim (Consultant, DECRG), Kulsum Ahmed (Lead Environmental Specialist, ENV), Mukesh Chawla (Lead Economist, AFTH2), Alexander S. Preker (Lead Economist, Health, AFTH2), Kees Kostermans (Lead Public Health Specialist, SASHD), Samuel Lieberman (Lead Economist, EASHD), Agnes Soucat (Lead Economist, AFTHD), Jean-Jacques de St. Antoine (Lead Operations Officer, AFTH1), Dominic Haazen (Senior Health Specialist, ECSHD), Amie Batson (Senior Health Specialist, HDNHE), Meera Shekar (Senior

Nutrition Specialist, HDNHE), Peter Kolsky (Senior Water and Sanitation Specialist, EWDWS), Michele Gragnolati (Senior Economist, ECSHD), April L. Harding (Senior Economist, Health, LCSHD), Olusoji Adeyi (Coordinator, HDNHE), Anne M. Pierre-Louis (Lead Health Specialist, AFTHD), George Schieber (Consultant, HDNHE), Katherine Tulenko (Public Health Specialist, EWDWP), Nicole Rosenvaigue (Senior Executive Assistant, HDNHE), Pedro Arizti (Ecomonist, OPCRX), Maria Eugenia Bonilla-Chacin (Economist, AFTH3), Feng Zhao (Health Specialist, AFTH1), John May (Senior Population Specialist, AFTH2), Jody Zall Kusek (Lead Monitoring and Evaluation Specialist, HDNGA), Peter Berman (Lead Economist, SASHD), Jan Bultman (Lead Health Specialist, ECSHD), G_rard La Forgia (Lead Health Specialist, LCSHH), Claudia Rokx (Lead Health Specialist, EASHD), Loraine Hawkins (Country Sector Coordinator, EASHD), Muhammad Pate (Senior Public Health Specialist, EASHD), Marcello Bortman (Senior Public Health Specialist, LCSHH), Aissatou Diack (Senior Public Health Specialist, AFTH2), Joana Godinho (Senior Health Specialist, LCSHH), Toomas Palu (Senior Health Specialist, EASHD), Sameh El-Saharty (Senior Health Specialist, MNSHD), Patricio Marquez (Lead Health Specialist, ECSHD), Eric de Roodenbeke (Senior Health Specialist, AFTH2), Emmanuel Malangalila (Senior Health Specialist, AFTH1), Peyvand Khaleghian (Senior Health Specialist, ECSHD), Paolo Belli (Senior Economist, Health, SASHD), John C. Langenbrunner (Senior Economist, Health, MNSHD), Shiyan Chao (Senior Economist, Health, ECSHD), Pia Rockhold (Senior Operations Officer, HDNSP), Menno Mulder-Sibanda (Senior Nutrition Specialist, AFTH2), David Evans (Health Specialist, EASHD), Christoph Kurowski (Health Policy Specialist, LCSHD), Firas Raad (Health Specialist, MNSHD), Magnus Lindelow (Economist, EASHD), Monique Mrazek (Economist, Health, LCSHH), Pia Schneider (Economist, Health, ECSHD), Gilles Dussault (former Senior Health Specialist), Roland Peters (Director, OPCS), Markus Kostner (Country Program Coordinator, MNCA4), Susan Hume (Country Program Coordinator, EACPQ), Preeti Ahuja (Country Program Coordinator, EAC1Q), Lilia Burunciuc (Country Program Coordinator, AFCZA), Myla Williams (Country Program Coordinator, ECCUS), Jill Armstrong (Country Program Coordinator, AFCET), Robert Floyd (Country Program Coordinator, SACPA), Tom Buckley (Adviser, TUDUR), Patrick Leahy (Manager, CHEPG), Robert Taylor (Principal

Financial Analyst, CASDR), Rita Klees (Senior Environment Specialist, ENV), Gail Richardson (Senior Operations Officer, OPCRX), Katrina Sharkey (Senior Operations Officer, AFC07), Maryse Gautier (Senior Urban Management Specialist, LCSFU), Meera Chatterjee (Senior Social Development Specialist, SASES), Sudip Mozumder (Senior Communications Officer, SAREX), Ruma Tavorath (Environment Specialist, SASES), Mohini Malhotra (Regional Coordinator, WBIND), Alexandra Humme (Partnership Specialist, WBIND), Barbry Keller (Operations Officer, AFCGH), Rachid Benmessaoud (Operations Adviser, SACIN), John Underwood (Consultant, OPCCS), Mario Gobbo (Principal Investment Officer, CGMGT, former Bank staff), Sanjeev Krishnan (Investment Analyst, CGMGT, former Bank staff), Emi Suzuki (Research Analyst, HDNHE), Rifat Hasan (Junior Professional Associate, HDNHE), Alexander Shakow (Consultant), and Yunwei Gai (Consultant).

Overall guidance to the team was provided by Jacques Baudouy (former Director, HDNHE), Nick Krafft (Director Network Operations, HDNVP), Joy Phumaphi (Vice President & Head of Network, HDNVP), Jean-Louis Sarbib (former Senior Vice President & Head of Network, HDNVP), James Adams (Vice President & Head of Network, OPCVP and Vice President & Head of Network, EAPVP), Danny Leipziger (Vice President & Head of Network, PRMVP), Xavier Coll (Vice President, HRSVP), Shanta Devarajan (Chief Economist, SARVP), Steen Jorgensen (Sector Director, ESDVP), Jamal Saghir (Director, EWDDR), James Warren Evans (Sector Director, ENV), Yaw Ansu (Sector Director, AFTHD), Tamar Atinc (Sector Director, ECSHD), Evangeline Javier (Sector Director, LCSHD), Emmanuel Jimenez (Sector Director, EASHD), Michal Rutkowski (Sector Director, MNSHD), Julian Schweitzer (Sector Director, SASHD), Guy Ellena (Director, IFC), Debrework Zewdie (Director, HDNGA), Kei Kawabata (Sector Manager, HDNHE), Akiko Maeda (Sector Manager, MNSHD), Anabela Abreu (Sector Manager, SASHD), Armin Fidler (Sector Manager, ECSHD), Eva Jarawan (Sector Manager, AFTH2), Fadia Saadah (Sector Manager, EASHD), Keith Hansen (Sector Manager, LCSHH), Ok Pannenborg (Senior Adviser, AFTHD), Bruno Andre Laporte (Manager, WBIHD), Elizabeth King (Research Manager, DECRG), and Susan Blakley (Senior Human Resources Officer, HRSNW).

Special gratitude is due to:

Government officials of client countries who generously provided us with valuable recommendations and guidance on how the Bank can better support their efforts to improve the lives of those who are most vulnerable, including: Ginez Gonzales (Minister of Health, Argentina), Norair Davidyan (Minister of Health, Armenia), Angel Cordoba (Minister of Health, Mexico), Julio Frenk (former Minister of Health, Mexico), Haik Darbinyan (Ministry of Health, Armenia), Levon Yolyan (Ministry of Health, Armenia), Ara Ter-Grigoryan (Ministry of Health, Armenia), Vahan Poghosyan (Ministry of Health, Armenia), Gohar Kyalyan (Ministry of Health, Armenia), Michael Narimanyan (Ministry of Health, Armenia), Samvel Kovhannisyan (Ministry of Health, Armenia), Suren Krmoyan (Ministry of Health Armenia), Derenik Dumanyan (Ministry of Health, Armenia), Sergey Khachatryan (Ministry of Health, Armenia), Eduardo Gonzales-Pier (Ministry of Health, Mexico), Mauricio Bailon (Ministry of Health, Mexico), Jaime Sepulveda (Ministry of Health, Mexico), Jorge Roel (Office of the Chief of Cabinet, Argentina), Gerardo Serrano (Office of the Chief of Cabinet, Argentina), Carmen Odasso (Office of the Chief of Cabinet, Argentina), Walter Valle (Ministry of Health, Argentina), Leonardo Di Pietro (Ministry of Health, Argentina), Oscar Filomena (Ministry of Health, Argentina), Deepa Jain Singh (Ministry of Women and Child Development, India), N. K. Sethi (Planning Commission, India), Shri Prashant (Ministry of Finance, India), Bouaré Mountaga (Ministry of Health, Mali), Amadou Sanguisso (Ministry of Health, Mali), Souleymane Traoré (Ministry of Health, Mali), Touré Cheikna (Mutualité Malienne), Traoré Mamadou Namory (Ministry of Health, Mali), Thiécoura Sidibé (Ministry of Health, Mali), Mahamadou Choulibaly (Ministry of Health, Mali), Ousmane Sylla (Ministry of Health, Mali), Sidi Yeya Cissé (Ministry of Health, Mali), Coulibaly Youma Sall (Ministry of Health, Mali), Cissé Djita Dem (National Council of Pharmacists, Mali), Dicko Aboubacar (SNV, Mali), Saleh Banoita Tourab (Ministry of Health, Djibouti), Simon Mibrathu (Ministry of Finance, Djibouti), Omar Ali Ismail (Executive Secretariat HIV/AIDS, Djibouti), Fatouma Kamil (Ministry of Health, Djibouti), Mouna Osman (Ministry of Health, Djibouti), Safia Elmi (Ministry of Health, Djibouti), Mohamed Ali (Ministry of Health, Djibouti), Samatee Said Hadji (Ministry of Health, Djibouti), Barihuta Tharcisse (Ministry of Health, Djibouti), Abouleh Abdillahi (Ministry of Health, Djibouti), M. Mahyab (Ministry of Health, Djibouti), Ali Hugo (Ministry of Health,

Djibouti), Farhan Said Bourkad (Ministry of Health, Djibouti), Bahya Mohamed (Ministry of Health, Djibouti), Mohamed Aden (Ministry of Health, Djibouti), Nasser Mohmad (Ministry of Health, Djibouti), Bourhan Ahmed Duni (Ministry of Health, Djibouti), Abdiuaoui Youssouf (Ministry of Health, Djibouti), M. Watta (Ministry of Health, Djibouti), Hassan Kamil (Ministry of Health, Djibouti), Simon Mibrathu (Ministry of Health, Djibouti), Mugisha Kamugisha (Ministry of Finance, Tanzania), Gilbert Mliga (Ministry of Health, Tanzania), Regina Kikuli (Ministry of Health, Tanzania), Faustin Njau (Ministry of Health, Tanzania), Gabriel Upunda (Ministry of Health, Tanzania), Herman Lupogo (Tanzania AIDS Commission), Christopher Sechambe (Tanzania AIDS Commission), Beng'i Issa (Tanzania AIDS Commission), Donald Mmbando (Tanzania AIDS Commission), Willing Sangu (Tanzania AIDS Commission), Ayoub Kibao (Tanzania AIDS Commission), Dr. Bushiri (Tanzania AIDS Commission), Hashim Kalinga (Tanzania AIDS Commission), B. Muhunzi (Tanzania AIDS Commission), Emmanuel Humba (National Health Insurance Fund, Tanzania), Abdelhak Bedjaoui (Ministry of Finance, Algeria), Mohamed Messouci (Ministry of Finance, Algeria), Hedia Amrane (Ministry of Finance Algeria), Ali Chaouche (Ministry of Health, Algeria), Leila Benbernou (Ministry of Health, Algeria), Cherifa Zerrouki (Ministry of Health, Algeria), Nacera Madji (Ministry of Health, Algeria), Leila Hadj Messaoud (Ministry of Health, Algeria), Benamar Rahal (Ministry of Health, Algeria), Benamar Regal (Ministry of Health, Algeria), Nassima Keddad (Ministry of Health, Algeria), Mosleh Bourkiche (Ministry of Health, Algeria), Ahmed Tani Abi Ayad (Ministry of Health, Algeria), Djamal Fourar (Ministry of Health, Algeria), Amar Ouali (Ministry of Health, Algeria), Faouzi Amokrane (Ministry of Health, Algeria), Zakia Fodil Cherif (Ministry of Health, Algeria), Houria Khelifi (Ministry of Health, Algeria), Djamila Nadir (Ministry of Health, Algeria), Djaouad Braham Bourkaib (Ministry of Labor, Algeria), Farida Belkhiri (Ministry of Labor, Algeria), Mr. Halfaoui (Ministry of Labor, Algeria), Mr. Muharso (Board of Health Development and Human Resources Empowerment, Indonesia), Dwi Atmawati (Board of Health Development and Human Resources Empowerment, Indonesia), Dewi Nuraini (Board of Health Development and Human Resources Empowerment, Indonesia), Rachmi Untoro (Ministry of Health, Indonesia), Rini Yudi Pratiwi (Ministry of Health, Indonesia), Dr. Erna Mulati (Ministry of Health, Indonesia), Kirana Pritasari (Ministry of Health, Indonesia), Eka Susi Ratnawati (Ministry of Health, Indonesia), Setiawan

Soeparan (Ministry of Health, Indonesia), Ida Bagus Permana (Ministry of Health, Indonesia), Anhari Achadi (Ministry of Health, Indonesia), Dedi M. Masykur Riyadi (BAPPENAS), Mr. Hadiat (BAPPENAS), Mr. Haryo (BAPPENAS), Mr. Haryoko (PHP, Indonesia), Antarini Antojo (PHP, Indonesia), Sudianto Kamso (University of Indonesia), Sri Moertiningsih Adioetomo (University of Indonesia), Laksono Trisnantoro (University of Gajah Mada, Indonesia), Rossi Sanusi (University of Gajah Mada, Indonesia), Istiti Kandarina (University of Gajah Mada, Indonesia), Regina Satyawiraharja (Atma Jaya University, Indonesia), Usep Solehudin (Yayasan Pelita Ilmu – Youth Clinic), Kartono Mohammad (Koalisi untuk Indonesia Sehat), and Mr. Soekirman (Koalisi Fortifikasi, Indonesia).

The following global partners for their generous advice and contributions:
Anders Nordstrom (WHO), Anarfi Asamoa-Baah (WHO), Andrew Cassels (WHO), Denise Coitinho (WHO), Timothy Evans (WHO), David Evans (WHO), Salim Habayeb (WHO), Liz Mason (WHO), Eva Wallstam (WHO), Marie Paule Kieny (WHO), Monir Islam (WHO), Paul van Look (WHO), Dan Makuto (WHO), Steffen Groth (WHO), Jihane Tawilah (WHO), Edward Maganu (WHO), Noureddine Dekkar (WHO), Joe Kutzin (WHO), Gerard Schmets (WHO), Ignace Ronse (WHO), Xavier Leus (WHO), Sara Bennet (WHO), Max Mapunda (WHO), Mark Wheeler (WHO), Gerard Schmets (WHO), Menno van Hilton (WHO), Jacoba Sikkens (WHO), Nick Drager (WHO), Nicole Valentine (WHO), Christopher Powell (WHO), David John Wood (WHO), Brenda Killen (WHO), Richard Feachem (Global Fund to Fight AIDS, Tuberculosis and Malaria), Neil Squires (EU), Juan Garay (EU), Christopher Knauth (EU), Elisabeth Pape (EU), Frederika Meijer (EU), Paula Quigley (EU), Philip Constable (EU), Pascale Sztajnbok (EU), Walter Seidel (Europe Aid), Christian Collard (Europe Aid), Christian Flamant (AFD), Alain Humen (AFD), Finn Schleimann (DANIDA), Hans Martin Boehmer (DFID), Andrew Rogers (DFID), Louisiana Lush (DFID), Nick Banatvala (DFID), Michael Borowitz (DFID), Jane Pepperall (DFID), Julia Watson (DFID), Billy Stewart (DFID), Carole Presern (Foreign and Commonwealth Office, UK), Gauden Villas (Embassy of Spain, London), Meinholf Kuper (GTZ), Andre Cezar Medici (IADB), Annette Gabriel (KfW Development Bank), Helga Fogstad (Norad), Bjarne Garden (Norad), David Weakliam (Develoopent Cooperation, Ireland), Rob de Vos (Development Cooperation, Netherlands), Reina Buijs (Ministry of Foreign Affairs, Netherlands), Mar-

ijke Wijnroks (Ministry of Foreign Affairs, Netherlands), Anno Galema (Ministry of Foreign Affairs, Netherlands), Jacqueline Mahon (Swiss Development Cooperation), Bo Stenson (SIDA), Catherine Michaud (Harvard School of Public Health), David Dunlop (AusAID), Jim Tulloch (AusAID), Michelle Vizzard (AusAID), Frederic Goyet (Ministry of Foreign Affairs, France), Jette Lund (Royal Danish Embassy, Washington, DC), Rik Peeperkorn (Netherlands Embassy in Dar Es Salaam), Jean-Pierre Notermann (Embassy of Belgium, Mali), Karima Saleh (ADB), Jacques Jeugmans (ADB), Patience Kuruneri (AfDB), Peter Heller (IMF), Dan Kress (Bill and Melinda Gates Foundation), Armand Pereira (ILO), Michael Sichon (ILO), Assane Diop (ILO), Emmanuel Reynaud (ILO), Philippe Marcadent (ILO), Rédha Ameur (ILO), Julian Lob-Levyt (GAVI), Andrew Jones (GAVI), Akaki Zoidze (Georgia), Malegarpuru W. Makgoba (Zambia), Char Meng Chuor (Cambodia), Richard Greene (USAID), Al Bartlett (USAID), Karen Cavanaugh (USAID), Bob Emrey (USAID), Tim Meinke (USAID), Hope Sukin (USAID), Charles Llewellyn (USAID), Thomas Hall (USAID), Robert Clay (USAID), Lisa Nichols (USAID), Gregory Adam (USAID), Sergio René Salgado (UN Presidential Malaria Initiative), Pascal Villeneuve (UNICEF), Felicity Tchibindat (UNICEF), George Gonzales (UNICEF), Marie-Claire Mutanda (UNICEF), Rudolf Knippenberg (UNICEF), Peter Salama (UNICEF), Amel Allahoum (UNICEF), David Hipgrave (UNICEF), François Farah (UNFPA), Laura Laski (UNFPA), Dorothy Temu (UNFPA), Venkatesh Srinivasan (UNFPA), Kamel Sait (UNFPA), Zahidul Huque (UNFPA), Desmond Johns (UNAIDS), Pradeep Kakkattil (UNAIDS), Denis Broun (UNAIDS), Soumaya Benzitouni (UNAIDS), Joseph Annan (UNDP), Koita Nouhoum (CARE), Damayanti Soekarjo (CARE), Adjie Fachrurrazi (CARE), Glenn Gibney (PCI), Mr. Tolley (PCI), Lina Mahy (Hellen Keller International), David de Ferranti (Brookings Institution), Amanda Glassman (UN Foundation), Nils Daulaire (Global Health Council), Ruth Levine (Center for Global Development), Todd Benson (IFPRI), Eric Chevallier (Medecins du Monde), Elena McEwan (Catholic Relief Services), Carl Stecker (Catholic Relief Services), Vineeta Gupta (Stop HIV/AIDS in India Initiative), Suma Pathy (Stop HIV/AIDS in India Initiative), Ray Martin (Christian Connections for International Health), Cynthia Tuttle (Bread for the World Institute), Anna Taylor (Save the Children UK), Winifride Mwebesa (Save the Children USA), Harvey Bale (IFPMA), Patricia Scheid (Aga Khan Foundation USA), Tom Merrick (Hewlett Foundation), Atika El Mamri (Federation of the

Handicapped, Algeria), Salima Tadjine (Algerian Society of Research and Psychology), Mimi Rabehi (Association of People Affected by Cancer 'El-fedjr,' Algeria), Adel Zeddam (Algerian AIDS Association), Othmane Bourouba (Algerian AIDS Association), Mouloud Hamdis (Algerian Association for Renal Failure), Indrani Gupta (Institute of Economic Growth, India), Alok Mukhopadhyay (Voluntary Health Association of India), Dileep Mavlankar (Indian Institute of Management), Ritu Priya (Jawaharlal Nahru University, India), Atanu Sarkar (Energy and Research Institute, India), Ramnik Ahuja (Cofederation of Indian Industry), Dr. Hariharan (Indian Medical Association), Narottam Puri (MAX Health Care Institute, India), and Laveesh Bhandari (Indicus Analyticus).

The following Bank management and staff for their advice and recommendations: Vinod Thomas (Director General IEGDG), Geoffrey Lamb (former Vice President, CFPVP), Guillermo Perry (Chief Economist, LCRCE), Mustafa Nabli (Chief Economist, MNSED), John Page (Chief Economist, AFRCE), Robert Holzmann (Director, HDNSP), Hassan Tuluy (Director, MNACS), Ulrich Zachau (Director, LCRVP), John Roome (Operations Director, SARVP), Hartwig Schafer (Operations Director, AFRVP), Orsalia Kalatzopoulos (Country Director, ECCU4), Pedro Alba (Country Director, AFC09), Theodore Ahlers (Country Director, MNC01), Judy O'Connor (Country Director, AFC04), James Bond (Country Director, AFC15), Isabel Guerrero (Country Director, LCC1C), Emmanuel Mbi (Country Director, MNC03), Annette Dixon (Acting Country Director, ECAVP), Donna Dowsett-Coirola (Country Director, ECCU3), Axel van Trotsenburg (Country Director, LCC7C), Alastair McKechnie (Country Director SAC01), Charles Griffin (former Sector Director, ECSHD), Marilou Uy (Sector Director, FPDVP), Mayra Buvinic (Sector Director, PRMGE), Luca Barbone (Sector Director, PRMPR), Rodney Lester (Senior Adviser, FPDSN), Roberto Zagha (Senior Economic Adviser, PRMVP), Egbe Osifo-Dawodu (Sector Manager, WBIST), Dzingai Mutumbuka (Sector Manager, AFTH1), Laura Frigenti (Sector Manager, AFTH3), Jamil Salmi (Sector Manager, HDNED), Randi Ryterman (Sector Manager, PRMPS), Laura Tlaiye (Sector Manager, ENV), Elisabeth Lule (Manager, ACTafrica), Alain Barbu (Manager, IEGSG), Hans-Martin Boehmer (Manager, SFRSI), Alassane Diawara (Country Manager, AFMML), Roger Robinson (Country Manager, ECCAR), Gaiv Tata (Country Program Coordinator, MNCA3), Alexandre Abrantes (Country Program Coordinator, LCC5A), Tawhid Nawaz (Operations Adviser, HDNOP), Adam Wagstaff (Lead Economist, DECRG), Martha Ainsworth (Lead Economist, IEG), Jeffrey Hammer (Lead Economist, SASES), Michael Mills (Lead Economist, AFTH1), Benjamin Loevinsohn (Lead Public Health Specialist, SASHD), Tonia Marek (Lead Public Health Specialist, AFTH2), Julie McLaughlin (Lead Health Specialist, AFTH1), Suneeta Singh (Senior Public Health Specialist, SASHD), Chris Walker (Lead Health Specialist, AFTH1), Susanna Hayrapetyan (Senior Health Specialist, ECSHD), Mary Eming Young (Lead Specialist, HDNCY), Janet Nassim (former Senior Operations Officer, HDNHE), Nawal Merabet (Public Information Associate, MNAEX), Mikko Kalervo Paunio (Senior Environmental Specialist, ENV), Manorama Gotur (Senior Corporate Strategy Officer, SFRSI), Denise Vaillancourt (Senior Evaluations Officer, IEG), Sophia Drewnowski (Senior Partnership Specialist, GPP), Katja Janovsky (Consultant), Davidson Gwatkin (Consultant, HDNHE), and Judith Heuman (Consultant, HDNOP).

ANNEX C

The New Global Health Architecture

Emergence of a New Global Health Architecture: Trends Since the Mid-1990s

Global health is on the international policy agenda as never before. Over the last 10 years, humanitarian concerns about the health of the world's poor, the spread of pandemics such as HIV/AIDS and fears about outbreaks of SARS and avian influenza, and the recognition that health is a key determinant of economic growth, labor force productivity, and poverty reduction have made health a central pillar of most development policies. At the same time, health is increasingly viewed as a human right, the fulfillment of which places obligations on both developed and developing countries.

During the 1990s, the global community discussed ways of renewing emphasis and strengthening action to reduce poverty and improve the health of the world's poor. The culmination of these discussions—the Millennium Declaration and the Millennium Development Goals (MDGs)—reflects the prominence of health in the global policy arena: three of the eight MDGs relate directly to health; the poverty reduction MDG is affected when citizens are pushed into poverty by catastrophic health care costs or lost earnings resulting from ill health; and several of the other goals (e.g., education, sanitation) interact directly with health outcomes. In particular, HIV/AIDS emerged as a challenge to be addressed multisectorally as the international community became increasingly concerned about it as a development issue.

With these challenges, came a growing sense that the traditional system of bilateral agencies and international organizations acting as the primary development partners was inadequately prepared to assist the poor countries of the world scale up to achieve the MDGs. In the past decade, there have been profound changes in the organizations that play key roles in global health. Private foundations, such as the Bill and Melinda Gates Foundation, and large global funds, such as the Global Fund to Fight AIDS, Tuberculosis and Malaria (GFATM), and the Global Alliance for Vaccines and Immunisation (GAVI), have entered the scene with large amounts of grant money. Other disease-specific initiatives such as the Joint United Nations Programme on HIV/AIDS (1996), Roll Back Malaria (1998), and the Stop TB Partnership (1999) were also established and have brought new financial resources for specific diseases.

Never before has so much attention—or money—been devoted to improving the health of the world's poor. However, unless deficiencies in the global aid architecture are corrected and major reforms occur at the country level, the international community and countries themselves face a good chance of squandering this opportunity.

Taking Stock of HNP Financing in the World

The Donor Level

As a direct and positive consequence of health becoming a high-profile issue in the global arena and attracting new partners, development assistance for health (DAH) has increased from US$2.5 billion in 1990 (0.016 percent of gross national income, [GNI]) to almost US$14 billion in 2005 (0.041 percent of GNI) (figure C.1). As a proportion of official development assistance (ODA), DAH has increased from 4.6 percent in 1990 to close to 13 percent in 2005. Much of this assistance is targeted to specific diseases or interventions, which raises issues of funding imbalances and prioritization. As a result, direct disease funding now accounts for an increasing proportion of donor aid. The latest Global Monitoring Report shows that, while the share of health aid devoted to HIV/AIDS more than doubled between 2000 and 2004—reflecting the global response to an important need—the share devoted to primary care dropped by almost half.[55]

Most of the significant increases in development assistance for health come from bilateral donors, new global partnerships, and foundations, while contributions from the multilateral development banks and specialized UN agencies have been relatively flat. Indeed, financing from bilateral

Figure C.1: Development Assistance for Health, by Source, 2000–2005 (US$ billion)

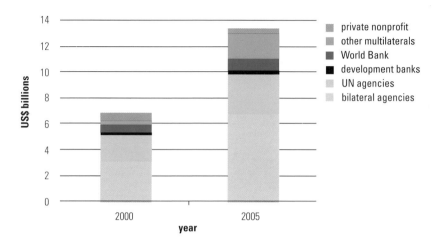

Source: Michaud 2007.

Notes: The category "other multilateral" includes the European Union, the Global Alliance for Vaccines and Immunisation (GAVI), and the Global Fund to Fight AIDS, Tuberculosis and Malaria (GFATM). The World Bank total includes only IDA lending.

donors accounted for more than 50 percent of DAH in 2005, and financing from new partners such as the Gates Foundation, GFATM, and GAVI accounted for almost 13 percent (Michaud 2007).

Although health-specific aid has increased, a significant gap persists between current aid volumes and estimated needs to reach the MDGs, for example. As shown in figure C.2, after a decade of decline in the 1990s in both real terms and as a share of GNI, ODA has indeed increased to some 0.33 percent of GNI in 2005. However, this level falls well short of the promised Monterrey targets of 0.7 percent of GNI and of the Millennium Project projections of 0.54 percent needed to achieve the MDGs (UN 2003, 2005). Other estimates of additional external assistance to help developing countries reach the MDGs range from US$25 billion to US$70 billion (Wagstaff and Claeson 2004). These shortfalls, when coupled with the low and inefficient spending at country level (discussed below), have serious implications for chances of achieving results.

The Country Level

Partially as a result of this increase in DAH, overall health spending in developing countries has also been increasing. Between 1990 and 2003, total health

Figure C.2: Net ODA as a Percent of GNI in DAC Donor Countries, 1990–2005, and Projected, 2006–2010

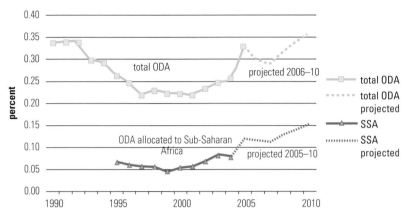

Source: Schieber, Fleisher, and Gottret 2006.

spending[56] in developing countries increased by more than 100 percent: from US$170 billion in 1990 to US$410 billion in 2003, or from 4.1 percent to 5.7 percent of developing-country GDP. However, despite these increases, domestic spending on health remains low and inefficient (table C.1).

Table C.1: Composition of Health Expenditures in World Bank Regions and Income Categories, 2004

REGIONS AND INCOME LEVELS	PER CAPITA GDP ($US)	PER CAPITA HEALTH EXPENDITURES ($US)	PER CAPITA HEALTH EXPENDITURES ($US PPP)	TOTAL HEALTH EXPENDITURES (% GDP)
East Asia and Pacific	1,457	64	239	4.4
Eastern Europe and Central Asia	3,801	249	552	6.6
Latin America and the Caribbean	3,777	271	608	7.3
Middle East and North Africa	1,833	103	270	5.6
South Asia	611	27	131	4.6
Sub-Saharan Africa	732	45	119	6.3
Low-income countries	533	24	105	4.7
Lower middle-income countries	1,681	91	298	5.4
Upper middle-income countries	5,193	339	689	6.7
High-income countries	33,929	3,812	3,606	11.2

Sources: World Development Indicators; IMF Government Finance Statistics.

Note: Per capita indicators weighted by population.

a. Revenue data reflect averages between 2000 and 2004.

b. Out-of-pocket health spending in Sub-Saharan Africa excludes South Africa, which, if included, changes the estimate to 26 percent of total health spending.

- Low-income countries spend less than 5 percent of their GDP on health, whereas middle- and high-income countries spend more than 6 percent and 11 percent, respectively. In exchange rate–based U.S. dollars, per capita total health spending was US$24 in low-income countries and almost US$4,000 in high-income countries, more than a hundredfold difference. Even after adjusting for differences in costs of living, the differentials are still on the order of 30 times (Gottret and Schieber 2006; WHO 2006b).

- Some 70 percent of total health spending is out of pocket in low-income settings, declining to 15 percent in high-income settings. In Africa, out-of-pocket spending accounts for almost 50 percent of total health spending on average and in 31 African countries, accounts for 30 percent or more of total health spending (WHO 2006b). For the poor, out-of-pocket spending is the most regressive source of health sector financing and also denies all individuals the benefits of risk pooling and financial protection.

In addition, some regions' reliance on external assistance to finance health and other sectors has serious implications for sustainability and countries' abilities to plan for the long term. For example, external assistance plays a more significant role in health sector financing in Africa than in any

PUBLIC (% TOTAL HEALTH EXPENDITURES)	OUT-OF-POCKET (% TOTAL HEALTH EXPENDITURES)	EXTERNAL (% TOTAL HEALTH EXPENDITURES)	TOTAL REVENUE TO GDP RATIO[a]	TAX REVENUE TO GDP RATIO[a]
39.8	51.0	0.5	19.1	15.1
67.6	26.5	1.1	28.6	16.7
51.0	36.3	0.7	23.0	15.9
48.8	46.3	1.1	27.3	17.0
18.8	76.1	1.6	15.0	9.8
42.1	46.3[b]	6.8	22.9	18.2
23.9	70.0	5.5	17.4	12.8
47.3	42.9	0.7	24.2	16.9
57.6	30.3	0.7	28.5	17.6
60.3	14.9	0.0	35.2	20.4

other region, accounting for some 15 percent of all health spending on average, while in other regions, it accounts for less than 3 percent. Further, of the 23 countries globally in which external assistance accounts for more than 20 percent of all health spending, 15 (65 percent) of them are in Africa (WHO 2006b). Moreover, in Africa, external assistance accounts for 55 percent of all external flows, while in the five other developing regions, worker remittances and foreign direct investment account for the bulk of external flows with external assistance accounting for only 9 percent (Gottret and Schieber 2006; WHO 2006b).

Low and inefficient expenditure patterns in low-income countries (LICs) are matched by their domestic resource mobilization capacity. Most LICs face enormous constraints in raising additional domestic resources: on average, LICs mobilize only 17 percent of their GDP from domestic resources (Gupta et al. 2004). Even if these countries could improve their capacity to raise resources domestically to finance health in an effort to scale up to reach the MDGs, massive increases in external assistance would be needed. Donors would still need to finance most of the gap.

Challenges in the New Global Health Architecture

The impact of increased resources on health has been mixed, especially considering the persistence of stark imbalances between rich and poor countries in terms of disease burden, the huge unmet health needs in most developing countries, and their lack of domestic resources to cope with these needs:

- Ninety percent of the global disease burden is in developing countries that account for only 12 percent of global health spending.

- High-income countries spent more than 100 times per capita on health than low-income countries.

- Developing countries will need between US$25 billion and US$70 billion in additional aid per year to remove the financing constraint to scaling up to meet the MDGs.

- Further, most countries in Africa are off-track on all of the MDG health goals. More broadly, in all Bank Regions but the Middle East and North Africa (MENA) and South Asia (SAR), most countries are off-track with respect to the child mortality goal.

It is in this context that questions have arisen about the effectiveness of health spending and, concomitantly, the integrity of the global aid architecture in health.

Effectiveness of Aid for Health

There are at least four important manifestations of ineffective health aid at the country level:

- *Aid is often not aligned with government priorities, and holistic health systems approaches are insufficiently funded.* As discussed above, health aid is often earmarked for specific purposes. Only about 20 percent of all health aid goes to support the government's overall program (i.e., is given as general budget or sector support), while an estimated 50 percent of health aid is off budget (Foster 2005a). As a result, many countries report difficulties in attracting sustained, flexible funding that can be used to support the health system: staff, infrastructure, training, management, and so on.

- *Aid can be unpredictable, short-term, and volatile.* In addition to being heavily earmarked, health aid can be very short-term and volatile (figure C.3). When the amount of aid a country receives is likely to change at short notice, it is impossible for Ministries of Health and Finance to make long-term plans—such as employing more doctors or nurses, widening access to HIV/AIDS treatment, or scaling up health service provision—without incurring major risks of sustainability of financing for these services. A related issue, which also creates difficulties for ministries of finance and planning, is that aid can be unpredictable (disbursements do not match commitments, even where the reasons are not related to performance).

- *Aid may be poorly harmonized, increasing transaction costs for government.* The high number of donors present in health, the large number of separate health programs, and large volume of resources may carry unpredictable risks and transaction costs unless they are well coordinated—both with each other and with government. A related issue is that the presence of multiple health partners may inadvertently undermine the government's broader efforts in the health sector. This is likely to affect the government's ability to deliver programs in other areas.

- *Integrity of the global health architecture.* In addition to problems with the effectiveness of aid flowing into the health sector, some of the challenges

Figure C.3: Volatility in Aid for Health, Selected Countries, 1999–2003

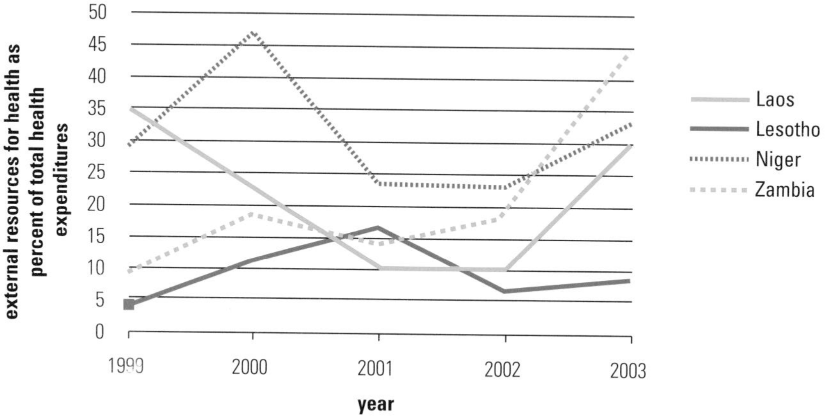

Source: World Health Organization 2006b.

of the new global health architecture stem from a lack of global governance and overlapping mandates of different aid agencies. Problems at the country level and the inherent complexities of the health sector also contribute to the quandaries concerning the effectiveness of external assistance for health.

Leadership at the Global Level

There are more major global stakeholders in health than in any other sector and literally hundreds of different flows of public and private funds to specific countries. Issues include:

- Various international organizations and stakeholders have overlapping and unclear mandates—no single organization coordinates global health policy, financing, implementation processes, or knowledge dissemination at country or regional levels.

- Global Health Partnerships (GHPs) were initially promoted as tools to better focus health aid in areas of perceived neglect and to *simplify* the aid architecture in health, and, as a consequence, make health aid more effective. However, many observers believe—and a range of studies suggest[57]—that this objective has not been achieved. It is recognized that GHPs have mobilized important new resources for major health threats and brought much needed political and technical focus to priority diseases or interventions. However, there is concern that the rapid creation of new institutions in health is difficult for countries to manage and further complicates donor harmonization efforts at the global level.

Finally, as in other sectors, donor governments find it politically advantageous to raise aid "vertically" to show their populations that their tax monies are being spent on "good causes." In particular, GHPs may intensify the "vertical" nature of health financing by focusing large amounts of new funding for specific, relatively narrow programs and interventions, creating separate financing and delivery silos, and leaving recipients little flexibility to reallocate funds according to their priorities or to fund health system costs, such as salaries. While this is an issue in all sectors, the consequences are particularly acute in health, because there is a need for flexible resources that can be used to support recurrent costs, other sectors that have a direct impact on health, and health systems.

Health Is a Complex Sector

Complexities in the aid architecture for health mirror the complexities of the sector itself. Creating and sustaining population health, providing financial protection from the consequences of ill-health, and managing, financing, and governing the health system are all difficult and costly.

- Numerous nonhealth-related factors affect health outcomes, necessitating complex cross-sectoral approaches.

- Health outcomes are reversible, if access to services is interrupted (unlike gains in education, for example).

- Individual behavior plays a critical role in health outcomes and is very difficult to influence or change.

- Measuring health outcomes—other than sentinel events such as births or death—and attributing causality to specific factors is inherently complex.

- The costly financial protection element of health financing is largely unique to the health sector (except for a few standard social protection programs such as pensions, unemployment insurance, and social assistance).

- The bulk of the funding needed is for *long-term recurrent* costs rather than the traditional donor-financed *short-term investment* costs, raising issues of sustainability and the need for countries to create adequate fiscal space in their budgets.

- The health sector is critical in terms of both its share of the public budget and as a major source of public employment.

- Well over a hundred major organizations are involved in the health sector, globally and nationally, far more than in any other sector.

- The private sector plays a substantial, often predominant, role in both the financing and delivery of health care services and is often absent from the policy debate.

- Market failures in insurance markets and in the health sector more generally require complex regulatory frameworks and limit governments' abilities to simply rely on market mechanisms.

From Consensus on the Problems to Coordinated Action at Country Level

A consensus on the challenges has emerged, and new steps have been taken to improve the effectiveness of aid for health and streamline the new global health architecture through donor harmonization and alignment with country systems. The Paris Declaration is a key reference point for improvements in health aid: as the framework for aid effectiveness in general, it also frames efforts to improve aid for health.

UNAIDS, together with the Global Fund, bilateral donors, and other international institutions, has committed itself to harmonization and alignment in HIV/AIDS through the concept of the Three Ones. These are: one agreed HIV/AIDS action framework for coordinating the work of all partners; one national HIV/AIDS coordinating authority with a broad-based multisectoral mandate; and one agreed country-level system for monitoring and evaluation.

Subsequent to the agreement of the Three Ones, the Global Task Team on Improving AIDS Coordination among Multilateral Institutions and International Donors (GTT) was established. In June 2005 it presented a plan to further coordinate the HIV/AIDS response, making specific recommendations to partner governments, the United Nations system, and the Global Fund to Fight AIDS, Tuberculosis and Malaria (though not to bilateral donors). In particular, the GTT recommended the development of a scorecard-style accountability tool to examine the performance of national partners in creating a strong HIV/AIDS response and international partners in providing support according to the GTT recommendations. The scorecard is being piloted by UNAIDS in a number of countries.

Stakeholders in the health sector have responded to aid shortfalls, aid effectiveness problems, and failures in the supply of global public goods for health through the development of innovative financing methods. These are: the International Finance Facility for Immunisation (IFFim), Advance Market Commitments (AMC), and UNITAID[58] (previously called the International Drug Purchase Facility). The innovative finance agenda is seen as an important component of a more robust and performance-driven approach to development assistance. This is particularly true, given the unintended impact that unpredictable aid has had on markets, most notably for pharmaceuticals and vaccines needed by the poorest countries.

The High Level Forum (HLF) was a series of three high-level meetings in 2004 and 2005 among key donors and some 20 countries that looked at many of the aid-effectiveness issues raised above. It also strengthened cooperation among WHO, World Bank, IMF, bilateral donors, global health partnerships, and other UN agencies and has helped create a *consensus for action* around the scaling up of the agenda in health.

As donors make good on their promises to scale up development assistance between now and 2015, many will wish to invest in health. Creating effective aid architecture in health—which delivers results—helps make the case that "aid works" and should leverage further resources for the sector and perhaps overall, while a dysfunctional health architecture does the opposite. One key challenge is to demonstrate the link between the aid effectiveness agenda and better health outcomes. The Paris Declaration emphasizes progress toward harmonization and alignment and has an in-depth monitoring and accountability process related to this objective. It does not, however, hold donors and countries accountable for development results in health or other areas.

Taking forward the harmonization and alignment agenda in health is about *managing complexity*—recognizing that diversity can help bring results and that the health sector benefits from a range of partners with different ways of doing business. As part of the post-HLF agenda, there will be efforts at the country level to develop instruments for mutual accountability between donors and countries. These efforts will be initiated by the health community but will look beyond the sector and aim to ensure alignment of health strategies and goals and other development objectives.

ANNEX D

The World Bank HNP
Results Framework

WHAT RESULTS ON THE GROUND ARE IMPORTANT? COUNTRY OUTCOMES					
STRATEGIC POLICY OBJECTIVE	FINAL OUTCOMES	HOW DO WE MEASURE THESE RESULTS? FINAL INDICATORS	MULTISECTORAL CONTRIBUTIONS TO INTERMEDIATE OUTCOMES/OUTPUTS	HOW DO WE MEASURE THESE RESULTS? INTERMEDIATE INDICATORS (REPORTING ACCOUNTABILITY OF SECTORS)	
(1) Improve the level and distribution of key HNP outcomes, outputs, and system performance at country and global levels in order to improve living conditions, particularly for the poor and vulnerable	I. Childhood mortality reduced (by income quintile) (MDG 4, Target 5 and MDG 7, Target 10)	U-5 mortality rate	*Water & Sanitation, Energy, Environment, Agriculture, Education, Gender, HNP.* Reduced neonatal, infant and under-five mortality and morbidity by increasing effective coverage with high impact interventions	*HNP reporting accountability.* (1) Immunization coverage (DPT3, measles, Hib, hepatitis B) (2) % pregnant women who have received a tetanus vaccine (3) % children with diarrhea that received ORT (4) % of children with ARI taken to health provider *Water and Sanitation reporting accountability:* (5) % population with access to improved water supply services *Energy reporting accountability:* (6) % of households with electricity (7) Energy from combustible renewables and waste (% of total energy)	

		HOW DOES THE BANK CONTRIBUTE TO THESE RESULTS?		HOW DO WE KNOW IF IMPLEMENTATION IS ON TRACK? PROCESS INDICATORS	
				BANK	
		BANK STRATEGY	COUNTRY	PROCESS INDICATOR	BASELINE
		A. Renewing Focus on Results (1) *Build statistical capacity* for client countries on priority HNP outcome indicators (disaggregated by gender and age) directly through Bank operations and/or supporting global partner's country support (e.g., MDGs). This includes the development of country-based frameworks for the collection of essential household HNP and multisectoral indicators. (2) *Pilot and evaluate impact of output-based and performance-based financing* for HNP-related projects/programs. (3) *Introduce results frameworks* for all projects targeting HNP outcomes, output, and system performance, including baseline data and output targets.	Number of active borrowers (alternatively, percent of countries by Region) who are able to measure causes of under-five mortality at disaggregated levels. Currently, fewer than a third of all low- and middle income countries have vital registration systems that are complete enough to monitor trends in the U-5 mortality MDG. Bank will seek to increase this to the number of countries with sound systems. National HNP outcome strategies and PRSPs with increased use of multisectoral approach to achieve results in HNP outcomes.	(1) At least 40% of new CASs targeting HNP results to be discussed with the Board in FY2009 and thereafter will identify capacity and systems building activities (Bank and/or coordinated with global partners) for monitoring and evaluating HNP results in government programs. (2) By FY2010, at least 14 active projects with most loan proceeds allocated on output-based financing. Impact evaluation plans in place for 60% of these projects or more upon approval. (3) At least 70% of new projects/programs approved by the Board in FY2008 and thereafter.	(1) Less than 10% of CASs targeting HNP results. (2) 4 active projects in FY2006. (3) Less than 25% of active projects as of FY2006 with satisfactory results framework.

			WHAT RESULTS ON THE GROUND ARE IMPORTANT? COUNTRY OUTCOMES		
STRATEGIC POLICY OBJECTIVE	FINAL OUTCOMES	HOW DO WE MEASURE THESE RESULTS? FINAL INDICATORS	MULTISECTORAL CONTRIBUTIONS TO INTERMEDIATE OUTCOMES/OUTPUTS	HOW DO WE MEASURE THESE RESULTS? INTERMEDIATE INDICATORS (REPORTING ACCOUNTABILITY OF SECTORS)	
	II. Childhood malnutrition improved (MDG 1, Target 2)	Percentage of children under the age of five who are underweight, stunted	*HNP, Water and Sanitation, Agriculture, Environment, Energy, Education:* Reduced child underweight and stunting by increased coverage with effective interventions	*HNP reporting accountability:* (8) % infants under 6 months who are exclusively breastfed (9) % of children who receive breastfeeding plus adequate complementary food (6–9 months) *Water and Sanitation reporting accountability:* See (5) above *Energy reporting accountability:* See (6) and (7) above	
			HNP, Education, Private Sector: Reduced under-five micronutrient deficit	*HNP reporting accountability:* (10) % children (6–59) months receiving at least one dose of Vitamin A supplementation (11) % households using iodized salt	
	III. Avoidable mortality and morbidity from chronic diseases and injuries reduced	Adult mortality rate (15– 60)	*HNP, Education:* Reduced prevalence of low birth weight	*HNP reporting accountability:* (12) % newborns with low birth weight	
			HNP, Education: Reduced exposure to risk factors of NCDs and injuries	*HNP reporting accountability:* (13) Smoking prevalence among teenagers and adults (14) % of adult population with BMI above 25	

	HOW DOES THE BANK CONTRIBUTE TO THESE RESULTS?		HOW DO WE KNOW IF IMPLEMENTATION IS ON TRACK? PROCESS INDICATORS	
			BANK	
	BANK STRATEGY	COUNTRY	PROCESS INDICATOR	BASELINE
	(4) *Periodic data collection and updates* (as appropriate to specific indicators) for at least 70% of the indicators included in project results framework and updated periodically in Implementation Status Reports (ISRs).	Ministries of Finance allocate resources to and within the sector on the basis of some measures of performance.	(4) At least 65% (annually) of all projects/programs approved by Board in FY2008 and thereafter.	(4) Less than 15% of active projects as of FY2006.
	(5) *Develop indicators* (including gender-based indicators) for priority HNP outcomes for which no agreed indicators exist (e.g., financial protection, governance in the health sector, and financial and fiscal sustainability).	Countries have "policy analytic capacities" within MOH or mechanisms for contracting out policy analyses, performance review functions.	(5) Develop indicators by end-FY2008.	(5) Does not exist.
	(6) *Improve results in existing portfolio.* Review and restructure existing HNP portfolio (project design and/or project development objective, PDO) to achieve satisfactory PDO or higher outcome at project closing.		(6) 75% for FY2009 and thereafter (each Region and total HNP portfolio).	(6) Annual average of 66% of projects closing with satisfactory PDO or higher (FY2005 and FY2006).
	(7) *Concurrent monitoring of overall active Bank portfolio performance and PDO indicators on HNP results.* Develop and implement central database with HNP project results based on ISR and project results framework data online for monitoring portfolio results and quality.		(7) Develop by end-FY2008; implement by end-FY2009.	(7) Does not exist.

| | | | WHAT RESULTS ON THE GROUND ARE IMPORTANT?
COUNTRY OUTCOMES | | |
STRATEGIC POLICY OBJECTIVE	FINAL OUTCOMES	HOW DO WE MEASURE THESE RESULTS? FINAL INDICATORS	MULTISECTORAL CONTRIBUTIONS TO INTERMEDIATE OUTCOMES/OUTPUTS	HOW DO WE MEASURE THESE RESULTS? INTERMEDIATE INDICATORS (REPORTING ACCOUNTABILITY OF SECTORS)	
			Infrastructure: Reduced mortality/morbidity due to road traffic crashes	*Infrastructure reporting accountability:* (15) % of road network with safety rating of 3 to 4 "stars" (on scale of 4)	
	IV. Improved maternal, reproductive, and sexual health (MDG 5, Target 6)	Maternal mortality ratio Total fertility rate Adolescent fertility rate Increased birth spacing	*HNP, Education, Infrastructure:* Improved coverage with effective maternal and peri-natal interventions	*HNP reporting accountability:* (16) % women with deliveries attend-ed by skilled health personnel (17) % women with at least one ante-natal care visit during pregnancy *Infrastructure reporting accountability:* (18) % of rural population with access to an all-season road	
			HNP, Gender, Education: Improve family planning and sexual health	*HNP reporting accountability:* (19) Contraceptive prevalence rate among women of reproductive age (20) Unmet need for contraception (21) Prevalence rate of STIs among adults and young people (15–24 years)	
			HNP: Reduced incidence of cervi-cal cancer	*HNP reporting accountability:* (22) HPV immunization coverage	

	HOW DOES THE BANK CONTRIBUTE TO THESE RESULTS?		HOW DO WE KNOW IF IMPLEMENTATION IS ON TRACK? PROCESS INDICATORS	
			BANK	
	BANK STRATEGY	COUNTRY	PROCESS INDICATOR	BASELINE
	B. Strengthening Health Systems and Ensuring Synergy between Health System Strengthening and Priority–Disease Interventions (8) Increase support to Bank country teams to *identify health system constraints (including gender-specific constraints) to achieving HNP results* and mainstream system-strengthening actions to overcome constraints in all new HNP operations (or other sectoral or global partner operations), including priority–disease interventions.		(8) Develop operations toolkit for rapid assessment of health system constraints for better outcomes (completed by end-FY2008) Complete identification of 7 countries by December 2007. Launch on-demand support in 4 countries by June 2008. Put on-demand support in place to Bank country teams in 7 countries by June 2009. At least 60% of projects approved in FY2009 and thereafter will include assessment of health systems constrains to reaching HNP results. At least 70% of those identifying constraints will include appropriate policy actions/investments to overcome them.	(8) Less than 25% identify health system constraints. Less than 45% include health system strengthening in areas of Bank comparative advantages.

| | WHAT RESULTS ON THE GROUND ARE IMPORTANT? COUNTRY OUTCOMES | | | | |
STRATEGIC POLICY OBJECTIVE	FINAL OUTCOMES	HOW DO WE MEASURE THESE RESULTS? FINAL INDICATORS	MULTISECTORAL CONTRIBUTIONS TO INTERMEDIATE OUTCOMES/OUTPUTS	HOW DO WE MEASURE THESE RESULTS? INTERMEDIATE INDICATORS (REPORTING ACCOUNTABILITY OF SECTORS)	
	V. Reduced morbidity and mortality from HIV/AIDS, TB, malaria, and other priority pandemics (MDG 6, Target 7 and 8)	Adult HIV prevalence among all antenatal women and among women 15–24 Reduce AIDS mortality: % of people living with AIDS who survive at least 12 months after a complete ART course	*Education, Infrastructure, HNP, Gender:* Increased HIV/AIDS prevention and case fatality reduction *HNP:* Increased HIV/AIDS ARV treatment	*HNP/GHAP reporting accountability:* (23) % young women and men aged 15-24 reporting the use of a condom the last time they had sex *Water and Sanitation reporting accountability:* See (5) above *Energy reporting accountability:* See (6) and (7), above *HNP reporting accountability:* (24) % men and women with advanced HIV receiving antiretroviral therapy (ART)	
			HNP, Agriculture: Increased malaria prevention and treatment	*HNP reporting accountability:* (25) % children who slept under an insecticide treated bednet (in malarious areas) (26) % of children with fever in malarious areas who receive antimalarial treatment (27) % of pregnant women in malarious areas who receive treatment or preventive treatment for malaria	

HOW DOES THE BANK CONTRIBUTE TO THESE RESULTS?		HOW DO WE KNOW IF IMPLEMENTATION IS ON TRACK? PROCESS INDICATORS	
		BANK	
BANK STRATEGY	COUNTRY	PROCESS INDICATOR	BASELINE
(9) *Put in place arrangements for collaborative division of labor* on health systems with global partners at global and country levels.		(9) Dialog in place for global arrangements by December 2007. Launch collaborative division of labor arrangements for at least 7 countries where projects/programs include interventions requiring expertise other than Bank comparative advantages (by December 2008).	(9) Does not exist.
(10) *Focus knowledge creation and policy advice (AAA) on Bank comparative advantage.* Increase proportion of country- and regional-level AAA, appropriate to requirements of LICs and MICs, focused on Bank comparative advantages.		(10) By end-FY2008, 50% and by end-FY2009 70% of new HNP sector AAA will be focused on areas of Bank comparative advantage in specific areas appropriate for LICs' and/or MICs' requirements (e.g., Health system financing, demand-side determinants of results, inter-sectoral contribution to HNP results, private-public collaboration).	(10) Less than 35% so focused.

			WHAT RESULTS ON THE GROUND ARE IMPORTANT? COUNTRY OUTCOMES		
STRATEGIC POLICY OBJECTIVE	FINAL OUTCOMES	HOW DO WE MEASURE THESE RESULTS? FINAL INDICATORS	MULTISECTORAL CONTRIBUTIONS TO INTERMEDIATE OUTCOMES/OUTPUTS	HOW DO WE MEASURE THESE RESULTS? INTERMEDIATE INDICATORS (REPORTING ACCOUNTABILITY OF SECTORS)	
		Reduced TB mortality	*HNP:* Increased TB detection and treatment	*HNP reporting accountability:* (28) % TB cases detected and cured under DOTS	
		Increased country readiness to detect outbreaks and prevent/contain address rapid onset of pandemic (e.g., avian influenza)	Increased proportion of low-income countries with a functioning sentinel surveillance scheme for influenza-like illness Increased proportion of countries with an integrated avian influenza pandemic contingency plan.	(29) Number of health facilities/providers who routinely report ILI to national authorities (30) % increase in the number of ILI reported annually (% to be defined for each country). (31) Number of specimens from sentinel surveillance sites examined and subtyped annually. (32) Evidence of secured source of funding for outbreak investigation as per the prerequisites of the integrated AI pandemic contingency plan (33) Evidence of simulation exercises being conducted in an integrated fashion together with veterinary authorities	
(2) Prevent poverty due to illness (by improving financial protection)	VI. Improve Financial Protection (Reduce the impoverishing effects of illness for the poor or near poor)	% population falling below the poverty line due to illness	*HNP, PREM:* Reduction of out-of-pocket expenditures in health for "insurable events"	*HNP reporting accountability:* (34) % out-of-pocket expenditures in health (for a basic package of services) as a proportion of total household income	

	HOW DOES THE BANK CONTRIBUTE TO THESE RESULTS?		HOW DO WE KNOW IF IMPLEMENTATION IS ON TRACK? PROCESS INDICATORS	
			BANK	
	BANK STRATEGY	COUNTRY	PROCESS INDICATOR	BASELINE
	C. Strengthening Bank Intersectoral Advisory Capacity			
	(11) Develop, pilot test, and implement *Multisectoral Constraint Assessment (MCA)* tool and process. Pilot test in a number of LICs and MICs.		(11) First tool developed by end-FY2008 and pilot tested in 2 MICs and 2 LICs by end-FY2009.	(11) Does not exist.
	(12) *Identify lending and AAA in CAS.* MCA-identified HNP-related Bank projects/programs/components in CAS.		(12) MCA will be used to identify 40% of projects/programs with HNP results included in at least 50% of new CASs discussed with the Board by FY2010 and thereafter.	(12) Does not exist.
	D. Increase selectivity, improve strategic engagement, and reach agreement with global partners on collaborative division of labor for the benefit of client countries			
	(13) *Increase use of harmonization and alignment* principles for Bank projects in IDA at country level.		(13) By FY2011, at least 81% of projects approved by Board will be based on country fiduciary systems or will have common fiduciary arrangement/rules for all participating donors.	
	(14) *Develop overall HNP fiscal space assessment in priority countries.*		(14) Develop and pilot fiscal space assessment methodology (completed by end of FY2008) Full fiscal space assessment in 7 priority countries in coordination with global partners.	(14) Does not exist.

| | | | WHAT RESULTS ON THE GROUND ARE IMPORTANT?
COUNTRY OUTCOMES | | |
STRATEGIC POLICY OBJECTIVE	FINAL OUTCOMES	HOW DO WE MEASURE THESE RESULTS? FINAL INDICATORS	MULTISECTORAL CONTRIBUTIONS TO INTERMEDIATE OUTCOMES/OUTPUTS	HOW DO WE MEASURE THESE RESULTS? INTERMEDIATE INDICATORS (REPORTING ACCOUNTABILITY OF SECTORS)	
			HNP, PREM: Increase in risk-pooling schemes (contributory or noncontributory)	*HNP reporting accountability:* (35) % of lowest quintiles households participating in risk-pooling schemes (contributory or noncontributory)	
			HNP, PREM: Reduction in income loss due to illness	*HNP reporting accountability:* (36) % of households receiving income substitution of ill breadwinner (37) % of workers receiving treatment for common productivity reducing illness (e.g., Intestinal worms, iron deficit anemia)	
(3) Improve financial sustainability in the HNP sector and its contribution to sound macroeconomic and fiscal policy and to country competitiveness	VII. Improve Funding Sustainability in the Public Sector from Both Domestic and External Sources	To be developed	To be developed	To be developed	
(4) Improve governance, accountability, and transparency in the health sector	VIII. Improved Governance and Transparency and Reduced Corruption in the Health Sector (MDG 8, Target 12)	Improved CPIA indicator 9a rating Reduced health workers absenteeism Reduced "under the table" payments Reduced excess payment for medical supplies	Decreased proportion of household total health expenditures paid on "under the table" payments Decreased percentage of off-the-international-market-price paid for medical supplies	To be developed	

Note: This global HNP Results Framework is presented as guidance for the Regions, yet essential to ensure its country-driven application and adaptation. The Framework is intended to serve as guidance and support for Regions to elaborate their own HNP strategy and for country teams to help them identify constraints to improving outcomes and performance at country level. The Framework should not be understood as a prescriptive, limiting instrument. The periodicity of the collection of data will vary. Not all indicators are measured annually. Countries conduct Health and Demographic Surveys 3 to 5 years apart.

		HOW DOES THE BANK CONTRIBUTE TO THESE RESULTS?		HOW DO WE KNOW IF IMPLEMENTATION IS ON TRACK? PROCESS INDICATORS	
				BANK	
		BANK STRATEGY	COUNTRY	PROCESS INDICATOR	BASELINE
		(15) *Review and reorient Bank grants (Development Grant Facility, DGF)* in HNP toward areas of Bank comparative advantages.		(15) By end-FY2008 5%, by end of FY2009 30% and by the end of FY2010 50% of Bank DGF grants will be allocated in partnerships related to Bank comparative advantages.	(15) Currently less than 1% of DGF grant financing is allocated to partners working on issues related to Bank comparative advantages.
		(16) Realign secondments and Trust Fund management in HNP sector with Bank comparative advantages.		(16) By end-FY2009, 80% of secondments to Bank and 80% of total Trust Fund financing managed by HNP sector will be in areas of Bank comparative advantages.	(16) Now 60% of secondments in HNP sector are in areas in which Bank has little comparative advantage.

ANNEX E

Multisectoral Constraints Assessment for Health Outcomes

Rationale I (for Countries and Country Directors)

The attention to outcomes brought about by the Millennium Development Goals (MDGs) exposed a critical gap in client–country and World Bank programs for Health, Nutrition, and Population (HNP). While it is universally acknowledged that reducing mortality, morbidity, fertility, and malnutrition requires multisectoral inputs and actions, little analysis has been done at the country level to systematically document the bottlenecks in different critical sectors, set out a framework for prioritizing actions, or assess institutional constraints. The proposed new economic sector work (ESW) instrument is designed to address this gap in the arsenal of client countries and development agencies. The proposed ESW will: systematically assess multisectoral constraints to achieving HNP results; provide a framework for prioritization of actions; and assess institutional factors and structures for facilitating coordinated actions by the prioritized sectors. For the World Bank country program, this new ESW product line will guide CAS development for multisectoral approaches to addressing the MDGs and other health outcomes, especially for the poor.

Rationale II (for the HNP Family)

Successful knowledge institutions (e.g., consulting firms or development institutions) put a premium on quality of knowledge, standardization of core competencies, and relevance to the clients. Within the World Bank, these success factors can be seen in the way groups like PREM and Social Protection select specific ESW lines that are high in quality, focus on the comparative advantages of the World Bank, and target not only line ministries, but primarily the Ministry of Finance (MOF). For HNP to achieve similar success, the current practice of an ad hoc and unstructured ESW program has to give way to much more selectivity, based on comparative advantage and serving the need of MOFs and Bank Country Directors in addition to Ministries of Health (MOHs). The new World Bank HNP Strategy has identified two clear lines of ESW business that fit the above success criteria. One line of ESW should focus on the crucial link between the MOH and the MOF by building simple instruments that address contingent liabilities for a country's budget created by the health sector, issues around fiscal space, and issues around the allocative efficiency and the welfare impact of the health sector. The second line of ESW, addressed in this note, relates to systematic assessments of multisectoral constraints to achieving health outcomes as well as institutional frameworks to ensure coordination of inputs by different line ministries. The ultimate objective of this latter line of ESW is to provide a technical and institutional prioritization framework for Finance and Planning Ministries (and input for Bank CASs) and to help elevate MOHs from service delivery structures to a higher role of stewardship.

Objectives of the Multisectoral Constraints Assessment

Given the complex multisectoral determinants of HNP outcomes, it is critical that decisions about investments in the different sectors be guided by evidence on distribution of these outcomes, assessment of the binding constraints in relevant sectors, a prioritization framework, and an assessment of institutional factors that can help or hinder multisectoral coordination and sectoral implementation. A fully fledged application of this new ESW instrument has the following objectives (rapid MCAs take on a subset of the objectives):

- *Identifying outcome targets* by reviewing and stratifying health, nutrition, and fertility outcomes at the national and subnational levels. Outcomes include mortality (infant, child, maternal, and adult), morbidity by cause of illness/injury, nutritional status, and fertility rates. Depending on the size and organization of the country assessed and the availability of data, the outcomes will be stratified by geographic groupings and socioeconomic status, including poverty levels, wealth groups, education, gender, and different sources of country-specific vulnerability factors (minorities, tribes, social castes, and so on).

- Investigate sector-specific constraints by documenting the presence or absence of critical inputs for achieving the targeted HNP outcomes. Inputs include, for example, immunization rates, access to and use of attended deliveries, use of iodized salts, knowledge of and use of modern contraceptives, source of indoor cooking and heating, access to clean water, success of vector control measures, and availability of roads for emergency transport of pregnant women. The selection of constraints to be investigated is a function of the HNP outcome in question.

- *Guide decision making* by using outcome and constraint assessments to develop a country-specific prioritization framework that outlines short-, medium-, and long-term policy actions by different sectors; develops alternative cotargeting maps and mechanisms that combine poverty and health outcome data; identifies institutional and operational constraints, as well as possible solutions for coordinated action; and lays out a menu of potential policy instruments.

A number of these objectives can be addressed with existing ESWs in some countries, especially if large ESWs were undertaken, but the approach tends to be ad hoc in nature and focus almost entirely on one sector (e.g., HNP or Environment). Moreover, rarely are all the relevant sectors addressed at the same time to allow for prioritization and synergy. Even more challenging is to find institutional assessments or options that look at practical ways of ensuring coordination in the production and targeting of multisectoral inputs. What MCAs can do for health outcomes in any country is to assess systematically technical and institutional constraints in order to create a prioritization framework for client countries and support World Bank country teams in addressing outcomes in the CAS process.

ANNEX F

What Is a Health System?

A "system" can be understood as an arrangement of parts and their interconnections that come together for a purpose (von Bertalanffy 1968).[59] What sets apart a health system is that its purpose is concerned with people's health. A health system has many parts. In addition to patients, families, and communities, Ministries of Health, health providers, health services organizations, pharmaceutical companies, health financing bodies, and other organizations play important roles. The interconnections of the health system can be viewed as the functions and roles played by these parts. These functions include oversight (e.g., policy making, regulation), health service provision (e.g., clinical services, health promotion), financing, and managing resources (e.g., pharmaceuticals, medical equipment, information). Describing the parts, interconnections, and purpose, Roemer (1991) defined a health system as "the combination of resources, organization, financing and management that culminate in the delivery of health services to the population." The World Health Organization (2000) redefined the main purpose in its definition of a health system as "all activities whose primary purpose is to promote, restore, and maintain health." In recent years, the definition of "purpose" has been further extended to include the prevention of household poverty due to illness.

A Complex System in Constant Flux

Many factors outside the health system influence people's health, such as poverty, education, infrastructure, and the broader social and political environment. Because they are open to influence from outside, health systems are known as open systems. A health system's various parts operate at many levels. Smaller systems may be self-contained and have limited scale and scope, such as those involved in running a clinic or a managing a health information system. Larger systems might involve the coming together of various smaller systems (e.g., clinics, hospitals, health promotion programs) to provide coherence at community or national level. Given the purpose, scale, and scope of a country's health system, it is not effectively controlled centrally, and changes in a system are not predictable in great detail (even if some parts of the system appear to behave predictably). This is partly because people and organizations innovate, learn, and adapt to change and partly because reorganization occurs continually in health systems in both formal and informal ways. These features have led systems thinkers to describe health systems as complex adaptive systems (Plsek et al. 2001). Understanding health systems as complex adaptive systems has important implications for approaches to influencing health systems to produce better health outcomes, or to do so in a more efficient or equitable manner.

Building on the definition of a health system, this annex describes the important functions of the main parts of the health system, highlighting some of the key issues for low- and middle-income countries. Interpreting the parts and functions of a health system can be done independently, but greater power comes in bringing the parts together to improve people's health and illness-related poverty. They are briefly examined in this annex. The annex concludes with further discussion of how to understand health systems as complex adaptive systems and the practical implications.

Health System Functions

Health service provision, health service inputs, stewardship, and health financing are the four main health system functions. Households' demand behavior as well as overall health sector governance largely determine how these functions perform.

Stewardship (overall system oversight) sets the context and policy framework for the overall health system. This function is usually (but not always) a governmental responsibility. What are the health priorities to which public resources should be targeted? What is the institutional framework in which the system and its many actors should function? Which activities should be coordinated with other systems outside the realm of health care, and how (e.g., highway safety, food quality control)? What are the trends in health priorities and resource generation and their implications for the next 10, 20, or 30 years? What information is needed and by whom to ensure effective decision making on health matters, including prevention and mitigation of epidemics? These questions are the core of the stewardship function. An additional central function of stewardship is to generate appropriate data for policy making. These range from public health surveillance data to health system performance and provide the basis for assessing health status, regulating the sector, and tracking health system performance, effectiveness, and impact. Stewardship remains a fragile function in many Bank client countries.

Public and private health service provision is the most visible product of the health care system. The best systems also promote health and try to head off illness through education and preventive measures such as well-child consultations. All these roles and activities mean that the system has to perform a wide range of activities. "Delivering health services is thus an essential part of what the system does—but it is not what the system is" (WHO 2000).

Health service inputs (managing resources) is the assembling of essential resources for delivering health services, but these inputs are usually produced at the borders of the health system. These inputs include human resources (produced mostly by the education system with some input from the health system), medications, and medical equipment. Producing these resources often takes a long time (e.g., a trained medical doctor, a new vaccine or drug). This function is generally outside the immediate control of health system policy makers who, nevertheless, have to respond to short-term population needs with whatever resources are available. An example of this problem is the current crisis of medical education in Sub-Saharan Africa.

Health system financing includes collecting revenues, pooling financial risk, and allocating revenue (strategic purchasing of services). We briefly examine them in this annex.

Revenue collection entails collection of money to pay for health care services. Revenue collection mechanisms are general taxation, development assistance for health (DAH, donor financing), mandatory payroll contributions, mandatory or voluntary risk-rated contributions (premiums), direct household out-of-pocket expenditures, and other forms of personal savings. Traditionally, each method of revenue collection is associated with a specific way of organizing and pooling funds and buying services. For example, public health systems are typically financed through general taxation, and social security organizations are usually financed through mandatory contributions from workers and employers (payroll contributions).

In most countries, health financing is a mix of general taxation, mandatory social insurance contributions, and household out-of-pocket expenditures (OOP). The relative importance of each source of financing varies greatly across countries. While OECD countries rely heavily on public financing (either fiscal or mandatory payroll tax), the importance of OOP is larger in middle-income countries (MICs), and it is the largest in low-income countries (LICs), where it often reaches 70 or 80 percent of total health expenditures. DAH is an important source of health financing in a number of LICs, mainly in Africa. However, DAH on average contributes only about 7 percent of all health expenditures in LICs, ranging from 3 percent in a few LICs to more than 40 percent in a few others.

Risk pooling refers to the collection and management of financial resources in a way that spreads financial risks from an individual to all pool members (WHO 2000). Financial risk pooling is the core function of health insurance mechanisms. Participation in effective risk pooling is essential to ensure financial protection. It is also essential to avoid payment at the moment of utilizing the services, which can deter people, especially the poor, from seeking health care when sick or injured. Each society chooses a different way of pooling its people's financial risk to finance its health care system. Most high-income countries follow one of two main models: the Bismarck model (Bismarck's Law on Health Insurance of 1883) or the Beveridge model (from the report on Social Insurance and Allied Services of 1942—the Beveridge Report). In most developing countries, multiple and fragmented forms of risk-pooling arrangements coexist. Population participation in risk pooling is lowest in LICs and among the poor. It is also low in MICs among the informal and self-employed population. Improving financial protection in Bank client countries requires a substantial effort to increase participation in risk pooling.

Fragmentation is the most distinctive characteristic of LIC and MIC health systems. Within each system, different types of risk-pooling arrangements coexist, creating a complex set of incentives for households trying to cover their health care costs. These incentives not only shape how households decide to face potential financial losses from health shocks, but also influence life-style and economic decisions such as whether to work in the formal or informal sectors of the economy. Reducing health system fragmentation is essential to improve performance and systemic capacity to serve and protect the poor.

Strategic purchasing. Strategic purchasing is the way most risk-pooling organizations (purchasers) use collected and pooled financial resources to finance or buy health care services for their members. In the practical, day-to-day interaction between purchasers and providers, the purchaser, within a regulatory framework, plays a key role in defining a substantial part of the external incentives for providers to develop appropriate provider-user interaction and health service delivery models.

"Systems" Thinking

When trying to intervene in any system, it is important to be able to distinguish whether its nature is primarily mechanical or adaptive. In mechanical systems, what results will occur in response to a given stimulus can be predicted, usually in great detail and under different circumstances. A mechanical system may be complex, like an automobile, but it does not show emergent behavior. Adaptive systems, on the other hand, have the freedom to respond to different stimuli in different and unpredictable ways and are interconnected with the actions of other parts of a system. Many human systems, including health systems, are adaptive. Health outcomes are not merely a product of a set of physical inputs, human resources, organizational structure, and managerial processes. They are complex adaptive systems that have the following key characteristics (Plsek et al. 2001):

- *Adaptable elements.* They can learn and change themselves. In mechanical systems, change is imposed, whereas under adaptive systems, changes can happen from within.

- *Context.* Systems exist within systems, and this context matters, because one part of a system affects another. In health systems, changing the financing system may change availability and performance of health workforce, the use of other inputs, and the relationship with patients. In adaptive systems, optimizing one part of the system may lead to poor overall system performance. In a hospital, for example, reducing the length of stay of patients in one ward may lead to queuing and readmission in other parts of the hospital, compromising overall quality or cost.

- *Inherent order.* Systems can be orderly even if there is no central control, often because they self-organize. Health systems are self-organizing; different types of provider organizations, associations, and behaviors emerge continually, either formally or informally.

- *Not predictable in detail.* Changes are not linear or easily predictable. For example, a large health program may have little impact, but a rumor may spark a strike or a riot at a clinic. Forecasting and modeling in health systems can be done to predict effects on health and poverty, but they are not predictable in detail because the elements and relationships are changeable and nonlinear, often in creative ways. The only way to know what complex adaptive systems will do is to observe them.

What are the practical implications of viewing health systems as complex adaptive rather than mechanical systems? In the first place, giving up a mechanical approach means spending less time on blueprints and detailed plans. It also means that it is less important to search for the "correct" health financing or organizational approach for a given country or a given context. It does mean the following:

- Understand the context, look for connections between the parts (e.g., between programs, between demand and supply, across sectors), anticipating downstream consequences and identifying upstream points of leverage.

- Focus on simple rules to produce complex outcomes. Balance three types of rules that: set direction (e.g., leadership and vision); set prohibitions (e.g., regulations and boundary setting); and provide permission (e.g., setting incentives or providing resources).

- Understand how organizational structure influences behavior. How ministries are organized, and how development assistance is provided matter a great deal. Health workers hired and trained under a centrally managed disease program will work differently from those accountable for all outpatient conditions and hired by a local health service organization.

- Use data to guide decisions. Constantly looking at how health systems perform is the best way to see how it is actually behaving and whether a project or new intervention is making a difference.

World Bank Partners in Health, Nutrition, and Population

Global Health Partnerships and Initiatives

African Program for Onchocerciasis Control (APOC)
European Observatory for Health Systems and Policies
Global Alliance for Improved Nutrition (GAIN)
Global Alliance for Vaccines and Immunisation (GAVI)
Global Forum for Health Research (GFHR)
Global Fund to Fight AIDS, Tuberculosis and Malaria (GFATM)
International AIDS Vaccine Initiative (IAVI)
International Lung Health Program – International Union Against Tuberculosis and Lung Disease (IUATLD)
International Partnership for Microbicides
Joint United Nations Programme on HIV/AIDS (UNAIDS)
Mainstreaming Nutrition in Maternal Child Health Program
Medicines for Malaria Ventures (MMV)
Population and Reproductive Health Capacity Building Program
Roll Back Malaria (RBM)
Stop Tuberculosis Partnership (Stop TB)
United Nations Standing Committee on Nutrition
West Africa Multidisease Surveillance Control
WHO Special Programme for Research and Training in Tropical Diseases (TDR)
WHO Special Programme of Research, Development and Research Training in Human Reproduction (HRP)

Process/Programs without Financial Participation

Child Health and Nutrition Research Initiative (CHNRI)
Disease Priorities and Control Program (DCP2)
Donors' Group on Adolescent Sexual and Reproductive Health and Rights
Global Alliance to Eliminate Lymphatic Filariasis
Global Alliance for Improved Nutrition (GAIN)
Health Metrics Network (HMN)
International Finance Facility for Immunisation (IFFIm)
Interagency Working Group on Youth
Micronutrient Initiative
Nutrition and Gender
The Partnership for Maternal, Newborn, and Child Health
Reproductive Health/HIV Interagency Working Group
Reproduction Health Supplies Coalition (RHSC)
Road Traffic Injuries Research Network
UNITAID

Global Institutional Partners

African Union (AU)
Asian Development Bank (ADB)
European Union (EU)
Food and Agricultural Organization of the United Nations (FAO)
Inter-American Development Bank (IADB)
International Labour Organisation (ILO)
Organisation for Economic Co-operation and Development (OECD)
United Nations Children's Fund (UNICEF)
United Nations Development Programme (UNDP)
United Nations Population Fund (UNFPA)
World Health Organization (WHO)
World Organisation for Animal Health (OIE)

Bilaterals/Partners

Canadian International Development Agency (CIDA)
Danida
Dutch International Cooperation
French Development Organization
German Agency for Technical Cooperation (GTZ)
Italian Development Organization
Japan International Cooperation Agency (JICA)
Norwegian Agency for Development Cooperation (Norad)
Swedish International Development Cooperation Agency (SIDA)
Swiss Agency for Development and Cooperation
United Kingdom Department for International Development (DFID)
United States Agency for International Development (USAID)
United States Centers for Disease Control and Prevention (CDC)

Foundations

Aga Khan Foundation
Bill and Melinda Gates Foundation
Ellison Institute
Ford Foundation
Hewlett-Packard Foundation
Rockefeller Foundation
Soros Foundation
United Nations Foundation
Wellcome Trust

HNP Contributions to Combating HIV/AIDS: Background Paper to the World Bank HNP Strategy

HIV/AIDS is a health priority for low- and middle-income countries (LMICs). HIV/AIDS is the fourth leading cause of death and disability in LMICs (Mathers, Lopez, and Murray 2006), and in many countries, particularly in Africa, the epidemic poses a major threat to their economic development. Although the global HIV incidence appears to have peaked, the number of new infections and deaths continues to rise (UNAIDS 2006). Recent financial and political commitments for combating HIV/AIDS have created new opportunities, but also new challenges. Much of the new funding is focused on increasing access to antiretroviral therapy (ART). In the last two years, the number of people on ART in low- and middle-income countries has more than tripled to 1.3 million by the end of 2005. Yet this represents only 20 percent of those estimated to need treatment (UNAIDS 2006). Scaling up HIV prevention and treatment in a sustainable way will depend on health systems that can deliver care, fiscal space, and the ability of the international community to provide the financing.

A comprehensive response to HIV requires action across many sectors. The health sector, however, has a unique and central contribution to make, especially in scaling up clinical aspects of prevention and treatment (e.g., voluntary counseling and testing, behavioral counseling for people with HIV, prevention of mother-to-child transmission (PMTCT), treatment of sexually transmitted infections, treatment for co-infections with tuberculosis and opportunistic infections, and ART), as well as for other public health functions such as disease surveillance and monitoring.

In 2005, the World Bank articulated its Global HIV/AIDS Program of Action (GHAPA) for supporting the global, regional, and national AIDS response. The Africa Region of the World Bank is developing an "HIV/AIDS Agenda for Action in Sub-Saharan Africa" to further articulate the Bank's role on HIV/AIDS in the Region most affected by HIV. The HNP Strategy is intended to complement these responses. This annex to the HNP Strategy:

- Identifies the main constraints of health systems in contributing to the fight against HIV/AIDS and ways of overcoming these constraints.

- Reviews the special challenges of financial sustainability in HIV/AIDS and health programs and identifies ways of overcoming these constraints.

- Outlines the key contributions that HNP sector can make to combating HIV/AIDS.

The Relationship between Health System Strengthening and Priority–Disease Approaches

The decades-old tension between health system strengthening approaches and priority–disease approaches has changed to a growing consensus that both types of approaches depend on the other to achieve their common goals (Peters et al. 2006; High-Level Forum 2005; Mills 2005; Stillman and Bennett 2005). It is also recognized that the old labeling of "vertical" versus "horizontal" schemes is not an accurate portrayal of either HIV/AIDS or health system strategies. Although many HIV/AIDS programs have created separate organizational units, with separate personnel, management, and accountability systems, the World Bank and other agencies have worked with countries to encourage programs to be broadly based and operate across sectors and civil society. By the same token, not all health system strengthening approaches are integrated "horizontally." Projects that focus on essential drug management or strengthening health information systems may be more "vertical" than HIV/AIDS programs when they use separate and hierarchical management and accountability structures, even if they function across diseases. In any case, important concerns remain about which approaches work best and how to find synergies between disease-specific and systems approaches.

Some have argued that priority programs such as for HIV or disease eradication should be able to strengthen health systems generally (Buve, Kalibala, and McIntyre 2003; Melgaard et al. 1999). Yet beyond the strength of expert opinion, there has been little evidence that these spillover effects actually occur (Peters et al. 2006). Some studies note that, although large disease control programs can be effective in addressing the specific problems they target, they can also harm the general health systems when they create duplicative and uncoordinated management entities, financing structures and reporting systems, or replace local priorities with those of donors, or distort salary and incentive structures and distract from other activities (High-Level Forum 2005; McKinsey&Company 2005; Stillman and Bennett 2005). In reviewing studies that examine approaches to strengthening specific programs and studies that attempt to strengthen a range of health services, Øvretveit and colleagues (2006) find little scientifically robust evidence for or against the view that disease-specific programs deflect overall health services from local needs. Nonetheless, they note that some strategies to deliver certain services, such as special payments to provide immunizations, can reduce the motivation to provide other services. They conclude that disease- or service-specific strategies on their own are unlikely to bring about the changes needed in health systems to achieve the Millennium Development Goals (MDGs).

Overcoming Health Systems Constraints

A number of recent studies have identified common types of constraints in health systems in low- and middle-income countries that affect both disease-specific and health systems (Hanson et al. 2003; Oliveira-Cruz, Hanson, and Mills 2003; Travis et al. 2004). These constraints can be examined by how they relate to the incentives environment for the health sector (table H.1). There is little strong evidence to indicate which constraints are most important, or what strategies are most effective in overcoming these constraints. The reason is that the studies that comprise the evidence basis for the reviews are mostly of limited scientific value, due to flaws in study design. The studies often do not define the particular strategies under investigation or cannot attribute change to the strategies pursued (Øvretveit, Siadat, and Peters 2006; Peters et al. 2006).[60]

Table H.1: Incentives Environment and Constraints for Health Systems in Low- and Middle-Income Countries

LEVEL OF INCENTIVES	EXAMPLES OF CONSTRAINTS
Individuals and communities	Lack of demand; limited access to information; lack of financial resources; exclusionary social norms; fractured or weak community institutions; low community participation; limited influence over providers, health bureaucrats, and political leadership; physical barriers to care
Health service providers	Limited staff; inadequate provider skills, poor training and technical guidance; weak motivation; weak supervision and management systems; poor compensation and rewards systems; poor physical work environment (e.g., inadequate drugs, equipment, and buildings)
Health sector	Weak sector leadership and vision; inappropriate sector planning and regulatory systems; weak accountability mechanisms; purchasing and provider payment systems unrelated to performance; poor collaboration with nongovernmental organizations and private sector stakeholders; reliance on donors and donor priorities
Macro environment	Insecure or unstable social and political conditions; macroeconomic instability; poor governance and corruption; trade and migration pressures; weak sectors critical to health (education, communications, agriculture, labor); weak systems for reconciling cross-sectoral development priorities; inefficient, unresponsive, and rigid government bureaucracies; confused or insufficiently supported decentralization strategies; poor physical environment (poor roads and communications infrastructure)

The HIV epidemic itself places additional pressures on weak health systems by increasing demand for health care and reducing the supply of health workers. It also reduces the supply of a given quality of health services at a given price, while increasing health expenditures (Over 2004).[61] This is likely to translate into higher national health care expenditure in absolute terms and as a proportion of national income. This leads to reduced non-HIV patients' access to other health services, unless additional expenditures are made to finance those services.

Health Financing Constraints

The contrast between the enormous unmet health needs of poor countries and the resources they have to pay for them is well recognized. In a recent synthesis of health financing in low- and middle-income countries, Gottret and Schieber (2006) find that developing countries account for more than 90 percent of the global disease burden, but only 12 percent of global health spending. Between US$25 billion and US$70 billion in additional aid per year has been projected as needed to achieve the MDGs. The Bank is concerned about a number of characteristics of development assistance for health (DAH), as described by Gottret and Schieber (2006), that are particularly relevant to HIV/AIDS:

- *Volatile and short-term aid.* The amount of DAH funds countries receive varies greatly from year to year, though the reasons may differ.[62] Although funding for HIV/AIDS has increased rapidly, due largely to funding from the Global Fund to Fight AIDS, Tuberculosis and Malaria (GFATM) and the U.S. President's Emergency Plan for AIDS Relief (PEPFAR), more than 70 percent of these funds are concentrated in about 25 countries, whereas donors have health programs in about 140 countries.[63] Volatile and short-term DAH makes it difficult for ministries of health and finance to make necessary long-term plans such as employing more doctors or nurses, raising wages, or expanding access to ART.

- *Funding distortions.* Fragmentation of donor assistance to health has created distortions in funding, making it difficult for governments to finance their system requirements for staff, supervision, training, management, and maintenance. For example, a government of Rwanda report identified how donor funding has helped create a sixfold difference in per capita health spending between provinces (Republic of Rwanda Ministry of Finance and Economic Planning, Ministry of Health 2006). Physicians working for nongovernmental organizations (NGOs) providing HIV/AIDS services received six times the wages of MOH physicians, compromising human resources and service delivery in the public sector. The Ministry of Finance (MOF) argues that funding for HIV/AIDS is "disproportionate" when there is little funding for child health or other strategic objectives. The MOH says "single-issue funds and single-issue projects are being used to disburse funds through centralized allocation mechanisms that do not respond to the relative importance of needs as perceived by patients and health providers." Paradoxically, as donors move to provide more general budget support, spending on health and HIV/AIDS may decrease if governments choose different allocation priorities, particularly if they feel that donors will provide other support for health and HIV/AIDS.

- *Allocative inefficiencies.* The large influx of funding for HIV/AIDS raises the question about whether the funds are used to provide maximum benefit. The recent emphasis on expanding access to ART has not been met by a similar expansion of prevention efforts. Although ART appears to have a net beneficial effect on preventing HIV infection, and both can be relatively cost-effective, preventive interventions will have a bigger impact on reducing new HIV infections and are more cost-effective (Bertozzi et al. 2006; Hogan et al. 2005; Salomon et al. 2005). The problem is particularly striking in PEPFAR, the largest funded program for HIV/AIDS, where prevention spending is falling and constrained by requirements for abstinence-until-marriage activities (Government Accountability Office 2006). If funding continues to increase for HIV/AIDS, and ART in particular, without concomitant increases in funding for other priorities, the question must also be asked if some funds would be better spent in other ways that can make a larger contribution to peoples' health or better address inequities. Alternative uses include programs targeted at the health of poor and vulnerable populations, other high-priority conditions that are relatively underfunded such as neonatal health, or desperately needed investments in human resources for health and other aspects of health systems.

- *Need to create fiscal space.* Large increases in public spending on HIV/AIDS or health initiatives that create future spending commitments must be considered in the context of governments' ability to provide resources from current and future revenues and donors' willingness to provide long-term funding. The problem is compounded if large expenditures are financed by borrowing, which requires additional revenue to service the debt and has potential to impair overall economic growth. In the case of Rwanda, only 14 percent of the donor spending on health passes through the government. This makes it very difficult for government to diagnose fiscal problems or plan a response to manage large influxes or reductions in short-term aid (Republic of Rwanda Ministry of Finance and Economic Planning, Ministry of Health 2006).

The Bank's Contributions in Financing for HIV/AIDS

The Bank will specifically contribute to financing HIV/AIDS programs and health systems in several ways:

- *Providing increased, long-term, predictable funding.* The World Bank is committed to leveraging and providing increased and predictable long-term

financing for HIV/AIDS and the health sector. This includes a commitment to financing recurrent costs of HIV/AIDS and health programs in
ways that help them increase their effectiveness and reduce wastage.
When the World Bank funds ART programs, it will seek to do so in the
context of long-term program funding, such as through Adaptable Program Loans or find new ways of funding cohorts of people on HIV treatment (e.g., 20-year horizon), rather than just through short-term projects.
Shorter-term project support for HIV/AIDS and health initiatives should
be selected and designed to meet shorter-term objectives, such as to test
innovations, help create new institutions, support transitions in ongoing
programs, or bridge especially unstable conditions.

- *Creating fiscal space and reducing distortions.* The Bank will work with client
  countries, the IMF, and other donors to help them develop ways of
  enhancing country capacity to absorb fiscal shocks and reduce their
  adverse effects. This would involve working with Ministries of Finance,
  other sectoral ministries, and donors to ensure better complementarity of
  external financing flows and domestic resource mobilization. External
  flows should facilitate and help catalyze domestic financial resource
  mobilization rather than increase debt or aid dependency. The Bank will
  also ensure that financing and reporting procedures support local systems
  and are harmonized with those of other donors, as outlined in the Paris
  Declaration on Aid Effectiveness[64] and the "Three Ones" for HIV/AIDS
  programs.[65]

- *Enhancing accountability.* The Bank will promote budgetary and financial
  reporting processes that accommodate and respond to the views of critical stakeholders within the country. These processes will need to account
  for the interests of the poor, vulnerable, and marginalized groups, including people living with HIV/AIDS, in order to increase accountability and
  enhance people's voice. These processes offer important opportunities
  for debating and resolving concerns about allocative efficiency and
  equity, and for public disclosure of information and decisions over policy,
  financing, and program direction.

- *New types of financing.* The Bank will provide financial, technical, and convening support to countries that request help with developing health
  financing systems that promote accountability, efficiency, and financial
  protection, and which form the framework for financing of HIV/AIDS

prevention, care, and treatment at the country level. The Bank will also test new approaches to its own financing of HNP and HIV/AIDS. Emphasis will be put on linking Bank financing to performance in purchasing HIV/AIDS and other health services, rather than rely on financing inputs. Such approaches accentuate the importance of using information and demonstrating results in HIV/AIDS and other health sector programs.

More Funding Is Not Enough

Although additional funds will be necessary for scaling up HIV/AIDS and other health services, additional funding can also play an important role in overcoming some health system constraints such as poor supply of drugs and equipment or weak demand for services (Hanson et al. 2003). However, there is an emerging view that funding alone is not sufficient to overcome constraints. Johnston and Stout (1999) argue that it is the continuous commitment to improvement, analysis of constraints, flexible implementation, and positive macroeconomic and governance environments that are most useful in strengthening health services. Lewis (2005) holds that the keys to effective absorption of funding for HIV/AIDS will require building up institutions and human capacity in the health sector, as well as broader governance capacity. Whitty and Doherty (2006) argue that the biggest barriers to fighting disease are not financing or political will, but the failure to match the recent investments in new drugs and tools with investments in training people and developing efficient systems to deliver them. This is exactly where the World Bank's HNP Strategy can assist countries to better tackle the HIV/AIDS and health problems they face.

Vision for HNP Contributions to Combating AIDS

In the "preferred future," countries' health sectors will make significant contributions to combating HIV/AIDS and improving their people's health, and the World Bank will help client countries:

- Improve health status among vulnerable groups and the general population, including achieving the MDGs. Curbing the incidence of HIV infections across all key subgroups and the general population is a vital part of this.

- Fashion effective, equitable, accountable, affordable, and sustainable health systems that provide a full range of preventive, curative, and rehabilitative health services and make full use of public and non-governmental health actors and engage with and contribute to institutions outside the health sector. The Bank shares the collective goals of universal access to ART for people with HIV, universal childhood immunization, antenatal care and safe deliveries for all pregnant women, provision of directly observable treatment for all TB infected, and full access to other elements of locally defined "essential packages" of care.

- Reduce the number of people plunged into poverty by health care costs.

- Help individuals and households to make informed choices about healthy life styles and use of health services.

The Bank's Contribution to HIV/AIDS through Health Systems

The focus of health system strengthening for HIV/AIDS is to improve and expand HIV prevention, treatment, and care via the health systems that deliver these services. The HNP Strategy outlines how the Bank will focus on strengthening aspects of health systems related to its comparative advantages in financing, creating the right incentives environment, working across sectors, and demonstrating and using results in the context of countries' human and economic development.

In addition to addressing financing of HIV/AIDS and health (discussed above), the World Bank plans to strengthen health systems to contribute to HIV/AIDS by:

- Integrating HIV/AIDS and health system programming to ensure that planning and financing of the health sector and HIV/AIDS programs support each other and do not create duplicative and competing structures. The Burkina Faso Health Sector Support and Multisectoral AIDS Project is an example of the way health sector and HIV/AIDS allocation decisions can be made collectively: a common lending instrument is supporting two pooled funds (one for the health sector, one for multisectoral HIV/AIDS activities), which will facilitate alignment of financing, management, and monitoring systems.

- Learning from the experiences of the AIDS Strategy and Action Plan (ASAP) service and the Global AIDS Monitoring and Evaluation Team (GAMET) program to provide task teams and country stakeholders with resources and tools to improve strategy development, engagement of civil society, and monitoring and evaluation.

- Funding interventions that are important to the HIV epidemic or the health situation that might otherwise be neglected because they are politically difficult for other agencies to finance (e.g., prevention and treatment programs for prisoners, harm-reduction programs for injection drug users).

- Refraining from funding popular programs that other agencies can finance with grants (e.g., commodities for ART and prevention of mother-child transmission) or activities for which Bank support systems are inadequate (e.g., clinical trials).

- Supporting systematic identification, monitoring, and evaluation of country-based Bank assistance to HIV/AIDS programs and the health sector to ensure that:

  - Country strategies, PRSPs, MTEFs, and sectorwide approaches adequately address HIV/AIDS and other priority health concerns, the interests of the poor, and health system requirements for delivering services. These strategies will need to be appropriately budgeted and aligned with the country's macroeconomic framework and have sustainable financing that does not skew balanced development of the economy. They will also need a focused and balanced approach to demonstrating results.

  - The proposed financing and implementation arrangements for HIV/AIDS and the health sector are supportive of the "Three Ones" and the Paris Principles on Aid Effectiveness.

  - Support to specific-disease programs or institutions is contingent on identification of any potential harm to the health system (or other health programs and prior establishment of appropriate risk-mitigation strategies.

In day-to-day operations, the World Bank has numerous levers of influence to support HIV/AIDS and the health sector at country level. Table H.2 outlines these levers and summarizes how they can be translated into specific actions.

Table H.2: Levers of Influence for the World Bank in HIV/AIDS and Health Systems at Country Level

LEVERS OF INFLUENCE	
Direct interventions	Bank actions in HIV/AIDS and health systems
Financing investments and operations	• Provide funding for agreed public sector programs that appropriately finance HIV/AIDS programs and health systems in the context of PRSPs and MTEFs. • Direct health sector financing, for capital investment (buildings, equipment) and recurrent costs (staff, training, drugs, supplies, and activities) for HIV/AIDS programs, development of health systems, and delivery of services.
Purchasing outputs/ outcomes	• Link funding to provision of health or HIV/AIDS services, or locally relevant performance targets, affirming that results have been achieved as basis for disbursement.
Expenditure control	• When financing inputs, ensure that fund disbursements conform with procurement procedures acceptable to the Bank. • Assure probity of Bank funds through audits.
INFLUENCING STRATEGIES	
Linking HIV/AIDS and health sector to public policy and financing	• Facilitate communication between Ministries of Finance and sector ministries for development of national strategies, planning, and evaluation to ensure that financing is sustainable and balanced across sectors and that the health sector and HIV/AIDS programs have a relevant role. • Bring together health with other sectors and civil society organizations over broader government reforms (e.g., civil service reforms).
Convening key actors	• Bring together critical players within civil society and government within country for learning, consensus building, strategy development, and planning for HIV/AIDS programs and the health sector in the context of PRSPs and MTEFs. • Network with experts and colleagues across countries to ensure that the best possible technical advice is considered. • Facilitate learning by critical players within country through communications, training, sharing materials, and dissemination of research and evaluation results.
Designing HIV/AIDS programs, health services, and their support systems	• Use project preparation and supervision to ensure the best available technical assistance, software, training, and support systems in the design or redesign of programs and support systems. • Focus Bank technical resources to strengthen policy and strategy cycles, financing systems, monitoring and evaluation systems, poverty concerns, and intersectoral linkages.
Monitoring and disclosing	• Ensure that appropriate plans for the monitoring and evaluation of health systems are developed, financed, and implemented and that the data are used for management and allocation decisions and for public disclosure and discourse. • Review performance of projects and HIV/AIDS and health sector programs for planning and disclosure purposes.
Providing knowledge and advice	• Commission or conduct studies on relevant HIV/AIDS and health policy and operational issues, such as impact evaluations of major programs and innovations. • Pooling and synthesizing information and experience on health systems, health financing, and links to HIV/AIDS with a focus on translating knowledge into local policy and practice.
Negotiating actions for disbursements	• Agree on actions for disbursement of Bank funds in the context of Poverty Reduction Strategy Credits that support HIV/AIDS and health sector objectives. • Ensure that agreed actions are taken by the borrower when a basis for Bank financing.

Notes

1. Interviews were conducted using a structured, open-ended interview technique, small group consultations, and consultations with partners at country and global levels. A questionnaire was sent to the Human Development (HD) Sector Management Units (SMUs) in all Regions, to the HNP Hub, the Global Program on HIV/AIDS, the World Bank Institute (WBI), and the International Finance Corporation (IFC) in March 2006. A consultation with the World Health Organization (WHO) was held in May 2006 in Geneva. Focus groups with randomly selected HNP staff (30 participants in all) as well as meetings with HNP teams at regional levels were organized to discuss the same set of questions. Two preliminary consultations with global partners were held on May 18 and 23 and in October and November 2006. Between September and November 2006, the strategy facilitation team visited nine client countries (Algeria, Argentina, Armenia, Djibouti, India, Indonesia, Mali, Mexico, and Tanzania) to consult with government, civil society, academia, global partners in the field, and Bank country office staff. Additionally, the strategy facilitation team benefited from abundant information and analysis provided by Bank staff, other multilaterals, bilaterals, and foundations. The team held various discussion meetings with groups of civil society in Washington, D.C.

2. Preker and Langenbrunner 2005; Angel-Urdinola and Jain 2006; Baeza and Packard 2006; Cotlear 2006; Dussault, Fournier, and Letourmy 2006; Gottret and Schieber 2006; Marek, Eichler, and Schnabl 2006.

3. Allen and Gillespie 2001; Berhman and Rosenzweig 2001; Galasso and Yau 2006; Jamison et al. 2006; World Bank 2006l.

4. Bell, Bruhns, and Gersbach 2006; Duflo et al. 2006; Görgens et al. 2006; Görgens-Albino and Nzima 2006; Lutalo 2006; Malek 2006; Marquez 2006; Moses et al. 2006; Wilson and de Beyer 2006a, 2006b; Wilson and Claeson 2006.

5. Additional sources: Birdsall, Kelley and Sinding 2001; Wagstaff and Claeson 2004; Campbell-White, Merrick, and Yazbeck 2006; World Bank 2006j.

6. *Development assistance for health* (DAH) consists of all resources aimed at providing financial support to developing countries to improve the HNP conditions of their populations. DAH includes multilateral organizations such as the Bank, bilateral aid, and private philanthropic aid. Annex C presents an overview of actors and trends in DAH in the last decade.

7. Global Fund to Fight AIDS, Tuberculosis and Malaria.

8. Behrman and Rosenzweig 2001; Bell, Devarajan, and Gersbach 2004; Bloom, Canning, and Jamison 2004; Bloom, Canning, and Malaney 1999; Croppenstedt and Muller 2000; Fenwick and Figenschou 1972; Fogel 1994; Gallup and Sachs 2000; Glick and Sahn 1998; Jamison 2006; Shariff 2003; Smith 1999, 2005; Thirumurthy,

Zivin, and Goldstein 2005; Thomas 2001; Thomas et al. 2004; Thomas and Strauss 1997; Wolgemuth et al.1982.

9. As measured by cumulative disbursements for all HNP sectoral classifications managed by the HNP Sector Board and other sectors.

10. The active portfolio has decreased by 30 percent since FY2001, mostly due to declining IBRD lending.

11. Share of AAA focused on health systems performance.

12. Defined as preventing households from the impoverishing effects of illness and other health-related life cycle events.

13. World Bank 2006d; Lewis 2005.

14. World Bank 2006d; WHO 2005.

15. World Bank 2006d; WHO 2006a.

16. Commitments for each of the three diseases fluctuate considerably from year to year. FY2005 data, the only data available at this time, should not be used to draw general conclusions about Bank financing for these diseases.

17. Fenwick and Figenschou 1972; Wolgemuth et al. 1982; Fogel 1994; Thomas and Strauss 1997; Bloom, Canning, and Malaney 1999; Smith 1999; Croppenstedt and Muller 2000; Gallup and Sachs 2000; Behrman and Rosenzweig 2001; Thomas 2001; Shariff 2003; Bell, Devarajan, and Gersbach 2004; Bloom, Canning, and Jamison 2004; Thomas et al. 2004; Smith 2005; Thirumurthy, Zivin, and Goldstein 2005; Jamison 2006.

18. UNICEF 2006a; Mathers, Lopez, and Murray 2006.

19. UNICEF 2006c.

20. UNICEF 2006b.

21. UNAIDS 2006.

22. Ibid.

23. WHO 2006a.

24. In terms of lending and/or policy advice.

25. Development assistance for health consists of all resources aimed at providing financial support to developing countries to improve health conditions of their populations. It includes multilateral organizations such as the World Health Organization, the World Bank, and UNICEF. It also includes bilateral aid and private philanthropic aid.

26. UNITAID is an international facility for the purchase of drugs that fight HIV/AIDS, malaria and tuberculosis. It was founded in September 2006 on the initiative of Brazil and France, and is to a great part financed by so-called innovative financing mechanisms, namely a solidarity levy on air line tickets.

27. International Finance Facility for Immunisation.

28. Throughout this Strategy, *health insurance* is used in its functional connotation (pooling of financial risk) and not as contributory insurance scheme à la Bismarck. Thus,

the use of the term "insurance" means any effective risk-pooling arrangement, including those financed out of general taxation (pooling at societal level), contributory payroll tax–financed social insurance, and private insurance (for-profit or not-for-profit). As discussed later, the Bank does not a priori promote, or discourage, governments and communities from choosing any of these arrangements. Specific preferences should be country-context specific. However, the Bank approaches policy dialog with client countries with a focus on policy and technical advice that provides options and supports their decision-making process for selecting and developing the most promising arrangements to achieve and sustain the strategic policy objective of improving access to services, and financial protection, particularly for the poor and the vulnerable in the specific country context.

29. *Verticalization* is defined as replication of key health system functions and duplication of support systems, each handling the needs (in parallel) of exclusively single-disease programs such as HIV/AIDS. Verticalization creates distortions that can sap the effectiveness of resources and makes a country miss an opportunity for spillover of priority–disease financing into systemic reform positively affecting many other diseases at marginal additional cost.

30. World Bank 2006d; Lewis 2005.

31. World Bank 2006d; WHO 2005.

32. World Bank 2006d; WHO 2006a.

33. Commitments for each of the three diseases fluctuate considerably from year to year, and FY2005 data should not be used to draw general conclusions about Bank financing for these diseases.

34. AMCs are intended to create a market-based mechanism to support research and production of vaccines for diseases that affect developing countries. Donors would guarantee a set envelope of funding at a given price for a new vaccine that meets specified requirements.

35. For example, the Global Fund to Fight AIDS, Tuberculosis and Malaria (GFATM) and the Global Alliance for Vaccines and Immunisation (GAVI).

36. For example, the Global Alliance for Improved Nutrition (GAIN), the Joint United Nations Programme on HIV/AIDS (1996), Roll Back Malaria (1998), and the Stop TB Initiative (1999).

37. Another 74 projects are expected to close by June 30, 2007 (38 HNP Sector Board managed and 36 other sector managed).

38. Realism is a measure of the extent to which task teams reflect potential implementation problems in their project ratings.

39. Proactivity is a measure of steps taken to put unsatisfactory projects back on track.

40. The IEG review is expected during 2008.

41. This time frame is used because AAA coding is accurate for those years. Earlier data are not captured properly in the Bank's data warehouse.

42. Only staff at grade GF and above are included in the analysis.

43. LICs for which official development assistance (ODA) and DAH represents a very small proportion of government/sector expenditures (e.g., India).

44. LICs for which official development assistance (ODA) and DAH represent a very large proportion of government and/or sector expenditures (e.g., Tanzania).

45. In-depth analysis of what a country health system is and how it works is outside the scope of this Strategy. Annex F refers readers to substantial analysis by the Bank and global partners.

46. Achieving results requires a combined effort from HNP, the Bank Poverty Reduction and Economic Management Network (PREM), Social Protection, Financial Services, Private Sector Development, Information Technology, and so on.

47. *System performance* is defined as systemic efficiency in sustaining or improving current HNP outcome and output achievements.

48. *Fragmentation* is defined as multiple small (inefficient risk-pool size) insurance providers that seldom complement each other and often present significant barriers for the portability of benefits when individuals need or desire to change from one to another insurer.

49. Household private out-of-pocket health expenditures are by far the largest source of health financing for most LICs, even for those receiving large DAH.

50. Soucat el al. 2004.

51. World Bank *forthcoming* b.

52. Cotlear 2006.

53. Ibid.

54. This section summarizes findings and recommendations of *Repositioning Nutrition as Central to Development: A Strategy for Large-Scale Action* (World Bank 2006l).

55. Share of DAH devoted to primary care dropped from 28 percent in 1999 to 15 percent in 2004 (World Bank 2006f)..

56. Includes external and domestic spending.

57. Caines et al. 2004; Caines 2005; McKinsey&Company 2005.

58. See note 26.

59. Most of the discussion and information in this section draws (and quotes) extensively from findings and recommendations of: *The World Health Report 2000, Health Systems: Improving Performance*, WHO 2000, Baeza and Packard 2006, and from contributions from the Health Services Team of the HNP Hub led by David Peters.

60. The common deficiencies in research design include: the strategies or intervention that are being pursued are not described in detail, so that it is hard to determine what the intervention actually consists of or whether it was implemented, and very different strategies are often given the same label; many strategies involve multiple components that are not specified or studied in a way that would indicate which component is essential, or where there are synergies between components; most studies do little to examine factors beyond the health system or the intervention itself that may

influence the results being examined; there are limited attempts to design studies that can actually attribute results to the strategy, including use of time series, before-after data, or comparison groups and randomization.

61. The effects in a given country will depend on factors such as its HIV prevalence, demographic patterns, costs of ART, availability of health insurance, supply of health workers, their perceived and actual risks of HIV infection, and the costs of providing services at the same level of quality (Over 2004).

62. These include the short-term commitments of donors—often no more than 12 months at a time—exchange rate fluctuations, and administrative delays by donor or recipient, and aid conditionalities.

63. GFATM grants typically have a two-year initial phase and a three-year second phase, with funding for the second phase conditional on acceptable progress in the initial phase, although grantees can apply for concurrent grants. PEPFAR was originally announced as a five-year program, with renewal under discussion.

64. The Paris Declaration on Aid Effectiveness includes a commitment to increase support for programmatic approaches that share the following features: leadership by the host country or organization; a single comprehensive program and budget framework; a formal process for donor coordination and harmonization of donor procedures for reporting, budgeting, financial management, and procurement; efforts to increase the use of local systems for program design and implementation, financial management, and monitoring and evaluation.

65. The "Three Ones" are a set of guiding principles for coordination of national partners and partners involved in HIV/AIDS control, and include: one agreed HIV/AIDS Action Framework that provides the basis for coordinating the work of all partners; one National AIDS Coordinating Authority, with a broad based multisectoral mandate; and one agreed country-level monitoring and evaluation system.

Bibliography

Allen, L., and S. Gillespie. 2001. *What Works? A Review of the Efficacy and Effectiveness of Nutrition Interventions.* Geneva: United Nations Administrative Committee on Coordination/Sub-Committee on Nutrition (ACC/SCN); Manila: Asian Development Bank.

Angel-Urdinola, D. F., and S. Jain. 2006. "Do Subsidized Health Programs in Armenia Increase Utilization among the Poor?" Policy Research Working Paper 4017, World Bank, Washington, DC.

Baeza, C., and T. G. Packard. 2006. *Beyond Survival: Protecting Households from Health Shocks in Latin America.* Palo Alto, CA: Stanford University Press.

Bardham, P. 1997. "Corruption and Development: A Review of Issues." *Journal of Economic Literature* 35 (3): 1310–46.

Bell, C., S. Devarajan, and H. Gersbach. 2004. "Thinking About the Long-run Economic Costs of AIDS." In *The Macroeconomics of HIV/AIDS*, ed. M. Haacker, 96–144. Washington, DC: International Monetary Fund.

Bell, C., R. Bruhns, and H. Gersbach. 2006. "Economic Growth, Education, and AIDS in Kenya: A Long-Run Analysis." Policy Research Working Paper 4025, World Bank, Washington, DC.

Berhman, J. R., and M. R. Rosenzweig. 2001. "The Returns to Increasing Body Weight." University of Pennsylvania. http://www.vwl.uni-muenchen.de/ls_komlos/tuebingen/articles/behrman.pdf.

Bertalanffy, L. von. 1968. *General System Theory.* New York: George Braziller.

Bertozzi, S., N. Padian, J. Wegbreit, L. M. DeMaria, B. Feldman, H. Gayle, J. Gold, R. Grant, and M. Isbell. 2006. "HIV/AIDS Prevention and Treatment." In *Disease Control Priorities in Developing Countries*, 2nd ed. New York: Oxford University Press; Washington, DC: World Bank.

Bhagwati, J., R. W. Fogel, B. S. Frey, J. Y. Lin, D. C. North, T. C. Schelling, V. L. Smith, and N. L. Stokey. 2004. "Ranking the Opportunities." In *Global Crises, Global Solutions*, ed. Bjorn Lomborg, 605–44. Cambridge, UK: Cambridge University Press.

Birdsall, N., A. C. Kelley, and S. Sinding. 2001. *Population Matters: Demographic Change, Economic Growth, and Poverty in the Developing World.* New York: Oxford University Press.

Bloom, D., D. Canning, and D. Jamison. 2004. "Health, Wealth, and Welfare." *Finance and Development* 41 (1): 10–15.

Bloom, D., D. Canning, and P. Malaney. 1999. "Demographic Change and Economic Growth in Asia." Working Paper 15, Center for International Development, Harvard University, Cambridge, MA.

Bustreo, F., E. Genovese, E. Omobono, H. Axelsson, and I. Bannon. 2005. *Improving Child Health in Post-Conflict Countries: Can the World Bank Contribute?* Washington, DC: World Bank.

Buve, A., S. Kalibala, and J. James McIntyre. 2003. "Stronger Health Systems for More Effective HIV/AIDS Prevention and Care." *International Journal Health Plan Management* 18: S41–S51.

Caines, K. 2005. *Key Evidence from Major Studies of Selected Global Health Partnerships.* London: DFID Health Resource Centre.

Caines, K., K. Buse, C. Carlson, R. de Loor, N. Druce, C. Grace, M. Pearson, J. Sancho, and R. Sadanandan. 2004. *Assessing the Impact of Global Health Partnerships.* London: DFID Health Resource Centre.

Campbell-White, A., T. W. Merrick, and A.S. Yazbeck. 2006. *Reproductive Health – The Missing Millennium Development Goal: Poverty, Health, and Development in a Changing World.* Washington, DC: World Bank.

Cotlear, D., ed. 2006. *A New Social Contract for Peru: An Agenda for Improving Education, Health Care, and the Social Safety Net.* Washington, DC: World Bank.

Croppenstedt, A., and C. Muller. 2000. "The Impact of Farmers' Health and Nutritional Status on their Productivity and Efficiency: Evidence from Ethiopia." *Economic Development and Cultural Change* 48 (3): 475–502.

DFID (UK Department for International Development). 2006. *Global Health Partnerships and Health Systems Strengthening.* London: DFID Health Resource Centre.

Dow, W., P. Gertler, R. F. Schoeni, J. Strauss, and D. Thomas. 1997. "Health Care Prices, Health, and Labor Outcomes: Experimental Evidence." Working Paper Series, Labor Population Program, RAND, Santa Monica, CA.

Duflo, E., P. Dupas, M. Kremer, and S. Sinei. 2006. "Education and HIV/AIDS Prevention: Evidence from a Randomized Evaluation in Western Kenya." Policy Research Working Paper 4024, World Bank, Washington, DC.

Dussault, G., P. Fournier, and A. Letourmy, ed. 2006. "L'Assurance Maladie en Afrique Francophone : Amélior l'accès aux soins et lutter contre la pauvreté." Health, Nutrition and Population Working Paper Series, World Bank, Washington, DC.

Eggleston, K., L. Ling, M. Qingyue, M. Lindelow, and A. Wagstaff. 2006. "Health Service Delivery in China: A Literature Review." Policy Research Working Paper 3978, World Bank, Washington, DC.

Elmendorf, A. E., and K. Larusso. 2006. "Human Resources for Health and World Bank Operations in Africa: A Review of Experience." Africa Region Human Development Working Paper Series 110, World Bank, Washington, DC.

Fenwick, A., and B. H. Figenschou. 1972. "The Effect of Schistosoma Mansoni Infection of the Productivity of Cane Cutters on a Sugar Estate in Tanzania." *Bulletin of the World Health Organization* 47 (5): 567–72.

Fogel, R. W. 1994. "Economic Growth, Population Theory and Physiology: The Bearing of Long-term Processes on the Making of Economic Policy." *American Economic Review* 89 (1): 1–21.

Foster, M. 2005a. "Fiscal Space and Sustainability: Towards a Solution for the Health Sector." Working Paper, World Bank, Washington, DC.

_____. 2005b. "Improving the Medium- to Long-term Predictability of Aid." Working Paper, World Bank, Washington, DC.

Galasso, E., and J. Yau. 2006. "Learning through Monitoring: Lessons from a Large-scale Nutrition Program in Madagascar." Policy Research Working Paper 4058, World Bank, Washington, DC.

Gallup, J., and J. Sachs. 2000. "The Economic Burden of Malaria." Working Paper 52, Center for International Development, Harvard University, Cambridge, MA.

Gertler, P., and J. Gruber. 2002. "Insuring Consumption Against Illness." *American Economic Review* 92 (1): 51–76.

Glick, P., and D. E. Sahn. 1998. "Health and Productivity in Heterogenous Urban Labour Market." *Applied Economics* 30 (2): 203–16.

Görgens, M., N. Cosby, J. Chipeta, and R. Govindaraj. 2006. "Malawi: Developing a National Multisector HIV/AIDS M&E System." Global HIV/AIDS Program, HIV/AIDS M&E Report, World Bank, Washington, DC.

Görgens-Albino, M., and M. Nzima. 2006. "Eleven Components of a Fully Functional HIV M&E System." Global HIV/AIDS Program, HIV/AIDS M&E Report, World Bank, Washington, DC.

Gottret, P., and G. Schieber. 2006. *Health Financing Revisited: A Practitioner's Guide.* Washington, DC: World Bank.

Government Accountability Office. 2006. *Global Health: Spending Requirement Presents Challenges for Allocating Prevention Funding under the President's Emergency Plan for AIDS Relief.* Report GAO-06-395. Washington, DC: United States Government Accountability Office.

Gruber, J., and M. Hanratty. 1995. "The Labor-market Effects of Introducing National Health Insurance: Evidence from Canada." *Journal of Business and Economic Studies* 13 (2): 163–73.

Gupta, S., B. Clements, A. Pivovarsky, and E. R. Tiongson. 2004. "Foreign Aid and Revenue Response: Does the Composition of Foreign Aid Matter?" In *Helping Countries Develop: The Role of Fiscal Policy.* Washington, DC: International Monetary Fund.

Haacker, M. 2004. "HIV/AIDS: The Impact on the Social Fabric and the Economy." In *The Macroeconomics of HIV/AIDS*, ed. M. Haacker. Washington, DC: International Monetary Fund.

Hanson, K., M. K. Ranson, V. Oliveira-Cruz, and A. Mills. 2003. "Expanding Access to Priority Health Interventions: A Framework for Understanding the Constraints to Scaling-Up." *Journal of International Development* 15 (1): 1–14.

High-Level Forum on the Health MDGs. 2005. *Working Group on Global Health Partnerships.* http://www.hlfhealthmdgs.org/ReportGHPWorkingGroup28Sep05 doc.

Hogan, D. R., R. Baltussen, C. Hayashi, J. A. Lauer, and J. A. Salomon. 2005. "Cost Effectiveness Analysis of Strategies to Combat HIV/AIDS in Developing Countries." *British Medical Journal* 331 (7530): 1431–7.

Izazola-Licea, J. A. 2006. "National AIDS Spending Assessments," presented at the Global Resource Tracking Consortium Conference, September 29, Geneva.

Jamison, D. 2006. "Investing in Health." In *Disease Control and Priorities in Developing Countries*, 2nd ed., ed. D. Jamison, J. Berman, A. Meacham, G. Alleyne, M. Claeson, D. Evans, P. Jha, A. Mills, and P. Musgrove. Washington, DC: World Bank; New York: Oxford University Press.

Jamison, D. T., J. G. Breman, A. R. Measham, G. Alleyne, M. Claeson, D. B. Evans, P. Jha, A. Mills, and P. Musgrove, ed. 2006. *Disease Control Priorities in Developing Countries*, 2nd ed. New York: Oxford University Press; Washington, DC: World Bank.

Johnston, T., and S. Stout. 1999. *Investing in Health: Development Effectiveness in the Health, Nutrition, and Population Sector.* Washington, DC: World Bank.

Kaufmann, D., and A. Kraay. 2003. *Governance and Growth: Causality Which Way? Evidence for the World, in Brief.* Washington, DC: World Bank.

Kelley, A. C. 1988. "Economic Consequences for Population Change." *Third World Journal of Economic Literature* 26 (4): 1685–1728.

Kolsky, P., E. Perez, W. Vandersypen, and L. O. Jensen. 2005. "Sanitation and Hygiene at the World Bank: An Analysis of Current Activities." Water Supply & Sanitation Working Note 6, World Bank, Washington, DC.

Kutzin, J. 2000. "Towards Universal Health Care Coverage: A Goal-oriented Framework for Policy Analysis." Discussion Paper, Health, Nutrition, and Population, World Bank, Washington, DC.

Leontien, L., L. W. Niessen, and A. S. Yazbeck. 2003. "Pro-poor Health Policies in Poverty Reduction Strategies." *Health Policy and Planning* 18 (2): 138–45.

Lewis, M. 2005. "Addressing the Challenge of HIV/AIDS Macroeconomic, Fiscal and Institutional Issues." Working Paper 58, Center for Global Development, Washington, DC.

———. 2006. "Governance and Corruption in Public Health Care Systems." Working Paper 78, Center for Global Development, Washington, DC.

Lopez, A. D., C. D. Mathers, M. Ezzati, D. T. Jamison, and C. J. L. Murray, ed. 2006. *Global Burden of Disease and Risk Factors.* New York: Oxford University Press; Washington, DC: World Bank.

Lutalo, M. 2006. "IFC Against AIDS—Protecting People and Profitability." Global HIV/AIDS Program, HIV/AIDS M&E Report, World Bank, Washington, DC.

Malek, D. 2006. "Australia's Successful Response to AIDS and the Role of Law Reform." Global HIV/AIDS Program Discussion Paper, Human Development Network, World Bank, Washington, DC.

Marek, T., R. Eichler, and P. Schnabl. 2006a. "Allocation de Ressources et Acquisition de Services de Santé en Afrique—Qu'est-ce qui est efficace pour améliorer la santé des pauvres?" Africa Region Human Development Working Paper Series 105, World Bank, Washington, DC.

Marek, T., C. O'Farrell, C. Yamamoto, and I. Zable. 2006b. "Tendances et Perspectives des Partenariats entre les Secteurs Public et Non-Etatique pour Améliorer les Services de Santé en Afrique." Africa Region Human Development Working Paper Series 106, World Bank, Washington, DC.

Marquez, P. V. 2005. *Dying Too Young – Addressing Premature Mortality and Ill Health Due to Non-Communicable Diseases and Injuries in the Russian Federation.* Washington, DC: World Bank.

———. 2006. "Preventing HIV Infection in Russia: Best Practices in Harm Reduction Programs." Global HIV/AIDS Program, HIV/AIDS M&E Report, World Bank, Washington, DC.

Mathers, C. D., A. D. Lopez, and C. J. L. Murray. 2006. "The Burden of Disease and Mortality by Condition: Data, Methods, and Results for 2001." In *Global Burden of Disease and Risk Factors*, ed. A.D. Lopez, C.D. Mathers, M. Ezzati, D.T. Jamison, and C.J.L. Murray. Washington, DC: World Bank.

May, J. F., M. Temourov, and I. Dupond. 2006. "Lutte contre la Pauvreté au Burkina Faso. L'Importance de l'écart Urbain-Rural des Indicateurs de Santé, Population et Nutrition." Africa Region Human Development Working Paper Series 96, World Bank, Washington, DC.

McKinsey & Company. 2005. *Global Health Partnerships: Assessing Country Consequences.* Seattle, WA: Bill & Melinda Gates Foundation.

Melgaard, B., A. Creese, B. Aylward, J-M. Olive, C. Maher, J. M. Okwo-Bele, and J. W. Lee. 1999. "Disease Eradication and Health Systems Development." *Morbidity and Mortality Weekly Report* 48 (SU01): 28–35.

Michaud, C. M. 2007. Data communicated by e-mail, January.

Mills, A. 2005. "Mass Campaigns versus General Health Services: What Have We Learnt in 40 Years about Vertical versus Horizontal Approaches?" *Bulletin of the World Health Organization* 83 (4): 325–30.

Moses, S., J. F. Blanchard, H. Kang, F. Emmanuel, S. R. Paul, M. L. Becker, D. Wilson, and M. Claeson. 2006. "AIDS in South Asia: Understanding and Responding to a Heterogeneous Epidemic." Health, Nutrition and Population Working Paper Series, World Bank, Washington, DC.

Murray, C. J., and A. D. Lopez. 1996. *The Global Burden of Disease.* Cambridge: Harvard University Press.

———. 1997. "Alternative Projections of Mortality and Disability by Cause 1990-2020: Global Burden of Disease Study." *Lancet* 349 (9064): 1498–1504.

OECD/DAC (Organisation for Economic Co-operation and Development/Development Assistance Committee). 2005. *Paris Declaration on Aid Effectiveness Ownership, Harmonization, Alignment, Results, and Mutual Accountability.* Issued at the Paris High-Level Forum, March 2, Paris, France.

Oliveira-Cruz, V., K. Hanson, and A. Mills. 2003. "Approaches to Overcoming Constraints to Effective Health Service Delivery: A Review of the Evidence." *Journal of International Development* 25: 41–65.

Over, M. 2004. "Impact of the HIV/AIDS Epidemic on the Health Sectors in Developing Countries." In *The Macroeconomics of HIV/AIDS*, ed. M. Haacker, 311–44. Washington, DC: International Monetary Fund.

Øvretveit, J., B. Siadat, and D. H. Peters. 2006. "Strengthening Health Services in Low-Income Countries: Lessons from a Rapid Review of Research." Draft, November 3, 2006. World Bank, Washington, DC.

PATH/UNFPA (Program for Appropriate Technology in Health/United Nations Population Fund). 2006. *Meeting the Need: Strengthening Family Planning Programs*. Seattle: PATH/UNFPA.

Peters, D. H., G. Bloom, M. H. Rahman, A. Bhuiya, B. Kanjilal, O. Oladepo, G. Pariyo, Z. Zhenzhong, and S. Sundaram. 2006. "Research for Future Health Systems." In *Global Forum Update on Research for Health Volume 3*, ed. S. Matlin, 133–37. London: Pro-Book Publishing.

Plsek, P. E., T. Wilson, and T. Greenhalgh. 2001. "Complexity Science: Complexity, Leadership, and Management in Healthcare Organizations." *BMJ* 323: 625–28.

Preker, A. S., and J. C. Langenbrunner, ed. 2005. *Spending Wisely: Buying Health Services for the Poor*. Washington, DC: World Bank.

Reddy, S., and A. Heuty. 2005. "Achieving the Millennium Development Goals: What's Wrong with Existing Analytical Models? Bureau of Development Policy of the United Nations Development Programme." http://www.millennium development goals.org.

Republic of Rwanda Ministry of Finance and Economic Planning, Ministry of Health. 2006. "Scaling Up to Achieve the Health MDGs in Rwanda. A Background Study to the High-Level Forum in Tunis, June 12–13, 2006."

Revenga, A., M. Over, E. Masaki, W. Peerapatanapokin, J. Gold, V. Tangcharoensathien, and S. Thanprasertsuk. 2006. "The Economics of Effective AIDS Treatment: Evaluating Policy Options for Thailand." Health, Nutrition and Population Working Paper Series, World Bank, Washington, DC.

Roemer, M. I. 1991. *National Health Systems of the World. Volume 1: The Countries*. Oxford University Press: New York/Oxford.

Salomon, J. A., D. R. Hogan, J. Stover, K. A. Stanecki, N. Walker, P. D. Ghys, and B. Schwartländer. 2005. "Integrating HIV Prevention and Treatment: From Slogans to Impact." *PLoS Medicine* 2 (1): 50–56.

Schieber, G., L. K. Fleisher, and P. Gottret. 2006. "Getting Real on Health Financing." *Finance and Development* 43 (4): 43–49.

Shakow, A. 2006. "Global Fund – World Bank HIV/AIDS Programs Comparative Advantage Study." Working Paper, World Bank, Washington, DC.

Shariff, A. 2003. "Links between Macroeconomics and Health: Relevance for the South

East Asia Region." Paper presented at the World Health Organization Ministerial Consultation on Macroeconomic and Health, Geneva, October 28–30.

Smith, J. P. 1999. "Healthy Bodies and Thick Wallets: The Dual Relation between Health and Economic Status." *Journal of Economic Perspectives* 13 (2): 145–66.

———. 2005. "Unraveling the SES-Health Connection." *Population and Development Review* 30 (Suppl): 108–32.

Soucat, A., W. Van Lerberghe, F. Diop, S. Nguyen, and R. Knippenberg. 2004. "Marginal Budgeting for Bottlenecks: A New Costing and Resource Allocation Practice to Buy Health Results—Using Health Sector's Budget Expansion to Progress toward the Millennium Development Goals in Sub-Saharan Africa." Working Paper, World Bank, Washington, DC.

Stillman, K., and S. Bennett. 2005. *System-wide Effects of the Global Fund: Interim Findings from Three Country Studies.* Bethesda, MD: Abt Associates, Inc.

Subramanian, S., D. Peters, and J. Willis. 2006. "How are Health Services, Financing and Status Evaluated? An Analysis of Implementation Completion Reports of World Bank Assistance in Health." Health, Nutrition and Population (HNP) Discussion Paper, World Bank, Washington, DC.

Thirumurthy, H., J. G. Zivin, and M. Goldstein. 2005. "The Economic Impact of AIDS Treatment: Labor Supply in Western Kenya." Working Paper 11871, National Bureau of Economic Research, Cambridge, MA.

Thomas, D. 2001. "Health, Nutrition and Economic Prosperity: A Microeconomic Perspective." Commission on Macroeconomics and Health, Working Paper WG1: 7, World Health Organization, Geneva.

Thomas, D., and J. Strauss. 1997. "Health and Wages: Evidence from Men and Women in Urban Brazil." *Journal of Econometrics* 77: 159–86.

Thomas, D., E. Frankenberg, J. Friedman, J. P. Habicht, N. Jones, C. McKelvey, G. Pelto, B. Sikoki, J. P. Smith, C. Sumantri, and W. Suriastini. 2004. "Causal Effect of Health on Labor Market Outcomes: Evidence from a Random Assignment Iron Supplementation Intervention." Paper presented at the Population Association of America Annual Meetings, Boston, MA, April.

Travis, P., S. Bennett, A. Haines, T. Pang, Z. Bhutta, A. A. Hyder, N. R. Pielemeier, A. Mills, T. Evans. 2004. "Overcoming Health-Systems Constraints to Achieve the Millennium Development Goals." *Lancet* 365: 900–906.

UN (United Nations). 2003. *World Population Prospects: The 2002 Revision.* New York: United Nations.

———. 2005. *World Population Prospects: The 2004 Revision.* New York: United Nations.

UN Millennium Project. 2005. *Investing in Development: A Practical Plan to Achieve the Millennium Development Goals.* New York: UN Millennium Project.

UNAIDS (United Nations Joint Program on HIV/AIDS). 2006. *2006 Report on the Global AIDS Epidemic: A 10th UNAIDS Anniversary Special Edition.* Geneva: UNAIDS.

UNFPA (United Nations Population Fund). 2004. *Programme of Action. Adopted at the International Conference on Population and Development, Cairo, 5–13 September 1994.* New York: UNFPA.

———. 2006. "UNFPA Global Population Policy Update." Newsletter *64.* http://www.unfpa.org/parliamentarians/news/newsletters/issue64.htm.

UNICEF (United Nations Children's Fund). 2006a. "Millennium Development Goals: Reduce Child Mortality." http://www.unicef.org/mdg/childmortality.html.

———. 2006b. "Millennium Development Goals: Improve Maternal Mortality." http://www.unicef.org/mdg/maternal.html.

———. 2006c. "Millennium Development Goals: Combat HIV/AIDS, malaria, and other diseases." http://www.unicef.org/mdg/disease.html.

Wagstaff, A., and M. Claeson. 2004. *The Millennium Development Goals for Health: Rising to the Challenges.* Washington, DC: World Bank.

Whitty, C. J. M., and T. Doherty. 2006. "New Tools to Fight Disease Should be Celebrated, But We Also Need the Systems and the People to Deliver Them." *Tropical Doctor* 36 (4): 193–94.

Wilson, D., and J. de Beyer. 2006a. "Male Circumcision—Evidence and Implications." Global HIV/AIDS Program, HIV/AIDS M&E Report, World Bank, Washington, DC.

———. 2006b. "Mozambique's Battle Against HIV/AIDS and the DREAM Project." Global HIV/AIDS Program, HIV/AIDS M&E Report, World Bank, Washington, DC.

Wilson, D., and M. Claeson. 2006. "Understanding the HIV Epidemic in South Asia." Global HIV/AIDS Program, HIV/AIDS M&E Report, World Bank, Washington, DC.

Wolgemuth, J. C., M. C. Latham, A. Hall, A. Chesher, and D. W. Crompton. 1982. "Worker Productivity and the Nutritional Status of Kenyan Road Construction Laborers." *American Journal of Clinical Nutrition* 36 (1): 68–78.

World Bank. 1997. *Human Development Network Strategy.* Washington, DC: World Bank.

———. 1999. "Investing in Health: Development Effectiveness in the Health, Nutrition, and Population Sector." Operations Evaluation Department, World Bank, Washington, DC.

———. 2001a. *An Analysis of Combating Iodine Deficiency: Case Studies of China, Indonesia, and Madagascar.* Washington, DC: World Bank.

———. 2001b. *World Development Report 2002: Building Institutions for Markets.* Washington, DC: World Bank.

———. 2002a. *A Sourcebook for Poverty Reduction Strategies.* Washington, DC: World Bank.

———. 2002b. *Supporting a Healthy Transition: Lessons from Early World Bank Experience in Eastern Europe.* Washington, DC: World Bank.

———. 2003a. "Health, Nutrition, and Population Sector Board Assessment." Quality Assurance Group, World Bank, Washington, DC.

———. 2003b. *World Development Report 2004. Making Services Work for Poor People.* Washington, DC: World Bank.

———. 2004. *World Development Report 2005. A Better Investment Climate for Everyone.* Washington, DC: World Bank.

———. 2005a. *Committing to Results: Improving the Effectiveness of HIV/AIDS Assistance.* Washington, DC: World Bank.

———. 2005b. "Education Sector Strategy Update." Human Development Network, World Bank, Washington, DC.

———. 2005c. *The Effectiveness of World Bank Support for Community-Based and –Driven Development.* Washington, DC: World Bank.

———. 2005d. *Improving Health, Nutrition, and Population Outcomes in Sub-Saharan Africa: The Role of the World Bank.* Washington, DC: World Bank.

———. 2005e. *Maintaining Momentum to 2015? An Impact Evaluation of Interventions to Improve Maternal and Child Health and Nutrition in Bangladesh.* Washington, DC: World Bank.

———. 2005f. *Meeting the Challenge of Africa's Development: A World Bank Group Action Plan.* Washington, DC: World Bank.

———. 2005g. *The World Bank's Global HIV/AIDS Program of Action.* Global HIV/AIDS Program. Washington, DC: World Bank.

———. 2005h. *World Development Report 2006: Equity and Development.* Washington, DC: World Bank.

———. 2006a. "Aid Effectiveness in Health." Paper presented at the Organisation for Economic Co-operation and Development Global Forum on Development, Pre-Meeting on Aid Effectiveness in Health, Paris, December 4.

———. 2006b. *Annual Report of Development Effectiveness 2006: Getting Results.* Washington, DC: World Bank.

———. 2006c. *Annual Report on Portfolio Performance Fiscal Year 2005.* Washington, DC: World Bank.

———. 2006d. Data collected from *Business Warehouse.* Washington, DC: World Bank.

———. 2006e. "A Discussion of the Results and Lessons Learned from Implementation Completion Reports (ICRs)—FY04–FY05." Working Paper, Human Development Network, World Bank, Washington, DC.

———. 2006f. *Global Monitoring Report 2006: Strengthening Mutual Accountability—Aid, Trade, and Governance.* Washington, DC: World Bank.

———. 2006g. "Health, Nutrition, and Population Portfolio FY06 Retrospective: Achievements, Shortcomings and the Need for Change." Working Paper, Heath, Nutrition, and Population, World Bank, Washington, DC.

———. 2006h. *Implementation Plan for the World Bank's Global HIV/AIDS Program of Action.* Washington, DC: World Bank.

————. 2006i. "Literature Review: Impact of Poor Health on Productivity and Earnings." Background note prepared for the Health, Nutrition, and Population Strategy, Human Development Network, World Bank.

————. 2006j. "Population and the World Bank: Background Paper Prepared for the HNP Sector Strategy." Working Paper, Health, Nutrition, and Population, World Bank, Washington, DC.

————. 2006k. "Provincial Maternal-Child Health Investment Project in Support of the Second Phase of the Provincial Maternal-Child Health Program." Project Appraisal Document P095515, World Bank, Washington, DC.

————. 2006l. *Repositioning Nutrition as Central to Development: A Strategy for Large-Scale Action.* Washington, DC: World Bank.

————. 2006m. "Strengthening Bank Group Engagement on Governance and Anticorruption." Development Committee Paper, World Bank, Washington, DC.

————. 2006n. "The Third Transition: Exploring the Impact of Changing Demographic Structures in Eastern Europe and the Former Soviet Union." ECA Regional Flagship Study, Working Paper, World Bank, Washington, DC.

————. 2006o. *World Development Report 2007. Development and the Next Generation.* Washington, DC: World Bank.

————. 2006p. "Enhancing World Bank Support to Middle-Income Countries," Board Paper, World Bank, Washington, DC, September.

————. 2007. *Public Policy and the Challenge of Chronic Noncummunicable Diseases: An Agenda for Action.* Washington, DC: World Bank.

————. Forthcoming a. "Seventh Quality of Supervision Assessment." Quality Assurance Group, World Bank, Washington, DC.

————. Forthcoming b. "India: MDG Issues in Poor States—Reducing Child Mortality in Orissa." World Bank, Washington, DC.

WHO (World Health Organization). 2000. *World Health Report 2000. Health Systems: Improving Performance.* Geneva: WHO.

————. 2002. *The World Health Report 2002. Reducing Risks, Promoting Healthy Life.* Geneva: WHO.

————. 2003a. *The World Health Report 2003. Shaping the Future.* Geneva: WHO.

————. 2003b. *Social Determinants of Health: The Solid Facts,* 2nd ed, ed. R. Wilkinson, M. Marmot. Denmark: WHO.

————. 2005. *World Malaria Report 2005.* Geneva: World Health Organization; UNICEF.

————. 2006a. "WHO Tuberculosis Fact Sheet." http://www.who.int/media centre/factsheets/fs104/en/index.html.

————. 2006b. *World Health Report 2006. Working Together for Health.* Geneva: WHO.

Yazbeck, A, and C. Hayashi. 2001. "How Well Are Bank-Supported Health, Nutrition, and Population Projects Designed to Benefit the Poor?" Seminar Report, World Bank, Washington, DC.

Index

Eco-Audit

Environmental Benefits Statement

The World Bank is committed to preserving endangered forests and natural resources. The Office of the Publisher has chosen to print *Healthy Development: The World Bank Strategy for Health, Nutrition, & Population Results* on recycled paper including 30% post-consumer recycled fiber in accordance with the recommended standards for paper usage set by the Green Press Initiative, a nonprofit program supporting publishers in using fiber that is not sourced from endangered forests. For more information, visit www.greenpressinitiative.org.

Saved:

- 30 trees
- 1,396 lbs. of solid waste
- 10,868 gallons of water
- 2,618 lbs. of net greenhouse gases
- 21 million BTUs of total energy